HOW TO CATCH
BIGGER PIKE

FROM RIVERS, LOCHS AND LAKES

HOW TO CATCH
BIGGER PIKE
FROM RIVERS, LOCHS AND LAKES

PAUL GUSTAFSON

and

GREG MEENEHAN

CollinsWillow

An Imprint of HarperCollins*Publishers*

Dedication

This book is dedicated to my mother, my wife, Sally, and to my son, Mathew,
without whose support, encouragement and patience
it would never have been written.

I should like to thank Steve Kilbee for putting up with me during
countless fishing expeditions, and Fred Buller and Alwyne Wheeler
for their invaluable advice and support. And not forgetting Robbie Brightwell
and Austin Ashman whose help over the years has been much appreciated.

First published in 1997
by CollinsWillow
an imprint of HarperCollins*Publishers*
London

© Paul Gustafson 1997

1 3 5 7 9 8 6 4 2

A CIP catalogue record for this book is available from the British Library

ISBN 0 00 218752 3

Design by Amzie Viladot

Illustrations by John Searl

Photographs supplied by Paul Gustafson, Greg Meenehan, Mark Williams, Still Moving Picture Company,
John Bremner, Tony Sargeant, Mick Rouse, the Irish and Swedish Tourist Boards and Anglers World Holidays

Page 6: Sunset over Farmoor Reservoir near Oxford

Colour origination by Colourscan, Singapore

Printed in Italy by
LEGO SpA, Vicenza

FOREWORD

by Fred Buller

Sixty years ago when I was a ten-year-old aspiring pike angler, pike fishing was just as exciting as it is today, but my word hasn't the sport changed since then. In those days, apart from one or two notable exceptions like Edward Spence's *The Pike Fisher* and John Bickerdyke's *Angling for Pike*, if you wanted to read about your sport you needed to buy general fishing books that included a chapter or two about pike fishing. Even the most famous of all our pike anglers, Alfred Jardine, never wrote a book solely on pike fishing. The nearest he ever came to that was with his book *Pike and Perch*.

As the present century draws to a close we pike anglers (and there are probably more of us in the Northern Hemisphere than any other kind of angler) can now resort to a whole library of pike angling literature, covering every known aspect of pike fishing. But it's not quite over yet – at least not until we take Paul Gustafson's new work into account.

Many contemporaries of 'PG', knowing of his skill, enthusiasm and dedication, will wonder why he took so long before 'coming out' with his own pike book. For many years now, PG has wisely resisted the temptation to contribute regularly to the angling press – an activity which drains an author of material that he would otherwise store up for a book. The reward for being shrewd and patient could be that his *How to Catch Bigger Pike* will one day find a place in the list of notable angling books and become a landmark on the subject.

It has been written by an angler who, ever since I have known him, has been hungry for knowledge of his subject. He has never stopped asking the older generation of pike anglers questions so that he could draw from their experience (before it was too late), to test against his own. You will therefore not be surprised to hear that he is more of a pragmatist than a romantic.

This book describes clearly and illustrates handsomly nearly all the known methods of pike fishing and will be needed by every improving angler who is still looking for another way to succeed. It is not only a tribute to the author but also the publisher, who has done everything possible to create a book whose quality is second to none in the field.

Frederick Buller.

Little Missenden, Buckinghamshire

INTRODUCTION

Izaak Walton called it 'the tyrant of the rivers, or the fresh-water wolf, by reason of his bold, greedy, devouring disposition.' Dick Walker said whenever he hooked one he felt as Jorrocks did towards his horse when he said: 'Come hup, you hugly brute!'

No other British freshwater fish species has the same aura, creates so much fear and commands so much respect as the pike. It has lived in Britain for millions of years, been the subject of tales that have been handed down for centuries, and been a part of epic battles that have lived on in memories of generations.

Huge, glass-cased specimens glare down from walls the length and breadth of Britain, with cold, staring eyes and rows of saw-like teeth, defiant even from beyond the grave.

It's the biggest native freshwater fish in the British Isles and a species that anglers long to catch, and talk about in reverential tones. We may rule on land but the pike is all-powerful beneath the waves, fearless and with neither adversary nor equal.

It's been said that you can't love pike; that they have cold, black hearts and that even the very best pike anglers can do no more than understand them. Yet anglers devote their lives to studying them, and some write books to explain the attraction they hold, to reveal what was hitherto unknown about these majestic fish, and to show how they can be outwitted.

But who is caught, then? The wily pike or the enthralled pike angler? The writers of books about pike, or the readers of them? For when a fascination for the species they call the king of freshwater fishes bites, it bites deep and doesn't ever let go.

FIRST STEPS
a pike fishing apprenticeship

Above: Every capture stays in the memory, whether it weighs 5 lb, like my first fish, or 35 lb, like this one, my personal best.

Everyone's past has a profound effect on their present and future, and for anglers, this is particularly true. From the first day that we pick up a rod and the first fish that we see and catch, we learn lessons that stay with us for the rest of our lives.

The circumstances of every capture are stored in the memory and brought into play when a similar situation occurs. Perhaps without being aware of it we are calling on experiences that stretch back to our earliest days to solve the latest fishing puzzle.

My first days of fishing were spent sitting alone beside a water, watching what was going on beneath the surface and seeing grown-up anglers leave home at dawn to return much later weighed down with their catches.

I was fortunate in that a lake lapped against the shore just a hundred yards from the bottom of my parents' home at Hinksey, in South Oxford, and it was there that I caught my first pike.

My fishing had been for perch, bream and eels until one day in autumn I got up early, collected my Pegley Davies rod and a bucket of minnows, which I had left to stand under a dripping tap in the bath, and ran down to the shore.

There were two green angling punts moored at the lake, and my tactic for catching fish was to drop a livebait on a size 6 hook against the side of the punt and let it swing under. Almost invariably it would be taken by a perch, sometimes a big one.

But this morning when I tried this approach nothing happened, so I pushed the punt a little way out. As the boat moved, I saw the tail of a huge fish lying below. I lowered the bait where I thought the head should be, and the minnow was taken.

The pike I caught was only about 5 lb, but I can still remember the excitement of its capture and the sense of discovery at seeing my first one. Despite the years that have gone by and the number of pike I have seen and caught since, every one I catch reminds me of that fish and the species still holds the same sense of wonder for me that I experienced on that day.

Throughout the summer, I went down to the shore early in the morning to sit and watch a large pike that would swim over the concrete shelf at the water's edge when the sun was out. I never fished for it. It used to fascinate me just to watch it, and I was quite content to sit there for hours.

I was once there when two men came back in a boat for their Sunday lunch after setting out early. Children weren't allowed out on the water in the punts, so they held a fascination for us and we waited eagerly to see what the anglers had caught when they returned. I watched the two men come ashore on this

Left: Spinning was a cheap and effective way of catching fish. All of my money went on lures – Ondex, Voblex and wooden jointed plugs – and all of my spare time was spent fishing.

occasion, and they had two very big pike in the bottom of their boat. These fish dwarfed my five pounder and I remember thinking that fish of that size were entirely out of reach for someone like me. I couldn't believe I would ever catch a fish that big.

I believe I owe my original instinct for fishing to my father, a keen and skilful angler whose favourite species became mine. One of my earliest memories is sitting with him while he was fishing for eels on the River Severn, near my birthplace at Shrewsbury, and when we moved to Oxford with my four brothers I watched him fishing the Thames for eels and spinning for pike.

To a young boy who wanted to explore the lake at the back of the house, but who had limited resources, spinning was a cheap and effective way of catching fish. All the money from my paper round went on lures – Ondex, Voblex and wooden, jointed plugs – and all of my spare time was spent fishing.

With school friends I learned all the best lies on the lake and practised casting until I could put a plug or spinner on a sixpence. Five of us fished a group of shallow lakes linked by a stream. These held huge numbers of small pike, and our early success with these fish and the lessons we learned by pooling our knowledge encouraged us to try further afield. With a haversack and a net we would spend days on a lake or cover miles of the local stretch of the River Thames and the tributaries that flowed into it.

There were older boys among my fishing friends, and when they learned to drive we went further afield, piling into an old VW Beetle. We fished the Evenlode at Woodstock and King's Weir on the Thames just outside of Oxford.

With the broadening of our horizons, the fish became bigger, and the number of species increased. By 1972, I had caught pike to 14 lb from the Evenlode, perch to

3 lb, and chub to 4 lb 11 oz, all on spinners. We would have carried on spinning to the exclusion of all other methods if it hadn't been for the influence of a character whom we met and who made regular appearances in our lives at intervals as the years went by.

He was an Irish navvy – we nicknamed him 'Pikie' – who worked now and then on the roads and lived in a hostel in Oxford. His tackle consisted of a big pike 'bung' float, size 2 single hooks, 35 lb line on a big sea reel and a heavy rod. Yet he caught plenty of fish.

Pikie seemed to be on the river almost every day, always in one of his favourite spots. He used to arrive in old, scruffy clothes and a tatty black mac that he wore on even the hottest day, and a rickety old bike that carried him and his battered tackle to the bank.

His trademark was his constantly runny nose with a dew drop on the end, and this kept putting out the cigarette stub, rolled from black shag, that was always pressed between his lips. He was forever trying to re-light this cigarette, his enormous, shovel-like hands shielding the lighted match from the wind, only to have it put out again when the next nose drip fell.

He seemed ancient to us, but when he died not long ago he was said to be in his eighties, so at the time he must have been no more than in his late fifties.

I remember watching the pike in Hinksey ditch, which ran along the bottom of my parents' garden. They would come to spawn in early spring, grouped in a shallow bay, very visible from the bank, and we would cast to them for ages to get them to take a spinner or a plug, but without success.

Pikie saw us struggling to catch these fish and suggested we get some livebaits and try with them. We came back the next day with a bucketful of lovely dace we had caught, and the first bait we cast among the pike was taken straight away. The fish weighed over

16 lb, a personal best, and we had four other doubles that morning.

I learned how to catch pike that weren't interested in chasing our spinners by using dace livebaits, and had my first success on a deadbait by accident, using a bait that had been allowed to lie on the bottom in a shallow bay while I ate my sandwiches. It was taken by a pike of 19 lb, still one of the hardest-fighting fish I have ever hooked

Spurred on by this success I tried to find out more about the method from angling books in the library, but little had been written about deadbaiting by the early seventies. Later when I talked to other anglers, Fred J. Taylor and Bill Giles among them, it was surprising how many had had the same experience, landing their first fish on a deadbait by accident.

As with the discovery of livebaiting, we became convinced that deadbaiting was now the key to success, and decided to spend a lot of our time fishing with them. We struggled for many months, because we didn't understand that deadbaits should be used when you have a good idea of where fish are, and not just cast at random. We used to hurl them out in what we thought were likely-looking spots, but our sense of fish location was not great. It was only when we began plumbing depths and working out why pike were in some swims and not in others, that we started to achieve consistent success.

A breakthrough came when we brought all three methods together. One of the best ways of locating fish was, and still is, spinning, and yet spinning didn't always take fish. Follows, swirls and plucks were often all that we could provoke with artificial bait. But once we had found pike-holding areas, we could use livebaits or deadbaits in the same spot, and this improved our catches immediately.

Spinning is a very good exploratory method because it will work straight away, but fish wise up quickly and success will be short lived. However, the knowledge of holding areas that spinning provides should enable you to catch larger fish when you change to a bait.

With the addition of deadbaiting to our armoury of methods came the need for stronger rods. I knew a couple of lock keepers who built their own, and when I had saved up the £25 each for two, ten-foot, 2.5 lb test curve Bruce and Walker fibreglass blanks, I pestered them until they agreed to make them up for me.

I can still see those men now, huddled in the keeper's hut on a cold, winter's day with the heater going full blast, whipping these rods and drying the varnish in front of the fire because I wanted to use them straight away.

But the confidence they gave me was immense. Before this, I had experienced problems with the reel falling off the worn, cork handle of my old rod – something that cost me several big fish. But these new deadbait rods had screw reel fittings, the first ones I had ever used, and armed with them I felt I couldn't fail.

I also caught a lot of pike after dark, particularly in summer, when sport could be slow during the day but came alive at night. Perhaps the best night fishing water we came across was the Big Coloured Pit, so called because it was still being worked for aggregate and had the clarity of soup. It was very deep – twenty-two or twenty-three feet in places – and fished in the daytime by South Cerney AC, who held matches there. They were after the bream, and regular angling pressure pushed the shoals far from the bank during the day.

When the matchmen packed up and it got dark, the bream came in for leftover bait and groundbait and to feed at the bottom of the shelf. The pike followed them. The bream always headed for one or two spots, so location was simple. I fished it with two friends, Steve Kilbee and Nick Webb, and in one session I had fish of 21 lb, 23 lb, 24 lb and 18 lb within twenty minutes.

Other waters produced fish only at certain times of day, and you could set your watch by some feeding spells. Once you got to know when they were, you could be at various pits at the hot times and catch big fish from several waters in one day, utilising fishing time to the maximum.

I even hooked a monster on the Thames. A good roach and bream angler, Norman Howes, helped me find it. He told me about a swim where he had fished for barbel and how he had been playing one of 8 lb when it had been taken by a pike that he estimated at over 30 lb.

I fished the swim and, after catching a couple of pike, had the big one on. But the hooks pulled and I was left wondering just how big it was. Two anglers on the far bank saw me playing it. The following weekend when I went back for another go, they were in the swim.

I asked them how they had got on and they said they'd caught the big one that I had lost the week before. I asked them if they still had it, hoping they'd put it in a sack ready for a photograph. They pointed to an immense body on the grass. It weighed 34 lb 8 oz,

and they'd killed it to have it set up. I found out later that, when they were told it would cost several hundred pounds to be done professionally, they threw the pike in a dustbin.

I told them what I thought of what they had done, and how long a fish of that size takes to grow to such a weight, but it was all in vain. The damage had already been done.

Word spreads quickly when you're catching fish, and other anglers appear at the water even when you think you've kept things quiet. The next thing the banks are lined with anglers and the fish take a hammering. When they come under extreme pressure, pike stop feeding during the day. They learn not to pick up deadbaits. They feed less frequently, and less food means they lose weight.

Perhaps this is why I like to fish waters unknown to other anglers, like the one that gave me my personal best of 35lb. And perhaps it's why I like the Scottish lochs – their remoteness, their wildness and the sense of isolation that is part of the experience of fishing them.

To see a Scottish pike hit a sink-and-draw bait in shallow water and turn and dash through weed, shaking its head from side to side and tail-walking to crash down into thirty or forty feet of water is an incredible experience. There's nothing as exciting as that.

Pike – the mystery and the myth

A measure of success, no matter how small, is crucial in the early stages of any angler's development if he is to stay a fisherman for life. Looking back, I realise I had just the right amount, at just the right time. Too many failures in a row would have drained my confidence, but on the other hand too much success would have taken away the challenge. A good fish followed by a few 'blanks' and then another good catch, and the lessons that came with each session kept my enthusiasm simmering.

When I try to analyse what attracts me to pike more than any other fish, I can only think that it's the enigma of the species. For millions of years they have remained unchanged by time because they have evolved the perfect predator's characteristics – a very big mouth, large teeth, excellent eyesight and great speed over short distance.

They are hunters and foragers, just as we are, and rule beneath the water's surface without any natural enemies, just as we do on dry land. Perhaps that is part of the fascination, that and the stories and speculation about how big they grow.

We know there are much bigger pike in this country than the present record of 46 lb 10 oz. It wouldn't surprise me to hear of a 55 lb fish from a food-rich stillwater with a good supply of game and coarse fish and no angling pressure. If the two or three waters that have this potential were opened to pike anglers at the right time of year, who knows what could happen.

RODS, REELS AND LINE

I can remember a time when a rod was just a rod – not a fashion statement. The colour didn't matter so long as it did the job of putting a bait in the right place, and a fish on the bank.

Today, you get laughed off the water if your rods don't match, aren't worth at least £100 each and aren't displayed in all their glory on a stainless-steel, designer-label rod pod.

I can't be doing with all of that. You won't find me polishing rods lovingly in the evenings. To me, they are tools, and if they get knocked about in the process, so be it.

I haven't taken my rods apart at the joints in fifteen years, and I probably couldn't get them apart if I wanted to. I haven't got time to put them away neatly in rod bags and holdalls. They go straight from the garage on to the roof rack of my car. When you have very little time available to you, you don't waste precious minutes tackling up and down.

Essentially, rods perform a simple task. Choose one with the right strength of blank for the size of bait you will be using and you won't go far wrong. Three budget-priced rods, even in glass fibre, that cover three different tasks are better than one, expensive carbon rod.

If you are in doubt what to go for, err on the powerful side because then you will stand a better chance of landing a good fish. But ideally, three types of rod will cover every pike fishing situation that you are likely to encounter.

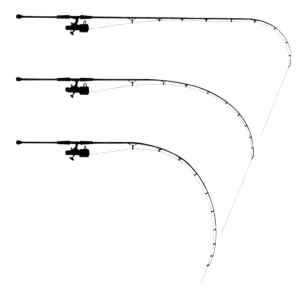

The heavy deadbait rod

A heavy deadbait rod should be capable of throwing out big baits like jack pike, large mackerel and big coarse fish. It should be able to cast a 1 lb-plus fish up to thirty yards, and make a very good rod for long-range casting, throwing a half mackerel seventy or eighty yards.

I have Armalites. They are heavy, but they sit on rod rests for most of the day so it's not as if you have to hold them for long. Armalites have quite soft actions, despite being semi-fast taper, and are sensitive and responsive when fish are being played. They are not 'broom handles,' so they are sympathetic with smaller fish.

A big pike may run a hundred yards or more with a jack pike sideways in its mouth before stopping and turning the bait. If you are going to be able to pull the hooks out of the skin of the jack, which is fairly tough, into the mouth of the quarry, which is quite bony, you need a rod heavy enough for the job.

Mine have a 4 lb test curve, semi-fast taper and are twelve feet long, two-piece, with a butt ring, three stand-off intermediate rings, and a tip ring. For long casting I find that the fewer the rings, the better, because friction is reduced. Rings no longer need to so numerous so the line follows the curve of the rod because good-quality, modern rod rings won't get grooved by line, as did the old chrome rings. The rings on mine are Seymo 200S Hardlons, a two-legged design that will stand up to knocks.

Don't be tempted into thinking that standard carp rods can do the job just as well. They are just not powerful enough because they are designed for throwing 2 oz and 3 oz leads. As pike anglers we are throwing 4 oz, 5 oz and 6 oz mackerel or a 12 oz pike as bait. Pike rods and carp rods are different animals, and you can't cut corners by getting them to double up.

Above left: Multi-purpose medium-range rods (far left and right) that I use for most of my fishing and lightweight spinning rods to work plugs.

Above right: Playing a mid-twenty on a medium-range rod. The through action of these models make them a pleasure to play fish, yet there is plenty of power to spare if needed.

The medium-to-close-range rod

The next rod in the trio is a medium-to-close-range, eleven-foot, two-piece model with a 3 lb test curve and a compound taper or 'through' action. Mine are made by Abu. These are ideal for flicking out small baits underarm on rivers, and are the rods I use for most of my fishing.

They're much lighter and easier to handle. I sometimes have a rod in my hand for nine, ten or eleven hours at a time, and can use one of these all day without it becoming uncomfortable. I can feel every knock and tap from a pike. They are even better when used with a multiplier.

I also use one for sink-and-draw fishing with trout or roach of 4 oz or 5 oz, and for livebaiting, though this rod will fish small mackerel, sardines and coarse baits perfectly well. It's a good, all-round, multi-purpose deadbait rod for medium to close-range work. The rings are Hardlons.

I have considered using lighter rods, but when you have to bully fish to keep them out of snags on weir pools or play them near sharp rocks on a big water, you can't stop them on anything lighter.

The light rod

The only time I would use a rod of less than a 3 lb test curve would be to do some light spinning, which is something I like but don't get enough time to do. I would use one of Abu's spinning rods for this type of fishing, part of a range I have designed with through actions, that perform well in a variety of situations and can be used equally well with multipliers or fixed-spool reels.

The right fittings

The biggest single bonus of making up your own rods is that you get exactly the fittings and dimensions that you want, from the number and spacings of rings, down to your name on the butt.

I have built all of my own rods, and the last one took me just forty-five minutes to ring and varnish. One thing that I never do is put my name on a rod. I was put off the practise many years ago when a bailiff came round to where I was fishing and told me it was a private water. He looked at my rod and wrote something down. 'I'm going to report you, Terry Eustace!' he said and walked away.

I've always been fond of Terry's Big Pit Pike Rods, but prior to that it was always because they are excellent fishing rods, rather than their usefulness in getting me out of a tight spot. I never did find out whether Terry at Gold Label Tackle got his collar felt for that!

The reel fittings I plump for are Fuji 18FPS screw reel fittings, which hold the reel securely without any chance of it dropping off. Add to that Fuji abbreviated rubber handles, which are warm to the touch, easy to maintain and non-slip, and Fuji butt caps and that's it. As far as I'm concerned, cork handles are a thing of the past. They become dirty very quickly, get damaged, and the cork absorbs water.

I go for rod rings with a very large diameter, as the larger it is, the longer they will take to block with ice in bad weather. I smear Vaseline in the rings in winter when conditions are bad.

Don't disregard fibreglass

On the subject of rod-making materials, I think it's high time there was a glass fibre revival. Like LP records, glass fibre was consigned to the scrap heap long before it had outlived its worth, and I for one wish I'd hung on to my glass-fibre rods.

It is still pleasant to play fish on a glass rod, it performs exactly the same tasks as carbon, and for one third of the cost. It may be heavier, but deadbait rods will be left in rests most of the day anyway.

What's more it takes knocks far better than carbon, which makes it ideal for boat fishing. Anyone who is looking for a good, cheap pike rod would do worse than contact Steve Burke at Specialist Angling Supplies, in Kent, who stocks a few glass rods.

I moved on from fibreglass because carbon blanks are very slim in diameter and suit my small hands slightly better. I can see rods becoming even lighter, thinner and, perhaps most important of all, more robust. The best may be still to come.

I also think we will see more anglers turning to telescopic rods, as the quality has come on in leaps and bounds. Some are superb, with an excellent action, very compact, ideal for when you haven't got a lot of space, easy to carry and quick to set up.

One development I have yet to see made commercially available is a one-piece rod, which would be welcomed by anglers like myself who never break theirs down. The weak point in any rod is the joint, or joints, and having tried a one-piece and found the action far superior to any two-piece I've used, I'd like to see them on sale. I don't know how many anglers would buy one-piece rods if they were commercially available, though I'm watching developments with interest.

Some anglers have strong views on whether rods should be finished with matt or gloss varnish. Mine have an anti-flash finish but I'm not sold on the idea that it makes much difference. I don't think a pike can see the glare of a rod while investigating a bait eighty yards from the bank. And even if it can, who knows whether a flash attracts pike, as it does on a spinner? In the end it's a question of taste.

The right reels

I can sum up the current state of reel design and manufacture by passing on two facts. The first is that the overwhelming majority of anglers want a reel to be black. The second is that tackle companies continue to make reels in silver, gold, electric blue, bright red and just about every other colour they can think of, decorated with crimson, white and yellow flashes.

Pike anglers want reels with big-drummed spools so that they can use them to cast deadbaits reasonable distances. They want handles that are durable and will stand up to regular use. And they want a free-spool facility.

But manufacturers don't give them what they want, right across the range of tackle. Instead they come up with gimmicks like reels with double handles and numbered clutch systems matched to breaking strains.

Only when the companies start asking anglers what they are looking for in a fishing reel and listening to their answers will we get something that meets all of our needs. Anglers are only too happy to tell them, and it's the companies listening that are doing the best business.

I use multipliers for a lot of my fishing because they suit certain styles better than fixed-spool reels, but for years I argued for a multiplier that allows you to back-wind.

You can convert most multipliers to back-wind by removing the anti-reverse dog mechanism, but I wanted an Abu 6500 that had started life with a purpose-made back wind and was made for left-hand wind and finished in black. I designed it and submitted the proposal, and finally, after all the discussions and negotiations, Abu have brought it out. It is the first sizeable multiplier to allow backwinding while playing a fish and, I believe, a major step forward in reel design.

The heavy mob

Just as there are rods that are heavy, medium-weight and light, so reels can be categorised and matched to a rod of the appropriate class. A heavy reel on a light rod will make it butt-heavy and ruin the action.

The heavy reels I use for medium-to-close-range work are Shimano 4500GT and 7000GT Biomasters, and Diawa SS3000 and PM4000. These are big, meaty reels that wouldn't look out of place sea fishing. They take 200 to 300 yards of 15 lb line – much more than you need for most styles of pike fishing, apart from drift fishing, or extreme-range casting with frozen deadbaits and 3 oz leads.

The wide spools are very long and tapered, so that more line is laid close to the surface, enabling longer casts to be made. In metal, the spools are more robust than the carbon or plastic, which I have had explode into fragments under pressure.

I load a bulk of old line, topped with 140 yards of fresh, strong monofil for deadbait fishing, so it almost reaches the spool lip. When the line is worn, after about six weeks, I turn it round by winding it on to a spare spool, so that the end that was buried is now uppermost.

Extra-large spools capable of carrying enough line to allow a float to be drifted out 200 yards or more can be bought, but I'm not prepared to fish more than 150 yards out because tackle control and effective striking then become a problem.

These big reels have fairly fast line pick-up, which you need for when fish run towards you. Wind down quickly and strike early, so that fish don't damage themselves by swallowing the bait.

A few reel grumbles

Large, torpedo handles offer a good grip on cold days and help with cranking into big fish. As you will have gathered, though, I don't like double handles. They get in the way, and I don't find them of any benefit.

Clutch drags are one of my pet hates. I never use them when pike fishing, preferring to screw them down solid and back-wind on powerful fish. When you wind down to strike a run from a pike, you need solid resistance to get those hooks home into that hard, bony mouth. If the clutch slips then you are going to lose that fish.

It's even worse when fishing at range, with enormous line stretch to overcome. You may get away with a bit of clutch slip when fishing for soft-mouthed species like carp and barbel, but not with pike. For my money, a clutch on a pike reel is about as useful as holes in a waterbed.

You can get rid of the anti-reverse while you're at it, too, as it's no use to anyone who backwinds.

Above: The old Shakespeare Sigma 060 reel had the best handle of any fixed-spool reel. The large torpedo handle provided a good grip and didn't succumb to pressure.

What I do like on reels is the free-spool facility, a trend set by Shimano's Baitrunner reels, and I would love to be able to buy a reel of similar size to those mentioned with a free-spool facility. Anglers have been asking for that combination for a long time, and I know of at least one company that has recently experimented with a reel along similar lines.

The original Baitrunner reel, the Shimano GT, has a spool and handle that is in my opinion just not man enough for the job of serious pike fishing. I've managed to bend mine out of shape, and while I'm quite hard on gear, strapping it to the roof of the car fully made up, I don't think this reel can take the knocks.

The alternative, of course, is to convert your own big reel to Baitrunner mode, or find someone who can. Several firms will sell you a Baitrunner kit conversion, and while I haven't tried carrying out the conversion or used the finished product, they seem to be a good idea.

The light brigade

The other fixed-spool reels I use are smaller, less robust versions of these heavy reels. They have lower line capacities than their bigger brothers and carbon spools, and are generally lighter and more pleasant to fish with. I tend to use these for spinning, because multipliers don't cast light baits or spinners well.

If you are fishing with anything less than 2 oz you would be better advised to use a fixed-spool reel. A multiplier will never run as freely as a fixed-spool with very light casting weights, because the weight of the lure won't overcome the inertia and friction when a spool turns on a spindle. A fixed-spool creates very little friction because line peels off the front.

Keep 'em clean

Unless you are one of the conscientious few, it's probably quite a while since you cleaned and oiled your reel. Reel maintenance is one of those things that all of us know we should do, but few of us find the time for, no matter how many articles we see about stripping down a reel and giving it a spring clean.

I'm no exception. It isn't until the reels sound a bit rough that I'll take the side plate off and give the insides a light greasing and a drop of oil... which happens only about once every five or six years.

It's worth taking the trouble, though. At the very least a noisy reel is annoying to use, and at the worst it could seize up while you are playing a fish. Then it will be the bad workman who is to blame, not his tools.

Magnificent multipliers

There's only one choice of reel for me for boat fishing, and that's a multiplier. It is much lighter, much easier to control using your thumb, and has a much more suitable retrieve rate than a fixed spool. It fits your hand like a glove and is light enough to use for the twelve or fourteen hours that summer fishing can involve.

With my thumb on the spool, I can feather the cast so that it lands lightly on the water, and feel every knock and twitch as the bait trundles along.

When lure fishing there's no danger of line-twist ruining sport, and when casting repeatedly for sink-and-draw fishing, line wear is reduced. Multipliers are ideal for the heavy lines need when fishing snaggy water because they cast them so much more easily than fixed-spool reels. And when it comes to maintenance, it's a simple matter of taking off the side plate.

Most have levelwinds to lay line evenly across the spool, and slow retrieve rates, so you are forced to reel in at the correct speed to suit a fluttered bait. There's no real need to cast far when fishing from a boat, so a fast-retrieve reel isn't necessary, except on the odd occasion when fish run towards you.

When multipliers were designed it wasn't with pike in mind, and so there are features on them that are

Left: Ignored by the majority of anglers in favour of fixed-spools, multipliers are easily the best choice for boat fishing and, with a little practise, are a joy to use.

not best suited to pike fishing, like star drags and clutches, and a permanent anti-reverse. I hope that the reel I designed for Abu will eliminate these problems.

Abu have the best on the market at the moment, the Ambassadeur 6501C, which is left handed, and in right-hand wind, probably the most popular reel in America. It is better suited to pike fishing than the 7000, which is too big, and the 5000, which is too small.

Abu's are still precision engineered and of superb quality. They are not cheap, but you get what you pay for. I haven't had to oil mine since I bought it more than twenty years ago, and it still works as smoothly as it did at the start.

They can take about 200 yards of 15 lb line, but I only put about 140 on because I know I won't need any more. You can buy spare spools for them and carry these loaded with fresh monofil in case the line gets frayed.

A reputation for being difficult

A lot of people are put off using multipliers. They have preconceived ideas about how difficult they are and soon get into trouble. The younger you are introduced to them the better, because they do take a little getting used to, but my son got the knack in ten minutes.

The way that you hold the rod when using one is another reason why some people turn up their noses. But, contrary to what people believe, it's just as comfortable to use the rod upside down as the other way up. You only need look at what sea anglers catch to realise that it works.

Most freshwater fishermen hold the rod in their right hand and wind with their left. That's what anglers want. It's the way they use a rod with a fixed-spool reel, yet manufacturers still produce multiplier reels that force their customers to swap hands when playing fish. We want to use our strongest hand to put pressure on the fish, but the handle is usually on the right.

Abu are one of the few firms producing multipliers that can be used the 'right' way round. It's time that common sense prevailed and anglers were offered a product that let them fish in the way that suits their natural preferences.

The ideal reel would be ambidextrous, but so far that hasn't got further than the drawing board.

I also use multipliers for fishing livebaits from boats, though the bait should be larger than an ounce or two, as multipliers don't cast well with anything less.

The only other reel I have seen used for pike fishing is the Alvey centrepin, which is best suited to trolling with lead-core lines. These have wide drums to prevent line-twist, which can put kinks in the wire. Anglers like Gord Burton use them regularly, but I don't. I get by with a multiplier for lead-core work, but centrepins are something I intend to experiment with in the future.

Getting on the right line

Line has a different role to play in pike fishing than in most other branches of the sport because the fish seldom see it or come into direct contact with it because it's so far from the bait.

There's no tactical dilemma involved in pike fishing. In other branches of angling, using heavier line means getting fewer bites, and using lighter line can mean landing fewer big fish. In pike fishing, though, casting and playing fish are the prime concerns, and so the requirements of pike anglers are different from those of carp anglers and match and pleasure fishermen. With a 30 lb wire trace on the end, there's no need to use a light main line to try to fool fish into taking the bait.

I have used lighter lines when long casting is required, and then I have gone down to 12 lb main line with an 18 lb shock leader, but that is only when the features I want to reach are out of 15 lb line casting range.

What qualities should line have? I look for one with a good, wet knot strength, and I look for high resistance to abrasion, for many of the lochs and gravel pits that I fish have rough boulders and bars that can sandpaper line to ribbons in a very short time.

I look for a line with a high resistance to ultra violet rays, which will cause an invisible weakening, particularly when fishing on long, sunny days in summer. And I look for a line with a resistance to wet oxidation, which causes it to deteriorate.

Although the thickness of line is not a prime concern, I like a line that doesn't glare or reflect light, with potentially fish-frightening consequences. But while a line doesn't necessarily need to have a low breaking strain to be effective, I like a line to be fine in diameter because this aids long casting, allows better bait presentation and reduces line drag when fishing on rivers.

Line diameter is something that has improved in leaps and bounds in recent years, to the extent that we're almost spoiled for choice. But the greater choice of lines has lead to a wider range being stocked by tackle shops, and so some are left on the shelf for longer.

When I buy line, I get it from the biggest, busiest tackle shop I can find, for I know that if I get a spool that's been on the shelves for months from a shop with a low turnover it could have lost as much as one-third of its stated breaking strain. And that loss is invisible. You pull some off the spool and it looks fine. It's only when you part company with a fish, and afterwards test some on a spring balance that you realise that your 12 lb line is breaking at 9 lb. Old line deteriorates fast when exposed to daylight, and a couple of outings can make its breaking strain drop dramatically.

It's high time that sell-by dates were introduced by fishing line manufacturers, and anything left on the shelves after the date has expired put in a bargain bin so that anglers can make allowances for strength loss and buy much heavier than they need.

What standard monofilament do I use? In the early days I used Platil, and then moved on to Maxima, which sinks well for deadbait fishing but doesn't take the knocks, especially when over gravel bars or submerged islands.

I then experimented with American lines, as the firms over there carry out a lot of research on how well lines stand up to wear and tear. I now use Berkley Trilene Big Game Specimen High Impact, in 15 lb, which has a diameter similar to Maxima 15 lb but wet knot strength of around 17 lb. I use this for gravel pit fishing, but bump it up to 20 lb for weir pools and lochs, and it's 20 lb that I put on my multipliers.

Berkley Trilene has excellent wet and dry knot strength, is very resistant to abrasion and very limp. It winds on to a reel almost perfectly

straight out of the box.
I buy it in 600 yard
and 1,000 yard spools,
and it isn't a great deal
more expensive than its
competitors.

But no single line
will do every job.
When I'm deadbaiting,
I like to use Maxima
because it sinks far
better than Berkley,
but if I am fishing
continuously over snags that are likely to cause
problems of abrasion, I will opt for Berkley and
apply washing-up liquid to the spool to try to
counteract its floating qualities. If I'm likely to
hit only the odd snag then I will try to get away
with Maxima.

One bulk spool will fill a number of reels
because there's no need to load more than 150
yards on to a reel.

Above: American lines have benefited from the research that has gone into how they cope with wear and tear.

Left: Berkley Trilene Big Game monofil line, which is coloured sorrel, is manufactured especially to cope with the stresses that fixed-spool reels exert during casting, retrieving and landing fish.

Braided lines

The recently-developed, HPPE braided lines have
a big future for pike anglers. I first tried them a
couple of years ago when a few brands were
imported from America but they weren't right;
they were prone to snapping on the cast or on the
strike, and suffered from bedding in on the spool.

But in the past few months as I write, the
quality has improved enormously, and there are
now several brands that are ideal for some types of
pike fishing. The chief attributes that braids have
over monofilament are their excellent abrasion
resistance, their knot strength and the fact that
they don't deteriorate in ultra violet light. They
are more sensitive when playing fish, having little
or no memory, and a much finer diameter than
monofil for the same breaking strain.

When fishing in strong winds or currents, a
fine-diameter line can make tackle control a great
deal easier. When drifting a bait under a float,
you can get the tackle to where you want it more
quickly with fine line because there is less drag.
When fishing into a headwind, a livebait can be
worked out from the bank without tiring.

The abrasion resistance of braids makes them excellent for sink-and-draw fishing, where repeated casting can damage lines. And braided lines don't need greasing to float, and this makes them ideal for livebait fishing as they do not weigh the bait down like thicker, heavier mono, and so allow it to work for longer.

I use two makes; Berkley FireLine and Berkley Gorilla Braid. The main drawback of braids is that they are not suitable for deadbait fishing because they float, which means they get towed by currents and pulled out of position by floating debris, and the bait dragged into weed. If you have to keep adjusting the line, you will keep pulling the bait out of position.

Also, the fine diameter causes problems when casting big baits, as this can make the line cut your finger like cheese wire, and cause problems with friction burns. But if you are using a multiplier, and casting a sink-and-draw deadbait, the spool takes all of the weight of the bait and the thrust of the cast, not your finger.

Can pike see colour?

As far as line colour is concerned, the only thing I know for certain is that the rods in a pike's eyes are equally attuned to picking out reds, greens and yellows, but least able to see blue. So baits dyed red, green and yellow should, in theory, be a good idea, as should lines that are blue.

Or perhaps it is better to use a line that is visible than one that is invisible, and that a completely clear line would be a disadvantage as fish that swim into line they can't see become spooked, whereas ones that swim round line are not. And no matter how visible or invisible a line is, it is always the wire trace that pike are more likely to see as they decide whether to take a bait.

I do know that if you use highly-visible lines when boat fishing you are alert to the danger of a fish running into another of your lines. And from the experiments that I have conducted, I haven't found bright lines such as fluorescent green, orange or yellow, present any pike scaring problems or to offer any disadvantages. I use the Berkley Extra Tough in fluorescent green whenever I'm fishing several rods on outriggers from the back of a boat, and I would recommend it for this.

Treating them right

I dress lines for livebait fishing with Mucilin grease, to make them float, whereas deadbait lines are treated with neat washing-up liquid and Fuller's Earth, for the opposite effect.

Trying to pick line quickly off the surface when float fishing then finding it has sunk into the weed is on a par with trying to sink a deadbait line that refuses to cut through the surface. Treating lines makes fishing less frustrating and improves tackle control. I mark the spools and keep them separate, so that they don't get mixed up.

At the sharp end

Some waters have underwater contours like the surface of the moon. If I'm forced to fish around gravel bars, submerged islands and rocky drop-offs, and they can all be fish-holding features, I run my fingers along the line at regular intervals during the session to search for signs of wear.

If I find the tell-tale signs of abrasion – any roughness to the touch or signs of shredding – I change the line, swapping spools with one ready-loaded. It's not worth risking losing a big fish for the sake of a spool of line costing £3 or £4.

In the USA, there's a neutral-buoyancy line that is oval in diameter. It cuts through the surface layer but stays just sub-surface. It's useful for fishing deadbaits in snaggy areas and on big waters with a lot of 'chop' and surface drift.

On Scottish lochs, the line needs to be kept high in the water if tackle losses are not to become a nightmare, especially when legering. I've seen anglers lose fish after fish with a standard rig that takes line along the rocky bottom.

Estate lakes, which are shallow and have a strong undertow which pulls line away from where it was cast, might also be easier to fish with such a line. I can see a great deal of scope for anglers here when someone decides to import it.

Lead core lines

When trolling over deep water is the only way of getting in touch with fish, I carry a lead-core line. The brand I use is made by Normark and sold in 100-metre lengths, marked off in a different colour every six metres to give a rough idea of the

Tying the knot

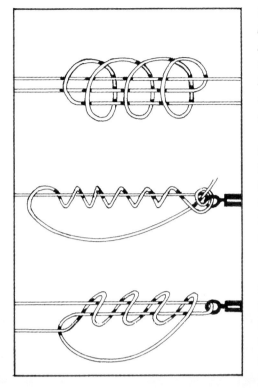

The strongest knot that I know of for joining line to the eye of a swivel or hook is the Grinner. And likewise, the Double Grinner is the strongest for joining two pieces of line.

When Fred Buller lost his legendary big pike on Loch Lomond, he didn't know that blood knots and half bloods strangle the line and decrease its diameter locally, weakening it so that it parts at less than the stated breaking strain.

Granted, it's more difficult to tie a Grinner, but it is well worth the effort as it comes close to retaining all of the line's strength. We are indebted to Dick Walker for giving us a knot that can do that.

The only times I tie a knot other than Grinner or Double Grinner is when joining line to the base of an empty reel spool, when I use a half blood knot, and

Top: The three-turn stop knot. Some people use monofil, but I don't like the thought of squeezing the line so for me it has to be a soft piece of pole elastic every time.

Centre: The straight half-blood – simple to tie but strangulation of the line against the eye is likely to lead to parting company with a big fish.

Bottom: Dick Walker's Grinner knot – well worth learning as it comes closer than any other design to preserving one hundred per cent line strength.

for tying a stop knot out of pole elastic, to set the depth of a sliding float. Since I have never had a fish take the last coil of line from my reel, I can say with hand on heart that this join has never let me down.

---

fishing depth. I have added to the markings by putting a dab of Tippex every five feet to give a better guide to how deep my bait is running when the line is out behind the boat.

It is made of thin lead, coated with a braid 'skin,' and keeps the bait deep. Trolled baits have a habit of riding up to the surface. Lead wire is ideal for this, if a little unwieldy to use. The only thing to watch for is kinks, which can cause the core to fracture if it is bent against itself too severely, and though line strength is not an issue, these sections won't run through the rod rings smoothly.

Trolling would never be my first-choice fishing method. When I fish a big water, I head for areas where I expect a big pike to be. I would much prefer to fish for that pike in a way other than trolling, but when there is nothing to help me

locate fish, or they are not where I expect them to be, I will resort to the method to cover water and to find fish in an otherwise barren expanse.

Once they are found, I will anchor and fish a static line with a deadbait, which is a more enjoyable way of catching pike, to my mind. There are those who enjoy trolling and have honed it to an art form, but for me it will always be something of a last resort.

I believe that the sort of fish I am after would prefer to pick up a static, dead or dying fish that it finds rather than use precious energy chasing a moving bait.

But make no mistake, trolling has accounted for some very big pike. If a bait flutters past a pike at the right depth and speed, it may not be able to pass up the meal. So the trolling gear goes with me.

TERMINAL TACKLE

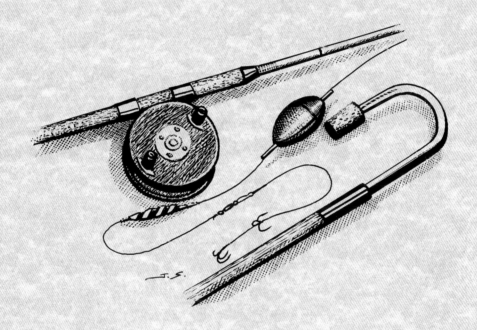

I have to put hand on heart and admit that I hate making wire hook traces. Some people love all that fiddling with bits and pieces, like making model aeroplanes from plastic kits, but for me trace making's a means to an end. I'd rather be fishing.

For that reason I tend to make my traces robust, so I can get them to last longer without kinking or wearing, and I won't have to sit down with the crimping pliers and box of bits quite so often.

Ways with wire

Wire is inherently unreliable stuff. If you get a kink in it, it breaks, and at way below the unkinked strain. Anglers who use light wire to improve presentation have to put up with it going as curly as a pig's tail, and useless for fishing, after landing one or two pike. So I never use less than 30 lb breaking strain wire.

I used to fish with 20 lb wire but it cost me a lot of fish because it kinks so easily. I don't believe I've caught fewer fish since switching to 30 lb. Even this thick wire has a diameter less than the equivalent nylon. It's not so supple as line, I'll grant you, but pike don't seem particularly fussy about what comes stapled to their food.

I use Berkley Steelstrand – a limp, seven-stranded wire that is a dark-bronze colour and unobtrusive. Some wires lose their colourng quickly so the silver comes through, but Berkley seems to maintain its colour well.

I've always thought wire rather expensive considering how easily it can be damaged. There must be scope for the development of a different trace material that is strong enough to be used over and over again, more supple than wire and yet durable enough not be bitten through by pike.

Wire does damage pike, and the sooner we find a softer material, the better. Carp anglers wouldn't put up with using a trace material that damaged the mouths and sides of fish during the fight and nor should we. I'd like to see the tackle trade come up with something better, and judging by the leaps forward being made in the manufacture of monofilament and braided lines, I think it won't be long before there is a more fish-friendly and practical alternative to stainless steel wire.

Crimping or twisting

As Shakespeare might have said, had he been an angler, to crimp or not to crimp, that is the question. Whether 'tis nobler to squeeze short sleeves of soft metal on to one's trace to secure hooks and swivels, or to twist the wire round itself after heating the end with a match.

I always crimp. It's stronger than twisting and it has never let me down, though the way you crimp is important. I flatten the crimp in the middle, and don't flatten the ends. This is so that if the hooks or swivel get bent back during the fight, there's room for the wire to move freely. Crimp too tight to the ends and the wire can fracture.

I use copper crimps made by Abu and a pair of crimping pliers with teeth of various sizes to match the size of crimp. It's important to pass the wire through each crimp three times, once on the way to the hook, once on the way back from the hook and then once again, with a short section of the free end doubled back inside the crimp, to tuck it out of harm's way. The end of a piece of wire is extremely sharp and capable of giving you a nasty cut if it catches your hand. It will also pick up weed and debris, so tuck everything in before you squeeze the crimp tight.

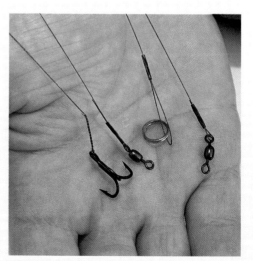

Left to right: Traces good and bad. Twisted, crimped too close, wide loop for spinning and the perfect trace.

Trace dimensions

Most of the traces in my bag are between eighteen and twenty inches long, with a few of fourteen to sixteen inches for free-roving livebait rigs. If the trace is too long with a livebaiting rig, the bait will be so far from the lead – which should be keeping it at the ideal depth – it may start riding up in the water. This can be counteracted by pinching a couple of swan shot on the trace to hold the bait down, but shorter traces solve the problem. The only ultra-long traces I use are for fishing the boulder-strewn waters of Scottish lochs, and then the traces will be twenty-four inches long merely to provide a longer, abrasion-resistant link.

If I'm using an uptrace for paternostering – see the diagram in Chapter Nine – to protect the line from being bitten through, the hook trace will be only about nine or ten inches and the uptrace the same. When livebaiting, the bait on a long trace can swim up in the water and tangle with the nylon above the uptrace. If a pike graps it then, it's goodbye to your rig, and perhaps goodbye to a pike, condemned to a lingering death. The trace

Above: Perfect traces rolled up ready to go. I will take up to forty traces with me, wound on a flexible rig roll and held in place with mapping pins. A cold river bank is no place for trace making.

should also be shorter than any weak 'paternoster' link that runs from swivel to bomb. If the bait reaches the sanctuary of the bottom, it will lie still and defeat the object of livebaiting.

Trace making is fiddly enough at home, but on the bank it's almost impossible, especially in cold weather. I take plenty of rigs, far more than I will need, wrapped around flexible, Gordon Griffiths rig rolls and pinned down with mapping pins.

If I'm heading for a water, such as a weir pool, where a catch of a couple of dozen pike could be on the cards on a good day, I will take forty traces with me to allow for those that will get kinked or lost.

The only time that I don't use rig rolls is when fishing in Scotland, or when it's raining, as rigs kept in a roll will get wet and have to be taken off and dried. For these occasions I use a plastic rig bin, which stops them getting wet and rusting.

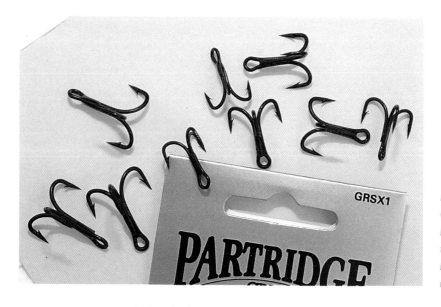

GRSX1

PARTRIDGE

Left: Partridge Extra Strong Outpoint trebles have small barbs and needle eyes. I've tried others but I keep coming back to these, which I use for much of my pike fishing.

Buy the best hooks

I've tried a lot of hooks in my time but there's only one make that has never let me down, and that is Partridge. I use their Extra Strong Outpoint trebles in black, Japanned, size 6s and 8s for deadbaiting. The size 6s are for jack deadbaits and the size 8s are my standard hooks for mackerel, sardines, coarse fish and small livebaits.

They were designed for 60 lb-plus salmon in Canada, and have slight outpoints, small barbs and needle eyes. They make excellent deadbait hooks – good and sharp, with fast-tapering points. They don't lend themselves to being sharpened, but I've never found the need. Once again, they are not cheap, but they are the best.

If you use hooks that are mechanically sharpened, you should ensure that they have needle-sharp points, or they have no chance of penetrating a pike's bony jaw. A few strokes of a diamond file will usually do the trick.

I occasionally use Partridge Parrot Beak single hook, through top and bottom lips of sink-and-draw baits, or through the root of the tail of a sardine, but I like the improved hooking capabilities that come from having two, treble hooks.

I also use the Parrot Beak single on traces for a trout livebait, using it with two trebles. The single goes in the dorsal fin, the bottom treble in the flank and the treble in the middle is left loose as a flier for better hooking.

When wobbling a trout deadbait, I use a size 4 or 6 single Parrot Beak through the top and bottom lips of the trout to retain it, and then push a piece of an elastic band over the point and past the barb to keep it in place. The other hook on the trace is a size 8 treble, which goes in the flank. It's important that the single hook goes through both lips of the trout, or the mouth will be forced open on the retrieve and presentation will suffer. If the mouth is open, the bait will spin, whereas I want it to flutter from side to side. And in snag ridden areas, there is less chance of a single hook getting caught up than a treble, with its two free prongs.

I also use Partridge Grey Shadow hooks for the Niflor Teflon coating that stops them from rusting. They've got longer points, slightly bigger barbs and wider gapes, which makes them excellent for livebaiting as they help retain the bait far better than hooks with micro-barbs. I also use them for bigger coarse-fish deadbaits because they retain them better than the Extra Strong Outpoint trebles.

They are very good on plugs and spinners, which are prone to attract rust. Few plugs come with the right size and quality of hook attached, and one of the first things I do when I buy plugs is change the trebles. Some anglers claim hooks should not be changed on plugs because those fitted give the plug its fish-attracting action. Plug firms put on hooks of a reasonable price and quality but no better than that, and I would

Right: You might think that one
swivel is as good as another, but
eye design is what holds the key

1 and 2: Diamond eye swivels
squash the line into a tight area at
the base of the eye as it's being
tied on, decreasing the diameter
locally which may lead to crack offs.

3: Snap links that work on the
keyring principle are well made and
shouldn't let you down.

4: But you can't play safer than with
a Mick McMahon design of link.

5: Berkley black barrel swivels are
bulit to withstand a 60lb pull.

6: Snap links on the loop and eye
principle have lost me big fish.

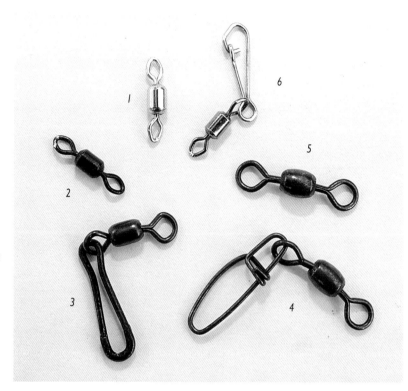

always improve the hooks, with something similar
that doesn't impair the action.

Many anglers now use semi-barbed treble hooks
in preference to fully barbed. But I have lost too
many fish on semi-barbed. With the rigs I use, a
run is struck immediately in eighty per cent of
situations. Pike won't be taking the bait
deep into their throats and there shouldn't be any
fear of fish damage. With my instant-strike rig,
pike are generally hooked neatly in the corner of
the mouth.

Sturdy swivels

You wouldn't think swivels could vary much,
but they do. Diamond-eyed swivels are bad news
in my opinion, because there isn't enough room
for line to seat itself. It gets squashed into a tight
area at the base of the eye as it is being tied on,
and when the knot is drawn together, that
shortage of space decreases the diameter of the
line locally and leads to crack-offs.

A good swivel should rotate under pressure, but
a lot of them grate and don't have much mobility.
A barrel swivel should have a snug fit between
the eye's stem and barrel, so that dirt and grit
can't get inside the barrel and cause wear. The

ones I use are Berkley black barrel swivels, which
are 60 lb breaking strain.

A *float for every occasion*

To say that pike floats are a bit behind the times
is rather like saying greenheart has probably had
its day as a rod-building material. Pike float
design is in its infancy. Look in a pike angler's
tackle box and you will probably see two types of
floats – thick, fat ones, and long, thin ones.
Imagine a match angler going fishing armed
with just two types of float. 'I've got my thick, fat
ones and my long, thin ones, so nothing'll get
past me today!'

As every matchman knows, to float fish
effectively you need a range in different shapes
and sizes to catch fish in a variety of conditions
and on several different waters. A pike angler is
no different. His float has the job of taking a bait
to where he wants to send it, acting as a bite
indicator and supporting a bait in the water.
There should be a huge range in the shops,
enabling anglers to present baits perfectly, but the
truth is, there are few different shapes for sale,
and anyone who wants something a little different
has to make his own.

That's what I do for most of my fishing. I tend to use small floats, as much of my fishing is deadbaiting, and floats for that style don't need to be big. Fishing Gazette 'bungs' have had their day. The only times I would use a big float are when fishing at range, when fishing on large, windswept waters like lochs or loughs, and in turbulent water below weirs, where visibility becomes a problem.

The colour depends on which direction the sun is coming from and the intensity of the light. With the light coming from behind me or from one side of me, I usually opt for orange-topped or red-topped floats. I don't find yellow easy to see. When the light is coming straight towards me and everything is in silhouette, I go for black, and when it is late in the evening and the light is fading fast, I change to floats with isotopes, especially if I'm planning to fish on into the darkness.

But one thing all of my home-made floats have in common is a tough coating of two-pack epoxy resin so that they will take all of the knocks that occur when driving from water to water with rods strapped to the roof rack, or when they're lying in the bottom of the boat, where they may get stepped on.

The fluted balsa float – this has an advantage over round-bodied floats in that it has concave surfaces, which help send a bait downstream

Left: The concave surfaces of a fluted balsa float trap the current, sending it downstream more rapidly than a round bodied float, imparting more movement to the bait than a standard float.

against an upstream wind. With a fluted balsa, the current gets trapped in one or more of the flutes and sends the bait on its way. Fluted floats also give a bait a bit of movement, which adds to its pulling power. I use them in two-and-a-half inch, four-inch and eight-inch sizes.

The round polystyrene float – this is a bit smaller than a golf ball and is a sliding float used in stillwaters to hold up a live 3 oz to 4 oz trout or a deadbait. Some are made from ping-pong balls, which are cheap to buy and take paint well, making them very visible. Mine are red on top and brown on the bottom. I like to use them on

Above: Round-bodied floats for deadbait fishing in stillwaters.

Above: Sliding, cigar-shaped floats, ideal for livebaiting..

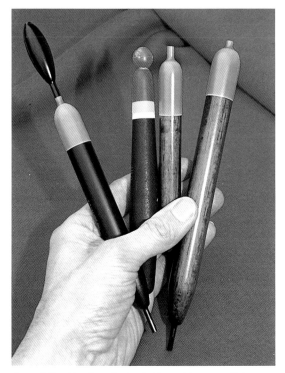

Above: Self-cocking floats for deadbaiting on big waters. Their weighted stems make them easy to cast and their fat profile and extra length help them remain visible even in a big wave.

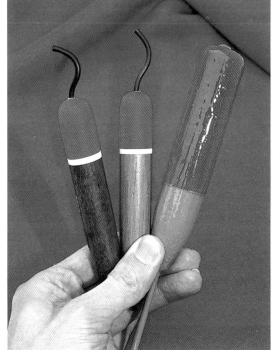

Above: Big water floats. The two trailing floats have a short length of bent tubing protruding from the top so that they lock on the line at the required depth. The third is a self-cocker for deadbait fishing.

backwaters of the Thames and the big marinas, where the flow is not strong and they can be used to carry a biggish bait slowly through a swim and right under the noses of hungry fish.

The cigar-shaped float – this is the one for trotting slowly in fast water. I use it as a sliding float for livebaiting. It's also good for fishing very

deep water and tripping a bait through. Made of expanded polystyrene, mine are in three sizes, four to eight inches in length. I couple the size of the float to the size of the bait. For most of my fishing I use one of about four inches long. Too big a float and a pike can't pull it under; too small a float and you get false bite indications from the bait. At the lower extreme, I have presented a tiny roach or gudgeon for pike swirling through shoals of fry by using a two-inch cigar float taking a single swan shot.

Pike are very delicately balanced in the water and if a float is too big it will upset this balance when they mouth the bait and move away with it, pulling them off keel and causing them to drop it. Sometimes they will be so hungry that they won't care, but on critical days when they are feeding half -heartedly, the size of the float can make a big difference.

The self-cocking float – for deadbait fishing on a Scottish loch I use these in a fat, cigar shape about seven or eight inches long and an inch and a half in diameter. They have to be this big to be seen above the waves. This design is attached bottom-end only as this makes them easier to cast long distances. Bottom-end attachment is too sensitive for livebait fishing, as the float gets pulled under and gives a lot of false indications. My self-cocking floats have a brass stem to add weight.

The sunken paternoster float – this is round, all-black, made of polystyrene, and of a size appropriate for the size of the livebait.
It will hold a bait off the bottom, where the pike can see it easily. However, there are ways of controlling the position of a bait without using a sunken paternoster.

This is one for special circumstances only, when a pop-up won't do the job, or for holding a bait in a known hotspot just beyond snags while keeping the line away from the tops of the obstructions.

The luminous float – if you haven't tried float legering at night, you haven't sampled one of the most exciting ways of catching pike. Seeing a luminous float slide away, and striking into a powerful fish somewhere down in the inky depths, adds a completely new dimension to your fishing.

My floats for this are cigar-shaped or round bodied, depending on the location, painted with luminous paint and with slots drilled in them to take night lights – usually isotope Betalights because they last the longest and so are cheapest in the long run.

Balloons – Finally, although I don't use drifter floats, if I want to get a bait out quickly into unfished water and have the wind at my back, I will resort to taking a few balloons with me and using them to drift the bait out. They get out a lot quicker than with a drifter and, after I have struck the balloon from paper clip attachment, I can go round to the opposite bank at the end of the day and pick the balloons up.

Stainless steel deadbait wobble bars

A lot of anglers are frustrated inventors. If they're lucky, a tackle manufacturer may take an interest in the idea and offer to pay royalties for each one sold.

I've been fortunate enough to have a couple of home-made products that I've used for years produced commercially. Dinsmore make the stainless deadbait wobble bars and the deadbait support links. I first used deadbait wobble bars in 1970 for fishing sink-and-draw. The early ones were made out of a length of mild steel cut to a size to suit the bait, had a hole drilled in them for the trace and were pushed inside the bait through the mouth.

They were attached to the trace by a link of wire, which was fixed to the eye of the top treble, leaving both sets of hooks free to be pinned to the bait in places that gave it a good action. If the bait got lost, the wobble bar came back because it was firmly attached to the trace by wire.

I've since used them to catch a huge number of pike, the biggest one 35 lb, which took a 4 oz brown trout fished sink-and-draw in three feet of water.

The advantages of having a weight inside the bait and not running on the line are that when you are reeling in, all of the action goes into the bait and not into a lead weight, which will swing from side to side. Leads make it difficult to cast accurately under trees and have a habit of becoming snagged when fishing over boulders.

You can fish at different depths and in restricted areas near to snags with a wobble bar, letting the bait flutter under obstructions, and when you hook a pike you are far more 'in touch' with the fish. It is particularly good for fishing in weir pools or anywhere where a lot of water needs to be covered. On gravel-bottomed rivers, a bait can be bounced along and made to look natural.

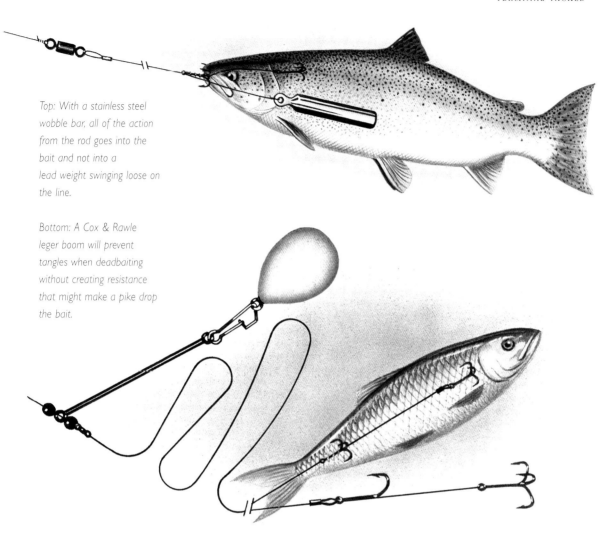

Top: With a stainless steel wobble bar, all of the action from the rod goes into the bait and not into a lead weight swinging loose on the line.

Bottom: A Cox & Rawle leger boom will prevent tangles when deadbaiting without creating resistance that might make a pike drop the bait.

Dinsmore sell the stainless steel bars in 0.5 oz, 1 oz, 1.5 oz, and 2 oz sizes for different sizes of bait, for working the bait deep or fluttering it across the surface. For a 5 oz roach I would use a 1 oz bar, and for an 8 oz chub a bar of 1.5 oz.

Deadbait support links

The deadbait support link, also made by Dinsmore, is a very light, black, plastic hook that takes all of the weight of the bait off the trace by using a spare loop of line, thus allowing the treble hooks to be pinned lightly into the bait and struck out cleanly. A full description is given in a later chapter.

Cox & Rawle leger booms

When the coarse fishing market can't provide me with what I want, I look to other branches of the sport, and this is how I came to use a sea fishing boom for pike. I wanted one that would prevent tangles when legering a

livebait or deadbaiting in rivers. I don't like having a metal swivel running freely on the main line, causing abrasion.

The Cox & Rawle boom consists of a length of plastic tube through which the line runs. It offers less resistance to a taking fish than pulling line through the eye of a swivel. It's particularly useful on silty waters when you don't want the line and trace being pulled into mud by the lead.

The lead is attached to a snap link at one end of the boom and the other end is stopped on the line by a bead and a swivel. I use 0.5 oz to 1.5 oz leads with it. It's the best anti-tangle boom I have come across. I don't know why they don't market it for freshwater fishing as well.

It's easy to overcomplicate rigs with a lot of unnecessary 'furniture' on the main line and trace, but unless the result is tangle free then your original aim won't be achieved.

A preference for pole elastic

When anglers mention stop knots, the word Powergum always seems to crop up, but I've never been happy with the effect it has on line. If you tighten it too much, it damages monofil, and I also find that it doesn't reel in easily through rod rings. It doesn't even cast very well.

When looking for a replacement, I came across soft, rubber pole elastics used by match anglers in a range of sizes. These present few of the problems that are associated with Powergum, are finer in diameter, grip just as well and are just as readily available. I buy a medium grade – colour-coded purple with a breaking strain of about 10 lb – and granny knot a short length to the line. I've tried lighter grades but anything less keeps snapping.

It reels through the rod rings easily and doesn't impede casting, and to move it I just wet the line and slide it to where I want it without doing any damage.

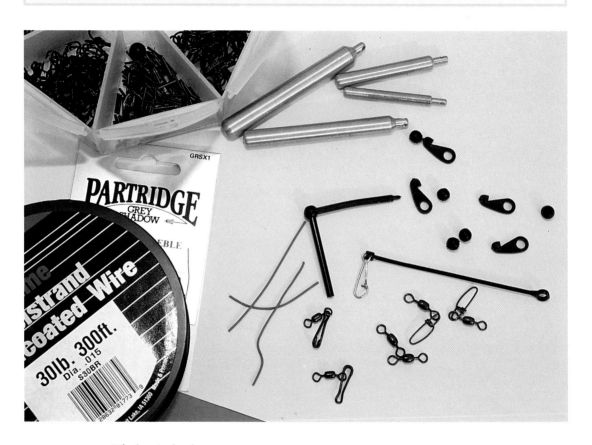

The best in beads

Dinsmore make a huge selection of beads, but I use two – both black, one with a very small hole and used above a sliding float, so that it doesn't jump over the stop knot; and a larger one to keep a boom or lead clear of the knot where the main line is tied to the swivel of the wire trace. I use plastic and rubber, both of which work well, but I haven't found floating beads to be of any extra benefit.

Lots of leads

Leads, like anglers, come in all shapes and sizes; some slim-line and built for speed, and others short and

Above: Booms, beads, barrel swivels and other bits and pieces essential for perfect bait presentation and tangle-free fishing.

dumpy. The question is, do we need so many alternatives? The shape and size of the best lead are dictated by the contours of the swim to be fished, the strength of the flow, if any, and the distance to be cast. In some swims a quarter-ounce drilled bullet will suffice, but in others a 2.5 oz Arlesey bomb will not be enough.

Generally, I use Arleseys half-ounce up to 2.5 oz with link swivels attached. If I want to hold bottom in an open area, then I use a lead flattened by putting it in a

vice and hitting it on both sides with a hammer. There are a multitude of shapes, powder coatings and anti-tangle devices, and no doubt some of them work, but I don't believe in complicating rigs unnecessarily because the less there is to a rig, the less there is to go wrong. I see very little advantage in using tubing.

The leger boom mentioned is important, as it holds the lead away from the main line. But use whatever you are confident with, and worry about what does and doesn't work when things start to go wrong.

A weak link

Snap links come in two types; those for people who like to live dangerously and those for people who play safe.

Some designs of snap link have been known to open when fish were being played. You need to look for links that cannot be pulled open by exerting pressure on the line. I will only use black Berkley Mick McMahon link swivels, which are Cross-lok designs and will never open by rod pressure alone.

I don't even use them for attaching plugs, when snap links are at their most useful. I prefer to form a large, open loop in the trace wire, going through the plug's eye, because the greater the amount of movement that the lure is allowed, the better the action. Many anglers who use plugs and lures don't realise how much they are impeding the action of their artificials by using link swivels. A big loop is a lot more successful, believe me.

Above: Proof that the deadbait support link works. A fish of 18 lb 8 oz caught at ultra-long range on a half mackerel.

Weaker line

I always carry a spool of old, weak nylon, of about 8 lb breaking strain, for making the loops that lasso the tails of bait fish and support them on deadbait rigs, and also as a weak link to the lead when paternostering.

Boxes within boxes

A big box means peace of mind. Everything I need for the day goes into one big, concertina-type tool box that I bought from a DIY store. It's well-made, and doesn't allow small items to jump from one compartment to another because the compartments fit snugly against the lid. It carries all of my terminal tackle for all of my fishing, and I know that if I've got this box, I've got all of the items I may need.

The box within the box is an hexagonal, semi-transparent Daiwa one with individual compartments with flap-up, snap-down lids, each of which contains the necessary items for making up traces – trebles, crimps, swivels and deadbait support links on link swivels, as well as beads and anything else tiny that threatens to roll away if given too much space.

I take it with me in case of emergencies and can lift it out and take it indoors when the dreaded time comes to make some more traces.

TOOLS AND ACCESSORIES

Left: Depth-o-plug, compass, thermometer and map. The items needed to successfully explore a new water may seem more useful for a day's orienteering, but careful notes made at the start will reap rich rewards later.

W hen it comes to accessories there is as much opportunity for bewilderment as in any other area of tackle.

Go into your local specialist tackle supplier and you will enter an Aladdin's cave of camouflage-coloured luggage, electronic wizardry and success-rate upping gadgetry all designed if not to catch fish, then at least to catch anglers.

It would be simple for us to turn our backs on all of it and say that none of it will help put more fish on the bank, but the truth is that in enabling us to use our time on the bank more efficiently, these products do make a difference to our level of success.

The knack is in being firm about what is and isn't needed and then sorting the best and most reliable items from the dozens of similar items made by different companies.

I try to have a firm idea of what I want before I go into a tackle shop and then match what is available to what I had in mind. Tackle dealers can be very persuasive and suggest that the alternatives they do have are just as good. You need to be brave and turn down something that is second best and go elsewhere until you find what you need.

I look at as many examples of one product as I can find, buy the best I can afford and look after it. If it's well made it will be a joy to use and will enhance the angling experience, if not your catches. Below is a list of what you would find if you rummaged around in my accessory bag.

The Depth-o-Plug

Starting with the business end of the list, a Depth-o-Plug is essential for anyone tackling a new water who doesn't want to resort to guesswork. It will help you to plumb depths to decide where to fish without having to resort to a pike float and sliding stop knot.

Basically, a Depth-o-Plug is a plastic tube with a scale of depth readings marked on the side. It goes on the end of your line and can be cast up to 70 yards. When it comes back, the level of the water inside the tube can be read against the scale to tell the depth at the spot where you have cast. You then pour out the water and cast elsewhere.

Those I've seen have been imported from America, and some have a thermometer inside. On a new water I like to work my way round the major swims, measuring the depth at regular intervals from one side of the swim to the other and back towards me, looking for any sudden drop in depth or rise on to a plateau. Make a note of any variation, how far out and at what angle, and also jot down the average depth so that you know which are the deepest swims on the water, for when the weather turns cold.

It's surprising how many anglers can't tell you what depth of water they are fishing in, or even which area of the lake is deep and which is shallow. Without this kind of information, you're relying on guesswork.

All of this work can be carried out in the close season, or when you have a couple of hours to

Right: Battered and battle-scarred, my bite alarms have seen a lot of heavy use in their lifetime but still give excellent service. They are the original Optonic alarms converted by Delkim and I would feel lost without them with me.

spare after work, It needn't encroach on fishing time. This will give you an advantage over other anglers as you build up an intimate knowledge of the contours of the water, to stand you in good stead later on.

Wide selection of alarms

Carp and pike anglers now have a bewildering array of bite alarms to choose from, with every imaginable function from simple red and green lights and a latching device that keeps them on after the line has stopped moving, to 50-metre paging devices which allow you to nip into the bushes to answer the call of nature without missing a run.

I tried a lot of alarms before I picked one that was reliable, robust and provided me with everything that I needed. Then I bought six of them and I've been using them every since. That was thirteen years ago and now they look bruised and battered, and have plenty of dents and scratches because they stay on my buzzer bars from one season to the next, but I wouldn't be without them.

They are the original Optonic alarms converted by Delkim, and if you are buying alarms now, Del produces an alarm that is just as good. The battery can now be changed without dismantling the whole alarm.

The alarms take extension leads which run to a sounder box that I hang in my car for night fishing when I can park near the water in foul weather. But the sounder box certainly isn't an alarm clock for when I go to sleep, which for caring pike anglers is the nearest thing to a criminal offence.

The alarms have volume and tone controls for when I want to keep noise to a minimum. Then I will turn them down as low as I can and sit close by. On normal volume and with regular use, I usually get twelve to fourteen weeks out of a set of batteries.

On gravel pits, where there is no flow and little debris to foul the line, I use Backbiter alarms and fish with the bale arms of my reels open. However, on rivers these keep getting set off by the current, so I use the Delkims and the Baitrunner facility on my reels with the bale arms closed.

Rod rests and buzzer bars

Most of the time my alarms are attached to rod rests rather than buzzer bars because it is only when I have a great deal of space, such as on a large, open, gravel pit, with pure gravel banks running for hundreds of yards, that I can angle the lines anywhere I want from the side-by-side arrangement without interference from bankside vegetation.

My buzzer bars are made of stainless steel, which takes the knocks. The front bar measures fourteen inches and the rear bar ten inches. This gives me a vee formation, with the rods pointing at different angles.

Above: On gravel pits, with no flow or debris, I use Backbiter alarms.

I like to keep the tips of the rods apart to cut down on tangles. When a fish kites towards the second rod, I have a few seconds more to sink the line. I like to have the rod tip pointing towards the bait, to cut down on line drag through sharp angles, but angled rods mean I can position baits further apart.

Overall, I prefer to use single rod rests because I am less restricted than by having the rods side by side. A lot of anglers who use buzzer bars let the direction they're set dictate where they will cast. Or if they do put a bait down the bank, the rod's still in their buzzer bar set-up, too far away. A pike will make a beeline for bankside vegetation, and may become snagged before they can apply any pressure to stop it.

The rear rod rest heads I use with a buzzer bar are stainless steel and U-shaped, made by a friend, which are welded to a bank stick. They fit the rod butts exactly, so that the rods can't be pulled into the water if the line gets jammed or wrapped round the handle.

For single rod rests, I use stainless rear rests made by Solar Tackle, which are very robust. I used to use plastic ones but they kept snapping, so stainless is worth the extra cost.

The bank sticks I use are Dinsmore Powerdrive, which have a screw thread to enable them to penetrate even hard banks, using a T-bar to turn them from the top. Some anglers prefer rod pods, but I find them big and cumbersome, especially if I need to move swims. For anyone keen to respond to what's happening on a water as conditions change and fish move around, I believe they're more of a hindrance than a help.

I also won't buy telescopic bank sticks with thumbscrews, as these will seize, break or rust sooner or later and become a source of irritation. Pinewood sell a telescopic bank stick that locks on a friction principle, so the height can be varied without the need for knobs or attachments.

Carry a notebook

You may not fancy the idea of taking a notebook with you when you go fishing, but if you want to build up an accurate picture of a water's contours, you need to note down the data rather than rely on your memory.

I draw a map of the water and its surrounding area, including inlets, outlets, submerged islands and any feature that will help pinpoint a productive spot on the lake.

If I'm keeping an eye on a water where excavation work is still in progress, there may be a chance to take pictures of it before it fills with water, which will be a great advantage in years to come. When it comes to knowing a water's contours, even an echo sounder can't compete with a chance to see a gravel pit before it is flooded.

The weather can help you to get to know a water better. Occasionally you will get a mixture of sunshine and cloud, with the sun bursting through the cloud momentarily at just the right angle to illuminate the contours of a clear water, showing underwater features you didn't know were there. With a notebook at hand you can add these to your plan and investigate them on future visits.

As you catch fish and spot others in the margins, make a note of where you saw or caught them, at what time of day, in what conditions, in which month of the year and on what bait – even down to the water temperature. They need only be brief notes but they will be enough to point you in the right direction in the future.

Lost without a compass

One of the best ways of locating fish on a gravel pit is to head for the north east corner, for reasons explained fully in chapter seven, yet finding these banks will be a problem without a compass.

Few anglers, even good ones, carry one, yet you can't tell wind direction accurately without a compass, nor whether a bank is sheltered from cold, easterly winds. Add an arrow pointing north to your map of the water so that you can include compass bearings in your calculations of where to fish given the wind direction over the previous few days.

When you've decided which bank to try, move in with the Depth-o-Plug and find out if you've got the right depth of water and if there's a feature that may hold pike.

Sunglasses and hat

Sunglasses have a three-fold use for anglers, apart from making us look hip and cool. They protect our eyes from reflected glare, they shield them from hooks and other sharp objects swinging

Barometers and thermometers

There's a direct correlation between atmospheric pressure changes, temperature changes and the chances of a successful day's fishing. A glance at the barometer and thermometer hanging on the garage wall every time you go out, and a note of what it read when you were successful, will give you an idea of the best conditions for fishing. Some people have garden ponds and peer into those before leaving to see how active the fish are. Others take the temperature when they arrive, and set great store by the readings at different times of day.

Certain waters respond best in particular temperatures and pressure cycles, and until you make a note of these and compare them with your record of catches, you won't fully appreciate how the pieces of the jig-saw fit together. There won't be one condition that brings pike on the feed on all waters. Each one will be different. But when you know which water will fish best under what conditions you can improve your success rate by letting past experiences of pressure and temperature dictate where you go and when, and what techniques to use.

All of the information you can put together will help with the overall picture, and the longer you carry out this research and the more thorough you are, the sooner you will see a pattern emerging. The most successful anglers only go out when they know conditions are right, and while they may miss out on an odd, maverick fish or two that doesn't obey the rules, they will save themselves a lot of time and trouble fishing when nothing is feeding.

After a while you get to know instinctively when conditions are just right, and you are going to catch something. If that happens to be in midweek when you have only a couple of hours to spare, so be it. It is better to fish for two hours when conditions are right than to wait for the weekend and fish all day when they are not.

around near our heads or flying back towards us when we lose a fish at the net, and if they are polarised, they enable us to cut out surface glare when spotting pike and hotspots.

In theory we could do without them, but it's surprising how much of a headache you can get

from the water after looking at the surface all day. It's a combination of the length of time, anything up to 16 hours a day in Scotland in summer, the strain of concentrating on a float and the problems caused by glare on the water's surface that cause the headaches and make polarising glasses essential for many fishing situations. There are a lot of good ones around these days, albeit at a price, with Ray-Bans and Optix being as well made as any.

To get the most from the polarising effect you should also wear a broad brimmed hat or cap, which will shade your eyes and keep your head warm. Baseball caps are excellent for this, and the best ones have neck protectors to keep the sun off your neck.

I like to wear a white hat in summer, to reflect the sun, and a camouflage one in winter, but I know some people are sticklers for always turning out in drab colours from head to toe. I was like that once myself. I went through a phase a few years ago of painting every item of tackle I had NATO green, right down to my flask. I even gave my stainless buzzer bars a lick of paint, too, but you live and learn.

Above: More enjoyment can be had by travelling light and casting as you walk, without the clutter of rod holdalls and bedchairs.

The trusty packaseat

Carrying gear to the waterside isn't a problem on a small stillwater, when a simple carryall can be used. But for river fishing, when a roving approach is essential, you may only be in a swim for a matter of minutes and may move swims dozens of times in a day. Your selection of tackle is scaled down because you're covering several miles of river, but you still need some sort of bag and perhaps a simple seat.

I have an original Efgeeco Packaseat, which is now seventeen years old, and it does both jobs in one. Made on a lightweight aluminium frame, it is large enough to take plastic boxes of terminal tackle, rig rolls, scales, sacks and so on, with pockets for bank sticks, but is still light enough to be swung over a shoulder without weighing me down.

The bait – half a dozen mackerel, a dozen sardines and a dozen freshwater fish – also goes inside. As I'm wearing waterproofs, the umbrella can stay at home.

A large part of the enjoyment of river fishing is travelling light and casting as you walk, unencumbered by bedchairs and rod holdalls. Anglers used to fishing stillwaters often can't make the transition to the roving approach required on rivers. They try to scale down their stuff but they can't bear to leave anything behind. Only when they've walked four miles and are too worn out to stand do they find the resolve to leave some of it behind on future trips or go back to fishing stillwaters.

Echo sounders and fish-finding devices

I wouldn't be without a fish-finder when tackling a big water I know little or nothing about. It's like having a third eye that can see beneath the waves. I use mine to sort out swims on vast strips of water like Scottish lochs or Irish lakes, or very big sections of river.

Most current models come in 20° or 53° transducers, though I find a 20° beam too narrow to give a useful picture, particularly over shallow water. The 53° gives a far bigger window. Sounders work by sending ultra-sonic signals through a transducer mounted on the back of a boat. These bounce back from whatever is below and return to the transducer to be translated into patterns on an LCD screen. Only trial and error will teach you how to interpret what you are looking at.

Some offer 3-D viewing, and the latest models have a side scanner that picks up signals from the side of the boat, increasing the area covered, and show objects on screen as hollow fish. Most of them have a grey-line feature that enables the user to tell how solid the bottom is, from soft mud to hard rock or something in between. Their built-in simulators allow someone unfamiliar with them to practise using them indoors until they are proficient enough to benefit when they get out on to the water.

From the LCD readout you can pick out a lot of features. Often, the places that look good from the bank turn out to be too deep or too shallow or have a bottom that isn't to the pike's liking. In lochs, I look for drop-offs near to a feature, or gentle slopes in rivers, and search the area around them or work down both banks of a river, putting the sounder on the left and exploring that side of

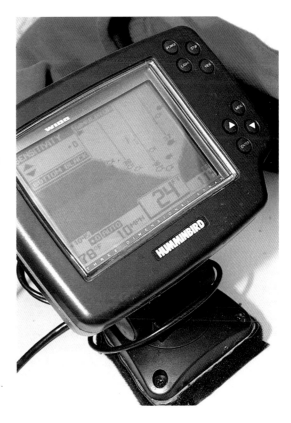

Above: I wouldn't be without a fish finder when tackling a big water. It's like having a third eye that can see beneath the waves.

the river and then coming back downstream on the far side with the sounder on the right.

Pike love snaggy areas because they give them cover from which to spring an ambush, and the closer you can get to these areas without losing tackle, the better. In rivers I like to fish around weed beds, lily pads and debris left over from old weirs, which I can locate with the fish finder.

I don't use it to find pike because there's no way of telling what species you are looking for. You might be dropping your deadbait in the middle of a run of game fish or a shoal of gudgeon.

In the early days, I wrote off areas that didn't show fish on the screen. On one occasion, I drifted over a perfect drop-off on Loch Awe, found nothing, and was tempted to move off to another feature. But I decided to stay put because I knew fish fed there at a certain time in the morning, before moving back out into open water. Right on cue, pike started arriving from other areas of the loch, visiting the swim to feed before moving back out into open water.

Fish finders are only as good as the person operating them, and getting good is a matter of experience. They are no more a short cut to success than learning to cast a long way or devising a new way of presenting a bait. Using them successfully is a skill that's well worth acquiring, and I have no qualms about taking one with me.

Fish-holding features come out of the blue

I use an echo sounder when a bankside feature suggests that there could be a fish-holding contour in that area, but I also like to have it switched on while I'm just travelling up-river, because features can turn up in the middle of nowhere.

I once came across an area with a sudden drop in depth on the Thames, where the bottom went from seven feet to fifteen. This depression held a massive head of bream, and it has produced some excellent catches of pike for me, but it was in an otherwise completely featureless and barren stretch of river. I later found out it was the site of an old weir pool that had been dismantled years ago, but if I hadn't had the echo sounder switched on as I motored upstream I would never have found it.

The model I use at the moment is a Humminbird Wide 3-D Vision, which will set you back between £500 and £600 at a specialist tackle shop or direct from the importers Cetrek Ltd, of Poole, in Dorset. They are very reliable, totally water resistant and very robust. Fitting them is easy and mastering the basics is simple. The real skill comes with practise.

Mine runs off a sealed-for-life, twelve-volt motorcycle battery, from which it will work for two or three days before needing a recharge.

Is a downrigger worth the outlay?

If you are seriously into trolling – and there are a lot worse ways of searching a large expanse of seemingly featureless water – it may be worth investing in a downrigger.

Basically a downrigger is a device that attaches to the gunwale of a boat and has a weight that will take a trolled bait down to a pre-set depth and keep it there. It is at its most useful on a concrete banked, man-made reservoir where the bottom is even, such as the two bowls at Farmoor. If the downrigger has to be adjusted continually to negotiate changing contours it can be awkward to use.

On one occasion at a trout reservoir, the pike were feeding 20 feet down in 40 feet of water, and anyone who had a downrigger and could troll a bait at that depth was more successful than those anglers pulling their baits through that feeding layer from below the fish, and only catching one or two.

Canon make the best ones, but they are rather expensive. You'll need to part with £300 for a really good one. This will have a control on it that allows you to regulate how deep your bait is running, something that cannot be achieved with certainty when trolling without such a device. A quick-release stacker, which is a pincer rather like a clothes peg, keeps the line attached to the lead ball at the right depth until a fish pulls it free.

I have one that slots into a platform I built on my boat because I have found downriggers work better when attached at the transom of the boat rather than the gunwales.

Considering the financial outlay, you will need to be using a downrigger a lot to make it worth the investment. The opportunities to fish even-bottomed waters for pike are rare, and even when they do present themselves it is rarely in the warm weather needed for pike in such deep waters to be active and intercepting a moving bait.

Binoculars for a clearer picture

Binoculars aren't just to watch the wildlife in between action. It's surprising how much more you can observe through a pair of 'bins.' Grebes feeding in one area at distance, fish topping or being chased, or pike swirling are all valuable clues. If there's a big head of fry on the water and the grebes are staying in one spot, it's a reasonable bet that one or two good pike are around.

On warmer days you may see a dorsal fin out of the water at the back of an island, especially in a flat calm, or a fish strike in the weed, and if you're float fishing you can fish at longer distance without eye strain using binoculars. In the course of a long day it also makes a welcome break to look around the water now and then just to see what's going on.

Maps for people going places

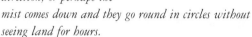

mist comes down and they go round in circles without seeing land for hours.

There is an excellent admiralty map of Loch Lomond (see A love for lochs) that charts all the depths and is very accurate. Trevor Moss at The Tackle Shop, in Gainsborough, sells it for around a fiver. I also use Ordnance Survey maps for any area of the country I am investigating, and these are sufficiently detailed to allow me to pinpoint a water.

For river fishing, Stanford's Map of the Thames

shows slipways, mooring points, car parks, lock gates, weirs, access points, footpaths, in fact everything you could want to know when tackling the river as a newcomer. There are other maps that show the features of rivers like the Hampshire Avon, Dorset Stour and River Wye in a similar way.

I coat my maps in clear vinyl so that it doesn't matter if they get wet. As maps are always being bent and folded, this also adds considerably to their life span.

Mine are fairly cheap Tasco 8 x 30 zip-focus ones. They do the job and stand up to getting knocked around, trodden on and dropped, which happens, inevitably, when you're fishing. I don't think its worth buying expensive binoculars because they come in for so much abuse, but it's definitely worth having a pair of some sort.

The ultimate landing net

Too many anglers have landing nets that will let them down at a critical moment. They wouldn't dream of using old line or rusty hooks but they keep using the same, shop-bought landing net with its frail, worn front cord and risk losing a big fish when it snaps, leaving them without a net.

I gave up on shop-bought landing nets years ago and made myself a sturdy net that can be repaired at the water. It has served me well ever since.

The arms are made of solid fibreglass and the spreader block of solid aluminium. Hollow glass-fibre arms snap or get trodden on, and nylon spreader blocks break. I've glued a cat's eye to the

block for ease of location at night and have a slot for an isotope for the same reason.

The arms measure forty-eight inches each and are made from the tops of two boat rod blanks. The ends of both have aluminium tips glued into them and have a cord of 60 lb to 80 lb nylon-coated wire – which will stand up to being prodded into gravel – secured in an aluminium cap that screws on the end. If the cord should break, it can be repaired on the bank by unscrewing one of the ends, unlike shop-bought nets, which cannot be saved.

The aluminium tips have two pieces of plastic tubing that bend over them to stop them sticking through the mesh and damaging the net.

The net is minnow mesh rather than bream mesh, which is heavy in flowing water, but the finer the mesh the easier it is to get hooks out. Mine is three feet deep and doubles as a landing net for eel fishing.

The screw-in handle is about five feet long and made of hollow fibreglass, as carbon fibre is more expensive and unnecessary, with an alternative two-and-a-half foot handle for boat fishing. If you still want to struggle on with the cord net you are using, invest in a repair kit from Dinsmore, so that if the cord breaks while you're on the bank, at least you won't be left without a net.

When I'm fishing a lure or sink-and-draw style and I'm likely to land a lot of fish that have a flying treble hanging loose outside their mouth, I use a net

with a border of three or four inches of a smooth, vinyl material around the rim, which doesn't catch on treble hooks. It was introduced by Abu last year and is the first purpose-made lure net with anti-snag material on the market.

Above: Solid aluminium spreader block and solid fibreglass arms. I gave up on shop-bought landing nets and made myself a sturdy one that is built to last.

Dual purpose unhooking mats

If I can get an item to do two jobs instead of one, I will. Keep sacks can double as unhooking mats on a reasonably soft surface like grass, and save on space when you're on the move. The best sort are zip sacks, which avoid all the fuss and time wasting of draw cords and knots.

A couple of firms make unhooking mats and sacks combined, and of these, ones by Wychwood and Specialist Angling Supplies are among the best.

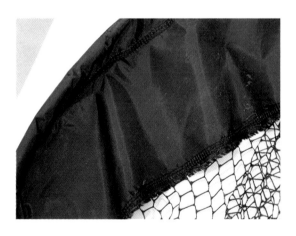

Above: A landing net with an anti-snag border prevents a lot of problems caused by treble hooks tangling with the rim.

Scales that are man enough

These should be accurate, easy to use and compact, as well as weighing to British record weight. Mine are 56 lb Salters, which are all of these things. I've yet to catch a pike that takes them to their limit.

But the future could well lie with digital scales, which are capable of weighing down to hundredths of an ounce. Salter have brought out a set that weigh in lb and oz as well as kilos and run off an HP2 battery. They do cost £80, but are strong and accurate and should last a lifetime if looked after.

Sling as a safety precaution

So long as it's big and soft and has two pieces of strong cord attached firmly, any weigh sling will do the job. Mine is made of nylon with a rubber lining and will weigh a fish of over 40 lb.

If a fish is particularly large or lively I like to put it back in the sling after weighing and photographing it, and use this to carry it down to the water. It only takes a trip or a stumble with a fish in your hands to lead to an accident that could cost the fish its life.

Essential forceps

In the words of the advert, 'don't leave home without them'. The safety of the fish you catch depends on your having at least one pair of artery forceps to remove hooks from gristly corners of mouths and inaccessible parts of the throat.

My eight-inch and twelve-inch forceps go with me on every trip. Both are of the straight kind, as I can't bear curved forceps. Have them ready to hand, use them quickly and get the fish back as soon as you can.

Invaluable knife and scissors

If you're preparing deadbaits like mackerel on the bank you'll need a very sharp knife to do the job. The old saying that it's easier to cut yourself with a blunt knife than a sharp one is very true. A sharp knife requires little effort, so there's less force involved and less likelihood of a slip and an accident.

My teeth will bite through light nylon but I draw the line when it comes to 20 lb, and so does my dentist. A strong, sharp pair of scissors are well worth having.

Hand towel for messy tasks

Some people think nothing of chopping up a mackerel, throwing the head and guts into the margins by hand, and then tucking in to their sandwiches. I'm not one of them. I may fish for a week at a time in Scotland, sleeping under the stars, but I still preserve a little self respect.

I always take a towel with me to clean my hands after preparing bait and handling fish. Apart from the hygiene aspect, wet hands on a cold day are as much fun as toothache.

Hands-free torch and headlamp

A hands-free light source makes a big difference when you're night fishing, for everything from unhooking fish to brewing tea. Petzl makes some excellent ones, in Mini, Medium and Mega sizes, with battery packs and headbands. The Medium size seems to have the best battery life.

All are waterproof and have a spare bulb in the torch head. I've used them for ten years and would recommend them heartily.

A powerful lamp attached to a motorcycle battery can be an aid to fish location if used in the

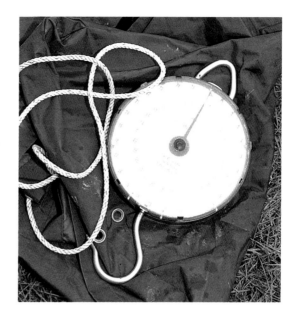

Above: A set of sturdy, accurate, easy to use scales will stand you in good stead. Make sure they're man enough for your dream fish.

clear, shallow water of a gravel pit after dark. When you turn on the lamp, pointing it directly down into the water from a boat in the shallows or from the bank, fish big and small are caught in its beam and stunned for a few seconds, like rabbits in a headlight beam.

They don't move, and in up to fifteen feet of water you can see several pike huddled in a hotspot that would be well worth trying another time. You even have time to guess their size before they move off. I once found a feature well out in a gravel pit that held six 20 lb pike. I know they were that size because I caught four of them the next day.

This tactic works best from a boat because the water is just a little bit deeper. It needs to be clear, though, but in the right conditions it's surprising how much it will pick up.

I will only use it as a last resort, though, when I'm really struggling on a water. I can see the purists among you wincing at the thought of chasing after fish with a powerful lamp, but is a light source any more unreasonable than a boat, for instance?

Only you can decide whether it's ethical or not, but if it means the difference between success and failure on a difficult water where location is the key, it takes a strong man to ignore it.

PIKE

– a fragile quarry –

Pike have got an image problem. It's not their fault, but somewhere along the line people — the non-angling public in particular – have got it into their heads that they are Britain's nearest thing to crocodiles.

Tales abound of these monsters of the deep engulfing ducklings, small dogs and the legs of swimmers; myths of huge, black-hearted fish from whom nothing and no one venturing into the water is safe. The only good pike is a dead pike, and anyone brave enough to catch and kill such a tyrant is a modern St. George slaying a dragon.

And the myth persists, even among experienced anglers, who should know better. Some matchmen still kill every pike that comes near them, and small boys step on them or kill them rather than face removing the hooks from their fearsome jaws, lined with row upon row of razor-sharp teeth.

The pike's a victim of a bad press. If he looked as cute and cuddly as a baby seal there wouldn't be a problem.

The irony of the image most people have of pike is that, far from being indestructible, armour-plated warriors, pike are probably the most delicate of coarse fish.

To everyone, anglers included, they look big and powerful, but the truth is that they can't stand rough handling. When removed from the water they are extremely vulnerable, especially in inexperienced hands. And the bigger the pike the more vulnerable it is.

When to strike

Pike anglers have to take their share of the blame for damaging pike. Part of the problem of their quarry's suffering stems from the fact that pike anglers use big baits that have to be turned by the pike through ninety degrees before they can be swallowed, and so the 'bites' or runs can't be struck immediately. In most instances, runs need to be left for a few seconds to allow the pike to engulf the bait.

There will always be a freak fish that takes a bait straight down, either out of habit or hunger. On some days, pike will wolf baits back, and on others they will rush off some distance with them before swallowing, especially if they have competition from other, perhaps bigger, pike. You can never know for certain how a pike will behave and what mood it will be in, and so accidents are inevitable.

I give pike no more than five to ten seconds before I strike, whether it's a screaming run or just a twitch, but even that can be too long. Judging the strike is a very individual thing. It's something that inexperienced anglers have to learn, water by water, and a certain proportion of the pike they hook are going to suffer because of it. Any system of trial and error will always produce its casualties.

I have fished for pike for most of my life and built up enormous respect for them. I would rather lose a pike, no matter how big, than deeply hook it. I don't like damaging fish, and having to retrieve hooks from deep inside a pike spoils my enjoyment because I have caused suffering – the last thing I want to do. If a big fish throws the hooks and gets free, it can always be caught again, but one that is damaged may be lost for ever.

It isn't the same in carp fishing. Carp don't run the same risk because single hooks are used and the strike is instant. Indeed, the fish often pricks itself when a bolt rig is being used, and the angler merely finishes the job by pulling the hook home. Treble hooks and time delays are unique to pike fishing, but the caring pike angler will find a way to avoid damaging his quarry.

Why does it happen?

There are three main reasons why pike are deeply hooked:
- Because the run was not struck early enough;
- Poor bite indication or detection;
- A poor rig, with hooks placed too far down a deadbait.

You alone can decide when to strike, and you must examine your motives for waiting longer than normal. As far as bite detection goes, you owe it to your quarry to use reliable alarms with fresh batteries and to stay close enough to your rods to reach them quickly.

Above: I would rather lose a pike, no matter how big, than deep hook it. Causing suffering to one is the last thing I want to do.

If you use Backbiter alarms, you should fish a tight line to the run clip so that it will sound at even the slightest dropback run and respond by releasing the line to even a small pluck, before a fish has time to swallow your bait. There are times when that is all the indication you get and if you don't get a sign that there is interest in your bait, everything may have been swallowed by the time you realise you've got a run.

That leaves rigs, and this is the area that I looked at when trying to overcome the problem of occasional deep-hooked fish. If a rig could be devised that could be struck almost instantly, swallowed baits would be a thing of the past.

Protection for pike

The motives for developing the instant-strike rig did not spring purely from a need for conservation. Pike on one of the waters I fished with friends were becoming cautious after they had been caught a few times. They would pick up a bait, swim a short distance then drop it.

We needed a rig that could be struck almost instantly, which would turn those aborted takes into captured fish. It was a question of where to place the hooks so that they could gain a hold in the pike's mouth immediately the bait was picked up.

Fishing at range

Fishing at range can also cause a delay to the strike, either through the amount of time it takes to wind down to the fish or because the strike is ineffectual. A proper striking technique is needed at long range if a fish isn't to gain an extra few seconds and swallow the bait.

After a few seconds, wind down hard, point the rod towards the bait and make a sweeping strike, bringing the tip of the rod from the surface of the water upwards. This will pick up any slack line and take a considerable amount of stretch out of it, too. The clutch should be locked solid to avoid any slipping of the spool, which would lessen the impact.

One strike may not be enough at range. The process may need to be repeated to keep in touch with the fish, by pointing the rod at the bait again, winding down and making a second, full sweep. Only then will you be in full contact with a properly-hooked pike.

At close range, with a softer, through-actioned rod, strikes are more of a pull than a sweep, to absorb the shock. Anything more than that can lead to a crack-off on the strike, especially if the fish moves away from you as the hooks go home.

The traditional positioning of hooks in a bait owes more to supporting the bait's weight in the cast than hooking a pike on the strike, and doesn't use treble hooks to their full potential.

I've never been happy with the depth to which hooks have to be impaled in a bait in order to keep it in place during the cast. It takes an almighty strike to then pull those hooks clear and into a pike's bony mouth when a run materialises, and at range, it is difficult to apply enough force even to pull the hooks clear of the bait.

We had noticed that a large proportion of the pike we played and lost still had the bait in their mouth, attached to one or more of the trebles. It made me realise that unless the hooks were struck clear of the bait they often failed to take hold in the mouth of the fish and that if I could find a way of supporting the weight of the bait by another means, the hooks could be nicked lightly into the bait and struck clear. I could also choose where to position the hooks so that an instant strike could be made.

The best way we found of supporting the weight of the bait was with a large loop of strong line. This was passed over the tail of the deadbait with a couple of half hitches to hold it in place. The other end of the loop was passed through one of the eyes of the swivel at the top of the wire trace, and held in place with a piece of folded, soluble PVA tape.

The PVA was in place because we didn't want a permanent attachment to the top of the trace, which might get in the way of the strike, but we needed something that would support the bait on the cast.

One early problem was that a lightly hooked bait could get pulled off the hooks when retrieved through weed, providing pike with free meals. There are times when a pike will pick up only one bait all day, so we wanted it to be the one we were using, not one that we had lost. We found a way to avoid leaving the bait behind; by passing the trace through the loop of line attached to the bait, so that when the PVA dissolved and the strike was made, the loop slipped down and caught on the trace and the bait came back.

At the start we used a pair of size 2 Edgar Sealey Parrot Beak single hooks on the wire trace, but lost a lot of fish on the strike. But when we switched to trebles the success rate improved enormously. A pike's mouth is more than a match for single hooks. The bony surfaces offer few hookholds, and you need more than one point to find a purchase.

But the principle worked. The hooks came out of the bait easily and into the fish, and by positioning them further along the bait, nearer the head, we were able to strike early and get a hookhold.

We could also cast soft baits like sardines further without the hooks pulling out. A few turns of fuse wire around the root of the tail made a holding place for the loop of line.

The only later modification was to switch from PVA tape to a purpose-made deadbait support link at the top of the trace, which supports the loop much better and brings a welcome end to fiddling with soluble tape with wet hands on rainy nights.

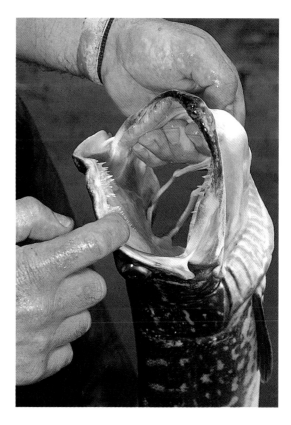

Above: With up to six hundred teeth in their armoury, pike don't take any prisoners when their powerful jaws clamp shut.

Livebaits need longer

No rig is completely 'instant strike', though. The only times when I've stood holding a rod and wound down and struck straight away is when fishing a tiny livebait in Blenheim, and on Theale Lagoon when fish were preoccupied with taking fry, and then it was because they were engulfing the bait instantly.

In most cases, deadbaits tend to be swallowed sooner than livebaits. Pike know that a fish is dead and is not going to escape and so they pick it up to swallow it straight away, whereas a livebait has to be caught and killed by grabbing it across the width of its body.

A fish taken head-on is less likely to be wounded fatally at the moment of being seized. Taking a food fish sideways enables a pike to puncture the internal organs, which are located along the belly, with the longer teeth of the movable, lower jaw, while the smaller teeth of the fixed, upper jaw act as a grip. Only then, when the fish has been killed, can it be turned to be swallowed, usually head first.

For this reason, takes while livebait fishing need to be given a little longer, say fifteen to thirty seconds. The bigger the livebait, the longer you may need to wait for the pike to take and turn it. Occasionally, when I have been fishing with a big roach or bream as bait, I've given runs a bit longer, but if you've ever seen a big pike taking a live fish you'll realise it can make short work of its prey. It may seize and wound a fish before it turns it to swallow its prey, but this happens quickly, before the fish can escape or another pike can move in and threaten to steal the meal.

Watching film of pike feeding in slow motion, I have seen that if the food fish is facing the pike as it approaches, it will try to dodge to the left or right of the pike to avoid being caught. The moment that it turns away, it is taken most easily, while it is side-on to the pike. Very few fish go upwards and over the pike's head, which is their best means of escape. It's nature's way of providing pike with enough sustenance, just as nature makes roach shoal up for safety in numbers.

Jack deadbaits

The physical size of a 2 lb or 3 lb jack pike bait dictates that any pike eating it has to be given longer, and I have waited from thirty seconds to two or three minutes for a fish to take one properly, depending on what the pike is doing with the bait.

The big difference between a take on a small deadbait and one on a jack pike is that successful hooking relies on your interpretation. When a pike takes a jack it sends vibrations up the line, often quite violent ones, and with experience these can be used to judge what is happening to the bait, and what the pike is doing. At some stage during the head-shaking and jerking on the end, there comes a moment when you just know that the bait is about to be swallowed, and you have to act fast.

The length of time this takes to happen varies from water to water, with the seasons, and with the mood of the fish. Sometimes pike will take the bait back to their lie and turn it and begin to swallow it. I wait for the run to stop, and I've known that to be 80 yards or more. Then I wind down gently to the fish so that I can feel the savage, mouthing actions and get an indication of when swallowing is beginning to commence.

There are exceptions to every rule, and I have had pike swallow jacks on the spot before now, so you need to be on your toes. No two fish will react in the same way, and no two takes are ever alike.

When a fish runs with a bait, be it a jack pike or a half mackerel, it usually goes directly away from you or, if you are fishing well out, straight towards you. You need to be sure that the bite indication system you choose will register both types of run.

Pressurised pike

Delayed striking isn't the only way that pike may suffer at the hands of unthinking anglers. To suggest that fish suffer from stress may seem like a fanciful notion to many, but there is no doubt that pike will not tolerate overfishing.

If pike are caught over and over again and harried, their growth is inhibited. You can see it happen whenever a new water that was previously closed or restricted to pike anglers opens its doors.

Above: An upper twenty on display before it succumbed to angling pressure.

The first people on the water enjoy the cream of the sport, but then catches tail off sharply as fish restrict their choice of food and feeding times to avoid being caught.

On a trout water I fished, the pike started by being caught on deadbaits and then switched to livebaits, and finally restricted their feeding to night time. The fish were still there, but bankside disturbance, baits crashing into the water and boats being rowed up and down all contributed to the spoiling of sport.

That's why I don't like fishing public waters. When the Oxford pits became fished really hard, I turned to waters that were more wild and which held pike that hadn't been caught before. I'm not interested in pike that have been caught lots of times by other anglers, only in 'fresh' fish.

So what will I do when all of the local gravel pits are being heavily fished? I will turn to the river, which has wild areas that have not seen an angler for years. There is enough water to keep me going until the end of my days, and provide me with good sport and a sense of the unexpected while gravel pit anglers are fishing shoulder-to-shoulder.

At the same time, I keep in touch with the gravel pit grapevine to find out which waters are becoming available. I have no more access to private waters than anyone else, but if I see a likely looking water that has been left fallow, or hear of one that has potential, I will contact the gravel company to see if I can gain access.

If I can find two or three likely looking waters, I will concentrate my efforts on these rather than try to spread myself too thinly by fishing a large number inconsistently. It can take as many as three seasons to get the best from a new water.

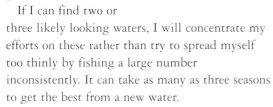

Above: On a gravel pit still being worked, pike can take refuge.

I have been known to find waters on Ordnance Survey maps and, if they look of a suitable age, find out who owns them and ask politely if I can fish. It's part of the challenge, and fishing a 'virgin' water is a unique and exciting experience. I wouldn't swap these waters for any number of over-fished venues, no matter what their record for big pike.

Private waters are fished on trust, and that's a trust I wouldn't abuse. I have permission to fish three or four extremely good waters but I do so sparingly. I may only fish them three or four times a season because they just can't stand the pressure, even though no one else fishes them except me.

When you are looking at why pike become stressed by being fished for by large numbers of anglers, you need to examine the place of pike in the underwater world. They are the supreme predator, having evolved over millions of years, the oldest fossil remains, found in western Canada, dating back at least sixty millions years. Remains in north Norfolk show there have been pike in Britain for at least five hundred thousand years, and they have few natural enemies. They

used to be taken by osprey, but if you see one of those once in a lifetime you can consider yourself privileged.

Pike are at the top of the ecological pyramid, and as such are more vulnerable to what can best be described as emotional stress. The more supreme the predator, the more harm it does to subdue that creature, and to make it aware that it isn't in command. I believe it's like caging a lion.

Less fishing space is better

Pike caught several times will change their feeding habits and seek out a place of refuge, but many gravel pits and lakes offer 'unrestricted access' to their banks.

It makes my heart sink when I hear that phrase. If you fish public waters and you want reasonable sport, find one with banks closed to anglers – where there is a nature reserve or an active gravel working – anything to reduce the amount of angling pressure and provide a haven for pike to get away from aerial bombardments with half mackerel all hours of the day and night.

Some waters are so wide that there's a section in the middle that no one can reach, or at least they couldn't until the invention of radio controlled, bait-towing boats capable of positioning baits accurately at hundreds of yards.

Drifter floats can only reach that water on a wind directly out from the bank. Otherwise the middle is a much needed place of safety for pike, and if there's a safe area somewhere on a water, pike will find it, feeding and staying healthy, and only venturing out when they're strong enough again to face the fray. The fact that the fish on that over-fished trout water I mentioned had changed their feeding habits suggests they had already tried the first alternative of seeking refuge and failed, and were now a long way down the short road to a rather sad, sorry and emaciated end.

Numbers of rods

If a large number of anglers on a water will have a detrimental effect on sport, then a smaller number of anglers armed with a lot of rods will be just as bad.

To some anglers, each rod is like a National Lottery scratch card – the more they have, the greater their chance of success. But the chances don't always increase in proportion to numbers of baits used. One rod in the right place is better than four in the wrong place, and is less likely to disturb the fish.

A lot depends on the type of water. On some I can fish several rods and on others only one. I have fished with more than two rods on occasion, but that's been when the fishing has been extremely slow. When fishing on a river I'm not prepared to use more than two rods, because the degree of technical difficulty is such that you can't handle more and still fish properly. If you get simultaneous runs on two or three rods when fish come on the feed, you face a dilemma. I've had two rods go at once, so it's going to be a lot worse with multiple rod set-ups.

With two rods, I've been able to pick up one rod, strike it and open the bale arm, then strike the other and play that fish. Once a fish has been hooked it will run off and then, feeling no resistance, stop, which will let you finish with the first fish. But multiply this by five or six and you have a recipe for disaster.

The greater the number of rods fished, the longer it will take to reach them all. In summer, and at night, pike can wolf baits back, and unless you are next to the rod, no more than ten

---

Sure handling

Handling pike is a minefield of problems. The toothsome predator myth which strikes fear into some anglers' hearts, and a good measure of incompetence, cause all the problems.

First and foremost, use an unhooking mat. Every serious big-fish angler should have one. You wouldn't like your skin rubbed around on gravel and nor does a pike. It should have enough closed-cell foam padding – which doesn't absorb water and become smelly – to cushion its body. So long as the design is long enough and soft enough, there's no need for buckles and flaps. I've never seen the point of putting flaps over a fish's body. They serve no useful purpose and remove the slime that is the pike's protective layer against infection.

If you get caught without a mat, look for an area of soft grass or use a weigh sling as a substitute. Repeat captures are becoming the norm and so we are going to have to start taking greater care of the pike that we catch or they won't be around for long.

Don't let a pike flap on the bank. The heavier the pike the greater the chance of it hurting itself as its body weight can cause damage to its delicate internal organs. If it jerks its head, put your hand under the head like a pillow to stop it hitting the ground, not on top of it, which means pushing one of its eyes against the ground. Ask yourself 'how would I like it?' and you won't go far wrong.

meters away, you will be giving yourself and the pike problems.

Gravel pits usually have only a few hotspots, and a couple of rods presented correctly are sufficient to fish effectively. Large numbers of rods are no substitutes for bad angling. Location is everything, and once you have pin-pointed the fish then two or three rods are more than enough.

Happy landings

Landing a pike should be a straightforward business, but a lot of people still poke around with the landing net before the fish is ready. It should be submerged and the fish drawn over it only when you feel that the pike is sufficiently tired to be netted.

Always bring the whole of the fish over the net before lifting. Once the fish is in the net, the rod should be placed on the bank and the fish lifted from the water by holding on to the mesh or arms, not the net handle, which is liable to snap and let the fish fall to the ground with a bump.

Left: The small barbs and needle eyes on Partridge Outpoint trebles are a substantial aid to problem-free unhooking.

Unhooking techniques

Big pike are easier to handle than small ones, partly because they tend to be quieter and partly because there is more room for manoeuvre in their mouths.

Lay the pike on its side and kneel astride it to prevent yourself leaning on it. If you are right handed, place your left hand under the gill cover at the front of the mouth and with a firm grip on the lower jaw, gently pull the jaw towards you to open the mouth. That way there's no chance of getting bitten.

There's a membrane under the jaw between the bones, so don't put your finger through it accidentally. Your fingers can rest against the membrane but you shouldn't use any force against it.

Using eight-inch straight forceps, grip the shank of the hook, turn the points towards you and tug them out. If the hooks are further back in the mouth, insert the forceps between the rows of pink gill rakers beneath the gill covers, being careful not to damage them as they are very fragile, and guide the forceps to the hooks while looking straight down through the open mouth.

If you have managed to deep-hook the fish, and the hooks are out of sight, put the trace under tension against the rod or by being held by someone else, and pull it until folds of skin in the pike's throat are drawn back, and the treble comes into view. Turn the treble upside down and tug it out. If it takes a bit of force to get it out, so be it. Just get on with it. If you can see it, then you can get it out. Whatever happens, if you find yourself

in that situation you'll be sure not to let it happen again. If ever there was a deterrent devised for people who leave runs too long before striking, then it's dealing with deeply-hooked pike.

Get a move on!

Wherever the hooks are and whatever the problem, get on with the job quickly and efficiently as it is better to remove the hooks with a quick tug and get the fish back in the water then to spend a long time teasing free the tiniest shred of skin. If you have someone with you, get them to pour water on the fish to prevent it from drying out.

If you've got a pike gag, throw it away. They do far more harm than good and are completely unnecessary. Sometimes, while going in through the gill rakers, the back of your hand just brushes them. You may be surprised how much the cuts will bleed. The rakers are coated in an anti-coagulant, which will stop the wound from healing for a short time, but the marks will be no more than grazes and you won't even be aware at first what has happened. If you seem to get cut regularly, buy a pair of gardening gloves and chop off the finger tips so that you can hold the fish firmly but still have the backs of your hands covered.

Everyone gets their fingers nicked or damaged now and then, no matter how experienced or careful they are. It is a good idea to have some plasters with you because open cuts need to be protected on the bank, especially with Weils disease around.

Keep pike as still as possible during the whole operation, for their sake as well as your own. The more a fish is allowed to move around, the more likely that you or it will become injured.

Beware of flying trebles

You would think that a pike hooked in the edge of the mouth would pose no problems, but get a loose treble wrapped in the mesh of a landing net and you have a situation potentially more damaging than a deeply-hooked fish as you struggle to get the hooks out of several layers of mesh.

Sometimes you don't see the 'flying' treble until the fish is in the net, and if that happens you should take the fish out of the net before unhooking it. If it spins in the net it could split its mouth on the tight trace or gouge its eye on the loose treble.

If it spins, stop the fish from moving around, cut the line above the trace to get the rod out of the way and with the pike held securely, get the mesh unpicked as fast as possible. The larger the mesh of the net the more difficult it is to unravel. Minnow mesh is a lot easier to deal with than bream mesh.

Landing the fish by hand isn't a complete solution, because if that loose top treble snags your jacket or, worse still, the back of your hand, one slip and you could have an angry, frightened,

Above: A gorgeous 22 lb pike caught from a Thames weir pool.

head-shaking fish tearing that three-pointed piece of sharp wire through your hand as it tries to escape. Carry a pair of wire cutters in your pocket. You'll be glad of them.

Be on your guard as the fish begins to tire and be ready to change tactics from landing by net to landing by hand. Play the fish out so that it isn't too lively in the edge. Small pike and those to about 15 lb can sometimes be unhooked over the side of a boat or in the shallows, as they are not going to be weighed or photographed. With big fish, it pays to use a net, and a good-sized one at that.

Why I won't use barbless hooks

I wish I could recommend barbless hooks as the pike fishing of the future, but while I have landed quite a few fish on them, I have also lost a good few. I'm not alone in finding barbless hooks difficult to get on with, and there are several famous names in pike angling, in particular Jim Gibbinson and Ken Crow, who have lost one too many fish on them and gone back to barbed.

Right: You must be on your
guard as the pike begins to tire
and be ready to change tactics
to suit the circumstances.

One fish sticks in my memory. It was a gravel
pit fish of about 25 lb, and when it launched
itself clear of the water it shook its head and the
trebles flew out. With it went all of my
confidence in barbless hooks.

I ease my conscience by reminding myself
that there's a school of thought that
claims barbless hooks, whether single or treble,
cause more damage than barbed because they
penetrate further, pushing deep into the
flesh-like needles.

I'm not sure whether that's the case, but the
fact remains that if you strike a fish early and
hook it in the mouth or scissors you can use
whatever sort of hook you want because that fish
isn't going to come to harm.

I would back anyone using barbed hooks and
striking quickly over someone using barbless, and
saying it doesn't matter how long they wait before
they strike. That's something that is heard too
often on the bank. A deeply-hooked pike
is a mistake, no matter what sort of hooks are
being used.

The right weigh

Purpose-made pike weigh slings are a different
shape from carp weigh slings. If you are after big
pike, you need the proper thing because folding a
fish in half will do nothing for its backbone and
put a strain on its internal organs. If fish were
meant to be shaped like boomerangs, God would
have made them that way.

Give 'em the sack

Keepnets are no place for pike. Split fins and sides
rubbed raw are the inevitable consequences. If you
must retain a fish, a pike sack or tube is the thing
to use. I always carry two sacks with me and they
double as an unhooking mat for roving fishing.

The big, zipped design is best. A fish can be
put in sideways on, and there is no draw cord to
tangle. Make sure the sack is big enough. A 20 lb
pike will be about 40 inches long. A sack material
is soft, but a fish can damage itself by rubbing
against a sharp object on the bottom in shallow
water. Wade out to deeper water where there is a
soft bottom, or tether the sack from a tree branch.

Pike tubes are excellent alternatives because
their rigid frames mean pike don't rub against
hard objects, opening areas to infection.

I have seen pike left in shallows overnight and
anglers come back to find herons and cormorants
have attacked them. It isn't fair to the fish. If it's
a really big pike and you want a photograph in
daylight then sack it overnight, but do it properly.

Fish handled carefully will be none the worse
for wear. I used to fish a pit where the first pike I
caught was almost always the same 8 lb jack. I
must have caught it eight or nine times, and I
think it knew I wasn't going to harm it.

On another water I was chopping mackerel
heads off baits and throwing them in the
shallows. I caught a pike and unhooked it and
when I put it back it swam over them, dropped
down and picked one up before going on its way.

And on the river, I've caught the same fish twice within minutes. Pike don't have a problem with being caught if they are treated properly and returned immediately. It's mishandling that make the fish lose condition.

I would liken handling pike to holding a racing pigeon. Put in the hands of someone who knows how to hold it, a pigeon doesn't struggle. The confidence of the handler is transmitted to the bird and it can sense that it's not going to be harmed. But hold it awkwardly and you transmit your incompetence and the creature will become agitated. There's a right and a wrong way to do everything.

Above: If you're going to get passers-by to take catch shots for you, a camera with a programme mode is a must. Anything more complicated is asking for trouble.

Posing for passers by

Pictures are not as important as the satisfaction of catching the fish and putting it back unharmed. It detracts greatly from the pleasure of the capture if a fish is damaged or has problems going back.

If you must take pictures, you owe it to the fish to have everything worked out in advance and to do the job quickly and efficiently. I have had a Nikon FM2 for twelve years and it stands up to being dropped and stood on and still produces excellent pictures.

I use mine for close up reference pictures of fish for identification, and pictures of waters and features. However, when it comes to getting a passer by to take a catch shot with it, you can tell by the puzzled look on their faces as they examine the unfamiliar buttons and knobs that things are going to go badly wrong. And they do, regularly.

So I've bought an autowind, autofocus Canon A1 Sureshot camera with a self-contained flash, which has a quality zoom lens of 35 to 70 mm and a programme mode that I can set before handing it over. Put it in the hands of someone who knows nothing about cameras, tell him where to stand and what to press and you will get good results almost every time.

Posing for self portraits

Self portraits require a little more preparation. Position bank sticks either side of the frame, just out of shot, and screw the camera into a bank stick with an adapter. A self-timer will give you about twelve seconds to position the fish, which should be laid on a sack with a corner covering its

eyes, something that often has a calming effect and stops it moving around. If you catch two fish at once, you could try placing them on your knees, which I did for a self-portrait of two 24-pounders that was considered good enough to grace the front cover of *Angler's Mail*.

As far as film is concerned, Fujichrome 100 gives colours that are very true to life. I buy non-process paid, 36-frame rolls and take it to my local developing lab, who turn it round in couple of hours, and it still works out cheaper than sending it away. It's got a good shelf life if you keep it in the fridge.

When holding fish for pictures, tuck your hands under the pike to show its proportions, without letting your fingers getting in the way, and hold it close to you to protect it if it struggles, and to avoid distorting its size in the photograph. Holding it towards the lens doesn't make it look bigger; it just makes it look weird and out of proportion, and either you or the pike are likely to be out of focus.

Choose a plain background with the sun in your face. Make sure the fish is clean of grass and leaves before you pick it up and that there are no distracting items of tackle showing in the corners of the shot.

Photos at night are harder to take. You will need to shine a torch on to the fish to focus and compose the shot. If there's a brolly or trees to

Above: Use gentle hands to return pike to the water.

provide background and reflect the flash, position the shot there, but always keep to distances specified on the flash information or you risk getting pictures that are too light or too dark.

Many happy returns

When a fish has been weighed and photographed – if it's big enough to warrant that – put it back in the weigh sling and then carry it down the bank to the water. When you put pike back, especially the harder-fighting loch fish, you should hold them in the water for a minute or two while they recover; this stops them from swimming off immediately. In Summer, fish will take longer to recover than in winter. At that time they are at their fittest, having had three or four months of good feeding to recover from spawning, and will fight their hardest. Couple this with the fact that oxygen levels are at their lowest and you will see why more time has to be taken.

Summer pike are more active and more athletic, so they are more enjoyable to catch. What they lack in size they will make up for in numbers and enthusiasm, but sacking them for a picture is not a good idea.

Before now I've hooked a big fish in summer and have asked someone to get my camera ready when I have still been playing it. It may have looked like overconfidence, but I wasn't trying to look cool, only to save time. Two or three minutes is the maximum time that pike should be out of the water in summer as in these conditions their body temperature is rising all the time.

Try to put them back in calm water, so that they can recover out of any flow. If you try to put them back in fast water they won't have enough energy to fight the current and will get swept downstream to die, belly up.

The same goes for very cold temperatures, when the air may be down to the minuses. Fins begin to freeze when it gets this cold, so don't mess about with sacks and pictures in these conditions, for the sake of the fish's well being.

Big pike are rare and beautiful creatures, so let's take good care of them. If we want these fish to grow and give other people enjoyment then we should look after them and return them in the same condition they were in when we caught them.

BAIT

The choice of baits available to pike anglers is enormous, and most of them have accounted for a fish or two at some time or other. From strange-looking exotic fish to strawberry-flavoured mackerel, someone, somewhere has tried them all. There's no doubt that they will all work on their day, and there will be days when pike will look at only one type of bait in one size and ignore everything else.

But the majority of the time, thank goodness, pike will take the old favourites, and if I were marooned on a desert island that happened to have a pike lake, I should be happy with a bucket of live brown trout and a bag of frozen sardines.

Why I plump for these two fish above any others, and when I would ignore them in favour of something else, form the basis for this chapter, for you need to know why pike prefer one bait to another to know when you can afford to leave the alternatives at home.

The changing face of livebaiting

There was a time when livebaiting for me meant catching coarse fish in advance of a session. Every piking trip had to be preceded by a few hours with a float rod in the hope of catching enough baits to last the day. It wasn't ideal. There were times when coarse fish were frustratingly difficult to catch, particularly in the depths of winter, and I didn't want to lose a day of pike fishing simply because I couldn't get livebaits.

There had to be a solution, and it came with the rapid growth of trout fishing as a sport and the demand for the species among fish eaters. Trout farms sprang up alongside all of the major rivers in the country, providing perfect livebaits for just a few pence each.

These fish are bred for the table, so anglers' consciences are clear as they are not removing precious stocks of native coarse fish. And there are fewer worries with transferring diseases, as trout farms are forever seeking and obtaining fish-moving consents from the Environment Agency.

Rainbow trout make excellent livebaits. They have a firm skin, with scales that stand up to handling and casting, and a soft flesh that is attractive to pike. They're a good source of protein, and I believe pike find them easy to digest. The fact that we eat trout rather than

roach or chub suggests they are bit of a delicacy. Their only drawback is that they have a tendency to swim high in the water when tired, like rudd, dace and roach, and if that happens they need to be taken off and a fresh bait put on. However, this habit can be used to good effect when legering livebaits as their desire to head for the surface keeps them off the bottom, and in view of any pike.

Brown trout are just the opposite. Their first impulse is to dive deep, and this makes them the best choice for float fishing, especially over deep water. Very little lead is needed to hold them down, which means they will stay alive for longer and not wear themselves out towing a heavy lead around. Crucian carp, bream and chub have a similar deep-diving tendency.

I am fortunate in living close to a trout farm that has a good stock of various sizes of trout. They also have both rainbows and brownies, and it is the latter that I particularly like for fishing in Scotland. Browns are much slower growing and so are more expensive – 45p each for a 3 oz to 4 oz trout compared with 30p for a similar rainbow. This is a good, manageable size, as the larger the fish, the more difficult it is to cast and control, and the bigger the float you need. In fact everything has to be stepped up, and then handling tackle becomes a problem. I buy a couple of dozen trout for a day's fishing and keep any leftovers alive for the next outing.

Is livebaiting necessary?

Even with the issue of coarse fish removal resolved by using trout, there still remains a question mark over livebaiting. The issue isn't so much a matter of whether it's cruel, which takes us into the realms of the 'do fish feel pain' debate, but whether it's necessary. If we can catch pike on deadbaits under any conditions, why not give up livebaiting for good?

Having fished both methods through several decades I can say with confidence that there are days when livebaits will out-fish any other method. Certainly, on a river when conditions are right, a livebait is in a class of its own. Location is of paramount importance when river fishing, and a great deal more water can be covered with a trotted livebait than with any other method. I can trot a bait up to 80 yards downstream under a float, searching the water as it goes down. It would take me a very long time to cover the same amount of water with a static deadbait.

I'm not what you could call an enthusiastic livebaiter. I would much rather use a deadbait. But I've seen how preoccupied fish feeding selectively can become. I've seen them at Theale Lagoon, crashing frantically into shoals of two-inch roach, mouths wide open, and one pike of over 30 lb in such a feeding frenzy that it beached itself in the shallows. I was able to weigh the stranded fish without having caught it, and it took the scales down to 30 lb 2 oz. Yet they refused everything we put in front of them, except small, live fish. There are times when nothing else will work.

The bottom line is, if you don't livebait, you're handicapping yourself. I would like to think I could catch the same number and size of fish on deadbaits that I do on lives, but that's just not the case. There are even some rivers, like the Trent, the Hampshire Avon and the Weaver, in Cheshire, on which you would be a lot less likely to succeed with a deadbait.

There are times when pike are in a torpid state, perhaps due to a series of heavy frosts or a prolonged spell of hot weather, and are not interested in feeding. They can often be persuaded to reflex-feed or grab a livebait out of aggression. A livebait must have much the same effect on the pike as a bluebottle buzzing around our heads. Sooner or later we have to strike out at it to bring an end to the annoyance. They will drop the bait as soon as it has been killed because they don't intend to eat it but if your hooks are in the right position and you strike early enough, reflex feeders can be hooked in the lip. A deadbait would have sat there all day without bringing any response.

Pike pick up attractive vibrations from livebaits, and they can feel those movements of the bait at much greater distance than they can see, making livebaits more effective. It always makes me smile when I read that a livebait should behave naturally to tempt a pike. It is precisely because these baits are behaving unnaturally that they are so attractive to pike, or more attractive than a fish swimming free and unrestricted as part of a shoal. Livebaits are vulnerable, and vulnerability to a pike means food.

I've cast a livebait caught from a water teeming with stunted carp and rudd into the middle of a shoal of hundreds of others that were identical and had the bait taken instantly by a 28 lb pike. There were so many small carp that you would have thought it unlikely that a fish would pick up mine. But I believe it did so because the bait was behaving unnaturally and giving out involuntary distress signals.

I've even cast baits into dense weed when pike have been lying there and they have been found surprisingly quickly. I believe they can home in on the tiny movements of the gills and fins of coarse fish using an unique sensory system that they have, known as the neuromast system, which is described in another chapter.

If someone comes up with an artificial lure that simulates these vibrations accurately, livebaiting could become obsolete.

What about coarse fish livebaits?

Trout supply almost all of my needs as far as livebaiting is concerned because coarse fish don't lend themselves to being hurled out a long way and to being cast repeatedly. But when I'm fishing from a boat or on a tributary of a river and don't need to cast very far then I will use roach and chub livebaits if I can get hold of them.

Some of the coarse baits I have used have been so big they would make a matchman swear, but big baits catch big pike and if that is what is required, then I will use them without any qualms. When I have experimented with big coarse baits I have found it almost impossible to go too big so far. River pike feed regularly on 2 lb bream and chub, so providing them with a bait of similar size is only giving them what they are used to.

Frank Guttfield was fishing the Thames a few years ago when a barbel of 6 lb that he was playing was taken by a very big pike that grabbed it across the head and the flank. It damaged the barbel so badly that Frank had to finish it off.

I have caught a pike of 26 lb that had a jack of over 6 lb in the back of its throat, and a friend who caught a pike of 13 lb 6 oz could see the legs of a coot sticking up from inside its throat.

Keeping and carrying livebaits

Left: Snap-lidded brewing bins and aerators will keep your live baits alive and lively from fish farm to home and then to the swim. Keep water levels low to lighten the load or your carrying arm may end up longer than the other.

When I visit the trout farm, which is only ten minutes drive away, I take with me two snap-lidded plastic buckets made for beer brewing, each with an aerator pump glued to the top. When I get them home I transfer the trout to the two, five-foot galvanised horse troughs that I keep in my back garden for livebaits and pump air into them through air stones from a power point in my garage. I can keep up to two dozen brownies quite comfortably in each for up to a month.

Both of the galvanised troughs that I use have pieces of nylon mesh stretched over the tops and stapled to two bits of timber, because I'm not the only fisher in the neighbourhood. I put a dozen trout in one evening and woke up the next morning to find nine lying on the lawn, picked out by cats that had several hours enjoyable fishing at my expense. I've had a visit from a beady eyed heron, too, that had my entire stock of brown trout for breakfast.

The important thing to realise is that trout have been fed very heavily on high protein trout pellets up until the time when they were bought, so their stomachs are full. Once I take them, I tend to starve them, for their own good. If I pick them up on a Tuesday and intend to use them that weekend, I won't feed them at all. In the past I have not fed them for two weeks without any detrimental effect.

Feeding them causes more problems than not because as soon as you give them something to eat, the tank becomes filthy. What goes in one end has to come out of the other, and you have to change the water on a regular basis.

Without food they can live quite happily on their own body fat for two or three weeks, and probably be healthier when you use them than when they arrived. Trout require clean, well oxygenated water much more than large amounts of food.

I have a tiny net from a pet shop to get the little chaps out, and I wouldn't be without it. Any trout left over at the end of the day go back in the troughs. If it's really cold in winter and there is a danger of the troughs freezing over, then I drag them into the garage to stop ice forming on them.

When carrying livebaits to the bank, I use the same buckets but with only three or four inches of water in the bottom if a long walk is on the cards. Gone are the days when I could lug a full bucket of livebaits across three or four meadows without breaking sweat. Pipe lagging taped to the handle, which is invariably made of painfully thin, rigid wire, makes carrying more comfortable.

I have even had days when trout livebaits have been ignored but when I put on a roach of 12 oz it was taken straight away. We had thirteen double-figure pike that day, all on big roach, and as soon as we ran out, sport was over. Big coarse baits do work, if your conscience will allow you to use them, and there are certainly times when nothing else will do.

Fish moving orders

Like it or not, bylaws state that you have to get a fish moving order from your local authority,

approved by the local
office of the
Environment Agency,
before you can take live
fish from one water to
another. You have to
state what you are
taking and where you
are going to use them.
If you haven't got an
order and you are
caught using live fish
from another water
there are fairly hefty
fines in place to
dissuade you from
doing so again.

Left: Sardines, smelt, sandeels, mackerel, pike, roach and trout. The choice of deadbait is a wide one, and all have different uses on different waters where pike show a preference for one type of bait over another.

A lot of trout farms now ask for fish moving order documents or consents when you go there to buy fish, and won't sell you trout without a form. Anglers do get away without them but it is best to obtain one. A single consent covers you for any number of fish for six months, and helps fight the spread of disease around the country. Some trout farms can't issue consents to take live fish because their stock is not designated disease free.

Legered livebaits

Most of the time, livebaiting means float fishing, but one tactic that is worth trying is legering with lives. Fished this way they don't move around much, which made me wonder why they are so attractive to pike. But the movement of the fins and gills is probably enough vibration for a big pike to detect.

The biggest pike often lie near the bottom, and when temperatures are low, they will be in deep water. We want to position a bait where they are lying, and it is easier to do that by legering than by float fishing. A float fished bait is only in the right spot for a moment before the current takes it away or the bait swims out of position, but a legered livebait can be kept where you want it without the need for repeated casting. Often when float fishing fails, legering succeeds, and creates much less disturbance because a rig only needs to be cast a few times in a morning.

If I know of a holding area and want to keep a bait in that lie or deep hole then I would use a

legered livebait. The outside of a bend in a river or a depression are just a couple of places where legering is a better option than float fishing. In difficult swims with lots of bankside vegetation to hamper casting, legering is again the prime method. Similarly when putting a bait close to snags like a half-submerged tree, or when trying to repeat a good cast, a legered bait is best. There are times when a legered livebait is the only method that will succeed. And my first choice of bait would be a rainbow trout.

Deciding which deadbait

If livebaiting is a useful alternative method for me, deadbait fishing is my bread and butter approach. It's the first choice in most situations and the method from which I gain most satisfaction while targeting big pike selectively.

Yet among many modern pike anglers it is a second-rate technique. Why use a dead fish when you can use a live one? Their image of deadbaiting is 'lob it out and leave it', but to see it as such is to overlook the number of different ways that a deadbait can be fished. Just as a good lure angler can search a stretch of water by bringing that lump of plastic or wood to life, so skilled sink-and-draw techniques can cover a whole pool on a river, enticing a pike to take by making the bait flutter and wobble attractively.

A lot depends on the choice of species of fish to use as bait, and here I've listed most of the alternatives, along with the times when they are at their best and why.

As a general rule I would say that deadbaits should be killed freshly or have been frozen soon after capture. However, I can't help thinking of an angler of my acquaintance whom I mentioned earlier, Jurassic Phil.

Everything he fished with was old, so it will come as no surprise to hear that his bait matched his tackle. He's the only angler I've ever met who didn't discard a deadbait when it split, but took out his sewing kit and stitched it back together with wool. You think I'm joking? I only wish I were, and the worst part is he used to catch pike on them, and big ones at that.

For Phil, deadbaits could be of any age or freshness, even rancid. For everyone else my advice would be deadbaits should be as fresh as possible.

Trout have their uses

Having read how highly I rate brown and rainbow trout as livebaits, you may be surprised to discover that I don't use them for static deadbaits. The reason is that I don't think they give off a particularly attractive scent when dead, and they certainly don't lend themselves to being frozen. They turn very soft and break up easily, so it's fresh or nothing, and even fresh are second best to other species.

However, when looking for a bait to be wobbled, it's a different matter. Their streamlined shape makes them move through the water very attractively on the retrieve, and their toughness when freshly killed means that they stand up well to attack. I have caught four or five pike on the same trout.

Left: Freshly killed brown trout make excellent wobbled baits. Trout are very flexible when first killed, before rigor mortis has set in and they go as stiff as a board.

Brown and rainbow trout are my first choice for wobbled deadbaits, especially when they weigh about 6 oz. I go for a slightly heavier bait when wobbling because a pike has to chase it to take it, often in fast flowing water, and I believe you need to offer a fish a decent meal to make the reward worth the energy expended.

Trout are very flexible when first killed, before *rigor mortis* has set in, more so than 'big-scaled' fish like roach and chub, and that suppleness gives the bait the movement throughout the body and in the tail that it needs to attract the attention of a big pike.

Freshly killed trout have been used to good effect at Underbank Reservoir and Damflask, in South Yorkshire, by Tag Barnes and Colin Dyson, fishing twelve feet down in forty feet of water, and the fact that they were freshly killed added to their attraction.

I take trout to the water's edge live, and kill them as I need them or just ten minutes before. It's the only way that you can ensure your deadbaits are truly fresh.

But sardines are best

So, if trout aren't my first choice for a static deadbait, what is? The answer is sardines. They are by far the best deadbait on rivers and will on most occasions out-fish anything else. Extremely oily, they give off a superb smell that gets wafted downstream to any feeding pike, drawing it up to the source of the scent.

What's more, they are extremely cheap and easily available, bought in kilo bags from your local market for about £2 for fifteen fish. The best ones I have used have been imported from Portugal.

You need to make sure they have been separated in the bag, though, because if they have been frozen in one big lump you will have to thaw the whole lot to get at the half a dozen you'll need for a trip. This process of freezing individually is known in the trade as 'freeflow'.

Beware of sardines that were frozen when less than fresh. The best baits will be bright and shiny. If there is a greenish tinge to the underside of the stomachs you know that they were frozen after being out of the water for a fair period of time.

I have used sardines and re-frozen them and still caught pike on them on the next outing, unlike smelts, which don't seem to lend themselves to being re-frozen. Mackerel stand up to this treatment okay, though.

If it's fresh sardines you are going for, look at the clarity of the eye to tell how good they are. Blood seeps slowly into the eye of a dead sardine, darkening it, so the more discoloured it is the longer the fish has been dead. Women in Greece used to give the eyes of fish on the market stalls a poke to make sure they were still attached because stallholders got to know that the eye was a gauge of freshness and started substituting ones from fresh fish to deceive their customers. Also, give the stomach a prod. A fresh fish has a firm stomach.

The one drawback to sardines is that they can't be cast very far. Their soft, oily flesh breaks up easily, so I try not to use them for long-range fishing on gravel pits but stick to close-to-medium work. There are three ways in which I fish sardines – float legered out of a boat, legered with a Cox and Rawle leger boom in rivers, and freelined using the deadbait support rig on gravel pits. Sardines are especially good after dark lobbed out underarm into the margins.

I take the bait to the water frozen in a plastic bag and partially thaw one sardine by dropping it in the margins while I am tackling up. I sometimes pinch a small amount of lead on the trace just above the root of the tail when I use a partially thawed bait, to make sure it has sunk.

I put one treble hook through the root of the tail and pin the other treble in the flank. Using the deadbait support rig enables me to cast sardines further and avoid losing them on the retrieve and giving the pike a free meal.

And mackerel are close behind

The only other deadbait that I use regularly is mackerel, which make excellent long-range baits that pike find very attractive. Their aerodynamic shape and extra weight mean they can be cast long distances freelined when frozen. The beauty of freelining is there is nothing to hamper the take or impede the strike, and the fight is not impaired by a heavy lead bouncing on the line.

Mackerel are very robust and stand up well to repeated casting caused by striving for range. If the first couple of casts go astray you can usually have another go without even needing to adjust the hook hold. The best way to mount the bait is with the deadbait support rig, with a loop of strong line around the root of the tail to support the mackerel and hooks pinned lightly in the skin.

I buy my mackerel in boxes weighing a stone from Greenslade's at Poole Harbour on the south coast. I buy ten stone at a time, for £4 to £5 a stone. I can pick the size of baits I want and I know that they are going to be extremely fresh. Even with the cost of the petrol down there it works out very cheap and provides me with much better bait than I would get from a fishmonger's, which always seems to have mackerel too big for my purposes.

I ring up Greenslade's in advance and ask them to layer the fish for me and to keep them apart. They have huge freezers down there and will put the fish in the back until there is a cool day, when I travel down to pick them up. It takes me just an hour and a half from Oxford with a good run and they're still frozen when I get them home.

I ask for twelve-inch fish and use three-quarters of that, chopping off the heads to use for pre-baiting. Some of the baits I chop in advance and freeze in bags of half a dozen, but mainly they are frozen intact and the chopping is done on the bank, as they are needed.

Any heads chopped off in advance can be thrown into a chosen area of a water I want to fish at regular intervals over three or four weeks leading up to the session. It's surprising how used to that food source pike become. They are waiting and hungry when you turn up with your rods.

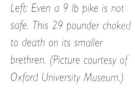

Left: Making a mackerel more streamlined by trimming it with a sharp knife will make it fly through the air without twisting when cast, keeping tackle tangles to a minimum.

Left: Even a 9 lb pike is not safe. This 29 pounder choked to death on its smaller brethren. (Picture courtesy of Oxford University Museum.)

Streamlining a mackerel

To prepare a mackerel for fishing, I chop off the head at an angle across the bait and then take off the corner, to give the bait a curved end where the head used to be. This lets more of the attractive juices seep out into the water, and prevents the belly from splitting. I also chop off the tail to within half an inch of the root, which makes it more aerodynamic and less likely to twist on the cast and cause tangles.

I will use a mackerel until the belly splits and then chop it up for prebaiting. Used baits will refreeze but I don't bother unless I'm short.

I go down to Poole to stock up in July or August, the peak time for English mackerel, and again in the winter. They have supplies all the year round as their boats travel far afield for fish, though it pays to be stocked up in advance of the winter's worst weather as this can keep the boats in port.

The boxes of frozen bait go straight into my chest freezer in the garage, apart from the few mackerel that I chop in advance, and some of it stays there for over six months and is still fine to use.

My chest freezer is a lot less than full size. If you're thinking of getting a freezer just for bait, don't make the mistake of getting a really big one as they need to be kept filled to work efficiently.

From the cradle to the grave

Pike first feed on pike from four or five weeks old, and later, small pike get eaten by bigger ones because they are plentiful and easy to catch. By the time it reaches a respectable size, a large pike may have seen off tens of dozens of smaller ones, so they are as natural a food source as any they are likely to encounter.

On a water without a big head of coarse fish but with plenty of pike, there may be little else in the way of food. In that case big pike will actively seek out smaller pike and will be in areas where they can obtain them.

On one water I fished there were reeds and rushes just in front of a deep trough, and small pike would sit in the reeds but very seldom venture out into deeper water. I caught one of

A pike when the time is right

There are times during the season when a small jack pike will outfish any other bait. At the back end of season, small male pike are drawn to big, hungry hen fish at a time when they have burned up a lot of energy in spawning. The cock fish can be so preoccupied with the urge to reproduce that they become an easy target. A big hen fish surrounded by males may turn on one and swallow it.

The time of year that this happens depends on the location of the water. On English rivers it is usually in February or March, whereas in Scotland it is more like March or April. Big Thames pike are suckers for a smaller pike at this time of the year, and they will also seek them out at other times.

When they're in that mood, a jack is the first choice bait. I once caught a 24 lb 8 oz pike from a Thames tributary on one, and at the back of her throat were the remains of another hapless suitor.

It's the distinctive smell of a small pike that triggers the reaction. Some anglers think only a whole fish will work as bait, believing it is the appearance that provokes the feeding urge, but a jack pike will work as bait whether whole, cut in half or even in steaks.

To fish a steak, pass a loop of nylon through the cavity where the guts were before they were pushed out, and use this to support the bait on the cast. Shape is immaterial to the attractiveness of the bait. The scent is everything.

Below: An upper double taken on a jack deadbait in March. At this time of year big pike seek out jacks.

about 2 lb on a sardine and, as I played it, an incredible bow wave appeared behind the fish, coming right in under my feet. The fish, one of about 13 lb, came shooting across the surface of the water and took the jack, but as it did so a fish well into the 30s grabbed the 13 lb fish across the side. I knew the hooks were nowhere near it's mouth so I tried to guide the big fish gently towards the net, but as I got it near it let go. Even a 13 lb pike is not safe when a very big one is hungry.

I've come across half a dozen such waters on my travels, and it always takes a while to understand what's going on. All you catch at first on conventional livebaits and deadbaits is small jack pike. The place seems to be overrun with them. You might even give it up as a bad job, but as soon as you offer a pike as a bait, by accident or by design, your results will be transformed.

Having whetted your appetite for catching pike on pike, however, I should warn you that feeding times are a lot less frequent than with standard food items.

If a big pike takes an 8 lb jack it could go for three to four weeks without needing to feed again. A pike needs to eat only four to five times its body weight in a year to maintain growth and keep healthy.

Above: Scrape a few scales from a small area of flank when mounting a pike deadbait on trebles. This allows the hooks to be nicked lightly in the flesh and struck clear cleanly.

Start by spinning

I've known waters with just a few large coarse fish that have failed to spawn. The pike were numerous and mostly small and had to feed on each other to survive. On a water like that, I would start by spinning for them and if I caught a number of less than 1 lb I would cut one in half and put it on a deadbait rig.

Pike are very tough-skinned fish, being small-scaled, and they need a bit of attention before being mounted on a rig. I chop off the fins to help with casting and scrape just a few scales from a small area of flank. This allows me to nick one of the hooks of the end treble in the skin. The other prongs sit on scales in an area that hasn't been cleared, so that they skid off on the strike. The other treble goes just in front of the tail root and is also nicked in very lightly.

Jack pike are such a good bait for big fish that it is tempting to suggest them as livebait, but experience has proven that they are too difficult to catch to order, and even when they can be caught, the tackle has to be stepped up to fish them effectively. Hooks, floats and leads all need to be bigger, and with that increase in size comes a

decrease in the chances of success. If jack pike can be caught, though, and there's a pike in the water big enough to make fishing with crude tackle worthwhile, then by all means persevere.

If I were going to use one I would keep it well off the bottom, out of the weed, and put it in a position where it could be seen clearly and was very vulnerable. I would also have at least 150 yards of line on the reel as a pike that takes a jack tends to run and run.

Clive Loveland and Allen Edwards fished for pike out of boats in Knipton Reservoir, near Grantham, in Lincolnshire, in the late sixties and landed some huge fish that fired the imagination of pike anglers for over two decades, the biggest weighing 39 lb. I'm sure that if pike were used more widely and more often by anglers we would see some huge fish start to come out.

Eels keep others at bay

As a dedicated eel angler with a fascination for the species, it takes a great deal of provocation for me to end up describing eels as a bloody pest. But that is a measure of how bad the problem has become in Scotland, where it is now impossible to keep a bait intact in the water on days, and nights, when small eels are active.

Roach have their place

If you'd asked me a short time ago what I thought about roach as deadbaits I would have said 'not a lot', as I'd never caught anything outstanding on one. But that was before a 26 lb 12 oz river pike took a 1 lb-plus roach that I was fishing sink-and-draw.

The truth is, if I had fished roach deadbaits more often perhaps I might have had more success with them than I have (see picture below), but as I am happy using sardines, mackerel and wobbled trout, I haven't felt the need to find an alternative to these baits. But if I were on a water where roach are the predominant species but which wasn't responding to sea baits, I would certainly give one a try.

I've also used them as pop-ups with air injected in their stomach, and swim bladder left intact, to stop them from sinking into blanket weed, creating a

Above: Avoid bursting the swim bladder when air-injecting deadbaits as the added buoyancy will help keep it clear of blanket weed on the bottom and visible to passing fish.

highly visible bait. And I use them in the mouths of tributaries or on gravel pits when the sun is out and pike come up to take plateau feeders. They make good trailing baits, too, towed behind a boat beneath a float, as I've done on Blenheim Palace lake.

Left: Eels have made a particular nuisance of themselves in Scotland by tangling wire traces and taking bait intended for pike.

In certain lakes in summer, eels are constantly making a nuisance of themselves by sucking the guts out of sardines, running away with baits intended for pike and tangling wire traces. There is only one pike bait that they won't touch, and that's another eel.

I'm a member of the Eel Anglers' Club and an ardent campaigner for putting large eels back, but it has become a positive pleasure to me to use a small one as bait in Scotland. Fishing an eel section certainly gets rid of the problem, for while pike have no qualms about eating each other, small eels won't consider eating their own kind, thank goodness. I never go to Scotland now without a couple of dozen eel sections in my freezer box.

Eels are so plentiful in these lochs that pike must feed on them regularly, especially when the eels are congregated in one place when making the most of a large, natural food source, like eggs from spawning fish. They are such a high protein food that it is too good for pike to ignore, and I'm sure they seek them out at certain times.

Waters in southern English also have large populations of eels. Broadlands Lake has a massive head of eels and brown trout, and plenty of big pike as well. On waters like this, eel sections are well worth a try.

Anything from a 1 lb to a 1 lb 4 oz eel is about the best size, though smaller ones still make good baits. The eel should be chopped into four-inch sections, which can be used over and over again without losing any of their attractiveness. I've caught three or four pike on one eel section, which is about as much as you can ask of any bait.

I mount mine straight on the hooks without using the deadbait support rig because there is nowhere to put the loop of line. This doesn't matter because an eel's skin is so tough that even hooks nicked lightly under it will stand up to the fiercest casting.

A 1 lb 4 oz eel is the limit, though. I'm not prepared to use anything of over that size. A 2 lb to 3 lb eel could be twenty to thirty years old, and I'm not prepared to kill something of that age just for an alternative bait.

Perch taken tail first

On the subject of alternative pike baits, it's often vital to match the species being used to the one most common in the water being fished. Perch come into their own as a bait when used on a water where they predominate, but when there are no more perch than normal, they are not as good a bait as a wobbled trout or a legered mackerel or sardine.

The species has made a comeback, and the huge increase in the population in recent times means they have to be considered as a bait as they are bound to figure in the diet of pike. Perch lie in similar areas to pike and live in close proximity to them so it is no surprise that pike target them. Considering how they are valued as a table fish on the continent it would come as no surprise if perch were to feature high on a pike's menu.

I can remember legering a sardine while fishing with my son on a backwater of the Thames and watching pike chasing perch but showing no interest in what I was offering them. But when I found a worm under a tree stump, caught a perch on my son's rod, and put that on as bait, it was taken as soon as I cast out, by a pike of 23 lb.

But while they make lively and hardy livebaits, with skins so tough that hooks need only to be nicked in lightly, as sink-and-draw deadbaits they are a dead loss as they go as stiff as a board as soon as they are killed. And as they don't smell particularly attractive, they don't make very good static deadbaits either.

Incidentally, there's a myth about pike that eat perch that claims they can only take them down head first. It's not true. Pike can also swallow them tail first, spiky dorsal fin and razor-pointed gill covers and all, though don't ask me how.

Smelt and sandeels

Sandeels make great distance baits because you can whack them out to features in a way that wouldn't be possible with other species. Their main drawback is that, while they can be freelined at close range, that is about their limit so far as freelining goes, because of their lightness, for they can only be cast short distances without a lead.

Smelts have a beautiful aroma of cucumber, and pink flesh that is very attractive to pike. When popped-up they stay buoyant for hours, and they are also good for paternostering. However, once thawed they don't lend themselves to re-freezing as the aroma disappears and the flesh turns very soft.

All manner of exotics

I'm often asked by anglers whether exotics work for pike, mostly by anglers who seem to think that the unusual makes up for bad angling. It's a popular myth that pike on waters fished hard with conventional baits will respond to strange creatures the like of which they've never seen before.

All manner of weirdoes, from tropical tank casualties to multi-coloured, spiky-finned sea fish have been tried, but to the best of my knowledge the anglers using them are still waiting for them to work regularly. The truth is that any bait is only as good as the angler using it.

It's tempting to think that pike on hard-fished waters will respond better to an unusual bait, but on pits in the Oxford area that have been pike fished regularly for over ten years, fish are still picking up mackerel and sardines. If ever there were an argument against popping down to the Asian market for a kilo of lesser forkbeard or raiding the aquarist shop's dustbin for black bullhead catfish, then that is it.

More important than the choice of bait are the method of presentation and putting the bait in the right spot. It's not the bait that 'blows' on a water, it's the way it is presented, and if a different tactic is used and the bait fished at a different depth or in a different style, then fish that rejected it the first time may be encouraged to take it the second.

Pike anglers can be the worst offenders when it comes to being inflexible in their approach. Many will throw out a deadbait and sit back for hours in the hope of a run when a paternostered, popped-up or wobbled deadbait would have brought instant results.

Or it could be the time of day, if pike have become wary of feeding in daylight and moved out of range to return at night, when fishing on into the dark could be the answer.

My advice to anyone determined to use exotics is fish one on one rod and a standard bait on the other, to compare their effectiveness. But personally I wouldn't bother with exotics unless I had first tried a variety of methods of presentation with conventional baits.

Flavouring and colouring baits

I've never felt the need to flavour or colour my baits, though some anglers do it a lot. If I want a bait that is highly visible, I will use a roach or dace, or pop a bait up, or wobble it to make it stand out more. There are so many ways of making a bait more noticeable that I don't think treating them is necessary. Some anglers will dye a bait and then fish it on the bottom. I have

Left: Flavoured and coloured baits will always be popular with anglers, but there are other ways of making sure your baits stand out and catch the eye of patrolling pike.

serious doubts about how much of a bait a pike can see when it is on the bottom. A pike's eyes are set so high on its head that they must lose sight of the bait when they get above it and close to it, which makes dyeing it a bit of a waste of time.

Some anglers swear that adding a coloured, plastic tag to trebles when using livebaits improves their catches. Most of the tags I've seen used have been red, which pike can see very well, but they are equally attuned to picking out greens and yellows.

In experiments in Holland, different coloured lights were shone in tanks and pike were found to be attracted to those that were red, green or yellow but least attracted to blue.

Red is a colour that occurs naturally on the fins of food fish like roach, and these are used to signal to each other, which means they are very visible under the water, although not visible above the surface by birds and other predators. If they are visible to other roach, they are particularly visible to pike because they hunt from below.

Yet Fred Buller's most successful plug is one that has a green back and a yellow belly, so I believe that any strong additional colour, whether it be red, green or yellow, may enhance a bait's attractiveness.

Of more importance is the size of the tag, because all freshwater is slightly cloudy, and for a pike to see a tag on a bait it needs to be big enough to stand out.

Be *prepared for the unexpected*

If there's one rule to bear in mind when choosing a bait for pike fishing it's always expect the unexpected. The majority of pike will take standard baits for most of the time, but there are always freak preoccupations, and fish with stomachs full of strange things.

On a water I fished with friends we all found sport slow until a big fish turned up out of the blue caught on a tench, which was only used because of a shortage of bait. Others followed when we tried the bait again, proving it wasn't a fluke. It seemed we were dealing with a preoccupation. They certainly didn't want what we were offering up until then.

Perhaps it was the size of the bait. The tench in that lake were numerous and all about 1 lb or just over. The fry in Theale Lagoon were only an inch or two in length yet they were being targeted by pike big enough to make you think they wouldn't consider it worth their while chasing things little bigger than whitebait.

If there's a moral, it's that it's always worth trying a bait that is naturally occurring, even if only as a last resort. If one species of food fish is there in large number, then the pike may not need to eat anything else, and this could hold the key to unlocking the mystery of why your line seems glued to your rod rings.

Sometimes it is only when the supply of the chosen food dries up that these fish are caught,

having been forced to broaden their diet. There may have been a lot of angling activity on that water for a number of years, yet these fish with tunnel vision as far as food is concerned, many of which are very large, will have avoided capture because no one was using what they were eating.

Pike like an easy life

Trout waters are slightly different. A lot of people, especially fly anglers who see pike as a menace, think that pike in trout waters feed only on trout. But that isn't necessarily the case. If there are many bream or roach in the water, then it is a reasonable bet that the pike will take the more vulnerable, slower-swimming coarse fish and ignore the trout.

Pike are basically lazy creatures looking for an easy life. They will seek to gain maximum reward from minimum effort, which means eating bream and roach. So although there are lots of trout, fishing with a trout livebait may not work.

In most situations, though, your standard choice of bait will suffice. It's only when pike get locked into eating one species and ignoring everything else that we have to rethink things.

And it's worth remembering that you can take experimentation too far, and neglect presentation and location, both of which are usually of more importance than choice of bait. Faith in the bait you are used to using is the foundation stone of successful fishing.

Upper Thames pike feed mainly on chub, and lower Thames on bream, while Severn or Wye fish take mostly roach, dace and eels. But I would back a sardine or half mackerel against any of these coarse baits in most circumstances.

I don't know if it's the stronger smell that sea baits give off, as they certainly must taste different from coarse fish, but with a few exceptions, sardines, mackerel and trout will score more heavily than any coarse deadbaits.

Just occasionally, though, something unexpected comes to light and makes us realise how little we know about the feeding preferences of pike. Farmoor I is a prolific, trout-fishing-only reservoir with a good head of pike and stocks of roach, bream, chub and perch of a suitable size for food. When big coarse fish die and float to the surface they are often picked out when they wash ashore and given to a local taxidermist, who examines the stomach contents when preparing the body to be set up. Over the course of a couple of years, several sizeable pike were opened up and all were found to be full to the gills with weed.

Farmoor I is a very rich water and the weed is not just empty green stuff but teeming with larvae and crustaceans. I can only suggest that those pike had cottoned on to the fact that they only had to eat this protein rich herbage to survive, and so avoid wasting energy chasing food that could swim away. Perhaps there is more to pike diet than we think.

GRAVEL PITS AND LAKES

Above: A 23 lb specimen taken on a half mackerel.

Gravel pits are like people – no two are ever alike. One will be good in the mornings but difficult in the evenings, and another will be moody in the morning but at its best late at night. But they all have behaviour patterns. Study them carefully and you will be able to anticipate their moods and arrange to be around when they are at their best.

If you fish a water around the clock for a number of weeks, you will be able to work out the feeding periods and to be on another water in the quiet periods.

In settled weather at any one time of year, it is sometimes possible to set your watch by the feeding spells of pike. And if you know when to be there and have access to two or three waters with consecutive feeding spells in one small area, you can be at each one at the 'hot' time and make the most of all of them.

Perfect timing

At one time I was fishing four waters near Oxford; the Education Pit, the Poplar Pit, the Nature Reserve and the Night Water. All were close to each other and had good bankside access, so I could drive right up to the swims. The fish

on the Education Pit fed at first light, for half an hour, and that would be it for the rest of the day. The Poplar Pit normally fished well from 11 am to 11.30 am, the Nature Reserve in the afternoons and the Night Water, logically, at night.

One Sunday a friend, Steve Kilbee, and I decided to have a 'pit crawl'. We started on the Education Pit and had pike of 23 lb, 24 lb and an eighteen-pounder at first light. We got to the Poplar Pit at about 10.30 am and had pike of 24 lb and 26 lb within the space of forty-five minutes. By noon we had moved down the road to the Nature Reserve and Steve had one of 26 lb, and that evening we fished the Night Pit and, within fifteen minutes of casting, I had a pike of 19 lb 6 oz. It doesn't happen like that very often, but when it does it's enormously satisfying and you know you are beginning to get it right.

But it's a mistake to fish too many waters. The more of them you fish, the less time you will spend on each one and the less well you will get to know each of them. It's best to concentrate on one or two until you know them intimately. If you then move on to other waters but find them

hard going at first, you can return to the ones you know for a confidence booster.

Above: A 27 lb 8 oz fish from the Nature Reserve, a water in which the pike fed most often in the afternoon when a south-westerly was blowing.

The popular choice for most pike anglers

Love them or loathe them, gravel pits make up a large percentage of the pike fishing available to most anglers, and as rivers gradually decline in level and quality because of the increasing demand for water, the role they play is likely to increase.

To fully understand them you need to know a little of the history of how and why they were created and how they differ according to the decade in which they were dug.

Most of those we fish now were dug in the 1970s and 1980s, when the building boom was at its height and gravel for roads and houses was in big supply. Rich seams in and around Berkshire, Buckinghamshire, Surrey, Hertfordshire and Oxfordshire were fully exploited by firms like Smiths Gravel, Peter Cullimore and ARC, with the result that large areas of land were turned into pits as companies extracted the gravel.

Huge complexes grew up around Reading, at South Cerney, down at Ringwood, and near Staines, as well up in Lincolnshire and down in

Kent… anywhere with gravel seams deep enough to be financially viable.

Oxford got a ring road to lighten the traffic in the city, and gravel for that dual carriageway came from pits that have since become famous-name fisheries, like the Thames Conservancy pit (TC) just yards from the road it created, Dorchester Lagoon and Queenford Lagoon.

So many gravel pits were dug in the seventies that when they had been worked out, many were left fallow as the extractors moved on to the next. They filled with rainwater and through seepage from underground springs, as the water table that previously infiltrated the gravel returned to its natural level. When winter came and heavy rain made swollen streams and brooks spill over into the pits, a new aquatic environment was born.

How they were dug

The way that gravel was extracted has a bearing on the contours of each water. Early pits were dug using drag lines and buckets to scoop up the gravel, creating long furrows side by side, like the lines in a ploughed field. This rather crude method means that pits dug in the sixties and early seventies have furrows along the bottom.

Any non-gravel items extracted were swept to one side in a random pattern, creating contours and bars, later to become important features. But these early pits are very different from later ones that were purposely landscaped by contractors, in line with new regulations.

Later, a more efficient method of extracting gravel was devised and pits were excavated using mechanical diggers called tracscavators, which need a dry surface to operate. So those dug in the eighties, right up to the financial crash and the end of the boom in

1987, were dug dry and didn't have furrows.

And now in the nineties, on the few pits being worked, methods are further mechanised and the bed of the lake much smoother, rising on to plateaux as the gravel seam lifts, and dropping where it runs deep again.

But no matter how good methods of gravel extraction become, the pits they produce will rarely be more than 30 feet deep because that's roughly gravel's extreme depth. The majority of pits in the Home Counties and Oxfordshire are between 9 feet and 15 feet deep. In Kent they removed the gravel but stopped when they reached the greensand layer because there was no commercial demand for greensand, whereas in

Top: A gravel pit dug dry, with its furrows and heaps of non-gravel items.

Bottom: An Oxford gravel pit dug down to its layer of blue clay.

Oxfordshire it was blue clay that they hit when the gravel had been taken out.

Pits dug purely for clay differ from gravel pits in that they can be as much as 140 feet deep. Clay occurs in much deeper seams than gravel. These very deep waters only fish well under the warm rays of spring sunshine and when the water has had a chance to warm up by the autumn, but not in mid-winter. A few years ago some friends and I fished Grebe Lake, at Crendon Underwood, near Bicester, which is a clay pit of this depth, and

struggled to get a run after November. Timing is the most important factor when approaching clay pits as the fish are in a state of semi-hibernation in the coldest weather and unlikely to respond.

Above: Pike from egg stage to three weeks old. After hatching, they attach themselves to weed for several days until their yolk sack has been absorbed and they are strong enough to become free-swimming and start to hunt for food.

How they are colonised?

In a newly flooded gravel pit, life enters from feeder streams that bring caddis and crustaceans, hog lice and shrimps – food for the first fish in a new water.

Often, gravel pits are connected by a series of small pipes used to keep the water level at bay while others are being worked. Small fish find their way in when streams flood over fields to one gravel pit, and then all the others become colonised. Damsel flies, sedges, and bloodworm spread as adults, on the wing, providing an excellent food supply.

Small fish and insects seem to appear almost instantly in recently flooded waters, providing the basis for a new ecosystem of aquatic life. The tiny fish begin their lives in the varieties of marginal weeds that sprout up as the gravel working stops and the water clears, over the course of two or three months.

If the pit has been dug dry enough for light to penetrate in the large puddles of shallow water, certain hardy waterplants may have got a foothold already. This weed provides the small fish that arrive with food and cover. Tiny fish can live out the start of their lives hidden in weed. Pull some up on any stillwater in summer and you will find insect life and minute fish sheltering in among the strands.

The plop of small pike

Daphnia multiply and provide food for small fish. Among them will be small pike. After hatching, they stay close to the weed in which they were born and live on a diet of daphnia, plankton and minute crustaceans. From four to five weeks old, they begin to feed on larger prey like chironomids and small fish, including their own kind, and by May and June they are taking large fry. I have often

sat by the water in summer and heard the resounding plops of tiny pike taking buzzers and damselfly nymphs off the surface in the marginal rafts of floating weed.

I believe that the first fish to learn to become cannibalistic may become the ultimate survivors. They manage to make it through the first winter by feeding on their own brethren, whereas other young pike often find food hard to come by and their mortality rate is much higher.

If the roach fail to spawn one year, then the pike that have learned to feed on their own kind are the ones that will survive. Why some do and some don't is still a mystery. If they get through the first two winters, they are over the most precarious time, and their likelihood of survival improves a great deal.

But nature does its best to help them, and its timing is exquisite. When the pike are a couple of months old the roach, perch and bream fry emerge from their eggs when they are of a perfect size for the young pike to eat.

When young pike are ready to leave the margins to seek bigger creatures in the depths, having outgrown the shallow water, they lose the characteristic, creamy yellow bars on their flanks. They now weigh about 7 lb, and this change in markings takes two or three years to come about. The bars are replaced by oval, dappled spots that are better suited to camouflage in the shifting light found in deeper water.

How fast do pike grow?

By the time a water is ten to fifteen years old, with a good fish population, it should contain a fair head of 20 lb pike. I caught a 23 lb pike in a gravel pit and sent a scale from it to Alwyne

Wheeler at the British Museum. He counted seven annual growth rings. The rate of growth is speeded up if the gravel pit is linked to older ones by drainage pipes or channels, which greatly aid the spread of fish. But even 50-acre or 60-acre, rich gravel pits rarely have more than four or five fish of 20 lb, which is about the upper limit, and there are very few waters with more than this.

Pike weights in gravel pits that aren't artificially topped up with trout or coarse fish seem to reach their size limit at 33 lb to 34 lb. If you've caught one of that weight, you've gone about as far as you can go on that sort of water. It takes a gravel pit with something very special for the weight of its pike to go above that – something like a plentiful supply of bream or a very large head of roach. Some commercially run waters stock large numbers of small food fish, like carp, that make good fodder and improve the growth rate enormously.

There have also been occasions when a pit has been backfilled and all of the fish have been concentrated into a smaller area, creating a bonanza for the pike. If you come across a pit being backfilled, do your utmost to get permission to fish it, because catches can be impressive and location is not a problem.

So, the age of a gravel pit is very important when trying to discover whether it holds big fish, but you can't tell how old one is by the number and size of trees on the banks. If it hasn't been landscaped, there will be very few shrubs. If there are mature willows, then it's a fair bet that it is between fifteen and twenty years old, but don't overlook a water just because it has near-barren banks. Plenty of those sort of waters have produced big pike.

Above: This is my second best river pike, a 26 lb 12 oz fish taken on a sink and draw roach while it was lying close to a bream shoal.

The amount of vegetation overhanging the surface and the clarity of the water dictate whether it is silty or weedy. Water surrounded by trees that lose their leaves tend to be silty and free from weed because the trees shade the light necessary for weed growth, and their fallen leaves cover the bottom, also hampering growth.

Some are so narrow and have such a luxuriant growth of trees on the banks that they form a canopy, blocking out much of the light. Less weed growth means fewer food fish and fewer pike. They may contain one or two small pike, but open pits are generally likely to be richer. Small, open waters can produce big fish, but don't spent too much time on them in the hope that they hold a monster. You'll know within two or three sessions if there's something special in there.

Gravel pits designed for angling

So many gravel pits were dug and left fallow in the seventies that it was possible to investigate them without anyone knowing or caring. The firms were too busy digging gravel to concern themselves about the pits they had left behind.

At South Cerney alone there were forty or fifty gravel pits in one small area, all of different ages and many untouched by anglers. All gravel pits produce their best catches in cycles, and those that didn't produce big fish when we tried them could be left for a few years until they were at their peak, such was the huge choice of waters.

But by the time the eighties arrived, purpose-built recreation waters were being created by gravel companies when extraction had been completed, in line with planning regulations and agreements signed when permission to dig for gravel was granted. They landscaped the pits, creating bars and islands for wildlife and nesting birds, planted vegetation above and below the waterline and flooded them to create wildlife sanctuaries, water parks and recreation centres for sailing enthusiasts, water-skiers and anglers.

What started out as an obligation to leave the area looking attractive soon became a chance to respond to a growing demand for sites suitable for outdoor activities. They found that if they built houses in the area and set up water sports parks for wind surfing and jet-skiing there was big money to be made at a time when the demand for gravel and the need to dig new pits was falling.

*Above: Waters that have had little attention from anglers
do exist, like the one in Gloucestershire that produced this fish
of 24 lb 8 oz.*

The situation now is that there are fewer new waters being created than for several decades but the rise in the popularity of pike fishing as the second most popular fishing species after carp has meant more anglers pursuing them. Where once you could visit a complex and stroll around several waters trying here and there unhindered, now there's hardly a gravel pit anywhere that hasn't got a line of brollies or bivvies sprouting like green mushrooms from its banks. And on such waters pike won't reach their full potential if they are being caught regularly instead of being left to feed and grow.

Pike angling pioneers

So the angler who wants good sport has to break new ground if he is to keep catching big pike. He needs to be the first one on a water, he needs to spend a lot of time fishing speculatively and put up with hours spent trying to get to grips with new places and, unfortunately, he needs to cover his tracks so that others can't follow.

I'm more secretive about location than I used to be. When waters were ten a penny I'd talk openly, but not now. The few pits that allow me solitude are very precious, because I know how hard it is to find new waters.

I like fishing pits that haven't seen an angler. Their challenge is a large part of the attraction of pike fishing, for me. And once I catch the fish I'm after, I seldom go back. The challenge is in finding somewhere untouched, exploring it, calculating the age of the pit and its potential, getting permission, working out how to tackle it, plumbing depths, finding features, calculating where the fish should be and putting them on the bank, hard-fighting and fin-perfect, untouched by any other angler.

For me, the preparation and planning is as exciting as the fishing, and the catching is just the icing on the cake. But when you land a fish from that type of water, having done your homework, you do get an incredible amount of satisfaction.

You don't get this if you let others do the preparation work for you, and just cast out and reel the fish in without understanding why you have caught it.

Waters that have had little attention from anglers do still exist. We once found a place so

Above: On my third cast with a sink-and-draw wobbled trout, this incredible pike came after the bait, broke the water as it took it and tore off. It pulled the scales down to an incredible 35 lb.

overgrown we had to cut our way through brambles and hawthorns to get to the bank, and then there were no swims or footpaths to make things easy. Yet it produced pike in the upper twenties for us.

I believe that almost all of the fish I have landed have never been caught before. You can often tell when a pike has been handled – abrasion marks down its side from hooks or wire, an old wound in the area of the jaw where a small layer of scar tissue has healed, or fins split by mishandling.

But virgin waters aren't easy to find. In many cases it takes more ingenuity and perseverance to get access to an unspoiled water than it does to catch the fish that are in it.

In search of new waters

Every close season I look at new waters and search for pits capable of producing big fish using Ordnance Survey maps for the area. Often they are the most remote, as this stops them from getting other anglers' attention.

My biggest pike came from a gravel pit I saw while driving around looking at waters. It was close to a stream, so I thought it might have a good head of eels and food fish, and it looked quite old judging by the size and maturity of the trees around it.

I knocked on the door of an old cottage nearby and asked the man who answered it if he knew anything about the gravel pit nearby. He said it belonged to him but he didn't have any fishing on it. I told him I was interested in pike and I explained that I wouldn't abuse his permission, drop litter, make a noise, drive on the land or do anything that would abuse his trust, and any fish caught would be put back.

He was a nature lover and had had the water dug initially to attract wildlife and birds. He didn't need money from anglers, being a rich land owner, so he had everything to lose and nothing to gain.

He said he would think about it for a few weeks, and I arranged to contact him at a later date. I didn't ring back sooner because people who get pestered invariably say no. I left it for six weeks, despite my keenness to get on the water. I find it easier to put my case face to face, and it's harder for someone to turn you down when you're

Above: Fish of 24 lb 12 oz and 24 lb 8 oz in consecutive casts from a clear gravel pit.

than three feet deep. On my third cast with a sink-and-draw wobbled trout, this incredible pike came after the bait, broke the water as it took it and tore off with it. The fight was short and dogged. One of my most memorable moments is when it rolled over in the net and I got my first glimpse of its size. It pulled the scales down to an incredible 35 lb.

I'm sure there were other big fish in there, but that experience had been close to perfection and I walked away and haven't fished the water since. I did consider it once, but the more often you go back the more likely that other anglers will find out where the water is.

Special occasions

If you get a chance to fish a water that is only open for a couple of days each year it is worth taking the one-off opportunity. Thorpe Park was like that once, allowing people on for lure championships or special occasions but being closed to angling for the rest of the time. There's a water near Reading that open its doors just once a year, and it produces 20 lb fish every time, weather permitting.

If you get a chance to visit a protected water, grab it with both hands. The pike are likely to be plentiful and in excellent condition, and not too difficult to catch. At other times, finding new waters can mean watching them being dug and earmarking them for attention once they have become fisheries. It takes two years for fish to become firmly established naturally in a new water. From then on, whether it breeds a monster is down to the shape of the pit and the balance between pike and food fish. I've watched a water near Stanton Harcourt for the whole of its 25-year history, and caught fish to 28 lb from it.

The size and shape of the water depends on the size and shape of the original gravel seam. The biggest pit I have come across was a mile and a half long, but others are only an acre. And while a big water is likely to be the better bet, there is no reason why a small one should not produce a monster. It is all down to food and pressure.

Some are five feet deep almost all over and others are 20 feet deep in places. You need to know how each one measures up. Some seem ideal until you find they have roosting points for

standing next to them than when you're on the phone, so I drove over and knocked on his door.

Again I explained how keen I was to fish, but he said he hadn't made up his mind and had to consult his wife. I found out in talking to him that we had a common interest in birds, and I think it was this shared love of nature that made him trust me and give me permission to fish.

Walking on to that water with my tackle felt like a victory already. I was being allowed on to a very special place that no one else had been near for decades. I plumbed the depth in various places and found nowhere of greater depth than eight feet, and the majority about five feet. The water was extremely clear, with a feeder stream at one end and an outlet at the other, and I could see a lot of coarse fish of a whole range of different sizes that hadn't been fished for in thirty years.

I got out my compass and headed for the north-east bank. The water was shallow there, no more

Above: A 24-pounder taken on a mackerel head.

Right: A 16 lb 4 oz pike taken on a half mackerel fished at close range.

cormorants, and the food fish have been all but wiped out, while others have big populations of bite-size food fish that provide pike with a well-stocked larder.

Some are coloured, where gravel extraction is still being carried out. These often have big populations of bream, and you can be sure that where there are a lot of bream of edible size, there are going to be a lot of pike. And others, particularly Oxford pits, are renowned for their stillwater chub, dace and roach, which breed successfully in them and so are present in all sizes. They form an important food source for pike and should be considered as a choice of bait.

Learning to read a water by what you can see above the waterline is a valuable skill, for it enables you to at least estimate the potential of somewhere you are considering fishing while doing nothing more suspicious than strolling round the bank.

Assessing pike fishing potential

So you're standing on the banks of a likely looking water on a warm, sunny day. What do you look for to assess its pike fishing potential?

Start by peering into the margins as you walk round. As we have said, any water that holds fair-sized pike needs a good supply of food fish of various sizes, so that pike of different sizes can find plenty to eat, and some of these will be visible in the margins or the shallows, especially if it is a warm day.

Some pits have a lot of big pike but nothing else because the only food fish are big, old coarse fish that have ceased to spawn, and with nothing smaller in the water, pike have nothing to eat apart from the jacks.

If it's a silt-bottomed water, it may have tench and carp in it, and if it's a weedy water it should have roach, rudd, tench and perch – worth bearing in mind when choosing baits.

Others are surrounded by farmland and get large quantities of nitrates washed in from the soil during rainfall, which will promote weed growth perhaps to the extent that the water won't be fishable other than on the surface until October.

The size of the water is a factor to consider, but don't be misled into thinking that a big water means big numbers of pike. I believe that a 120-acre water I fished had just twelve pike of over 20 lb in it. If a water such as this gets a lot of angling attention, and the fish are caught regularly, perhaps without people realising that they are the same ones, the brief burst of good sport won't last. The fish will find some way of eluding anglers, by changing their feeding times and habits and by moving into areas where anglers cannot reach them.

Built on chalk

Some pits aren't gravel pits at all but are formed when extracting chalk, which brings another set of circumstances into play. These tend to be very clear, like the famous southern trout streams, the Test and the Itchen, which run over chalk. Weed growth can be phenomenal, creating presentation problems.

Weed can grow to within feet of the surface, so a sunken-float paternostered or buoyant bait will be more visible. I have cast deadbaits into weed on such waters and caught fish, scaling up from 15 lb line to 18 lb to pull them clear. An air-injected bait fished on top of weed, a pop-up rig with the bait allowed to rise to near the surface or a shallow, float fished bait are other ways around the problem.

I like to tackle these waters early in the year, in February and March, before the weed has started to grow, or in October, when pike are still high in the water and the weed is beginning to die back. But whenever I fish, I will always go for a very visible bait, like a roach or a dace.

At the other extreme, waters that are very coloured present no weed problems but may have a thick layer of silt that can hide baits when presented near to the bottom. In the water we named the Big Coloured Pit, the fish were very pale, as they often are in murky water. Whenever you get a cloudy water there is always a bream shoal thriving in that environment, and this pit was no exception.

We found out by accident that this water had a deep layer of silt on the bottom. We were fishing there unsuccessfully when Jurassic Phil's tatty old umbrella was picked up by a strong gust of wind and hurled into the water. Most people would have given it up for lost but being someone with deep pockets and short arms when it comes to paying for new tackle, Phil had to have it back.

He tied a 3 oz bomb and two trebles to the end of his line and cast over it to drag it back. Only when he got the brolly, thick with silt, did we realise what the bottom was like and that our baits had been sinking deep into the stuff, out of sight of the pike. Pop-ups were the answer, and still are. Sometimes the solution can be found completely by accident, and the key to cracking a water can lie in one small discovery.

Where do you head for?

On a new water I always start in the north east corner, because that's where the warmest, south-

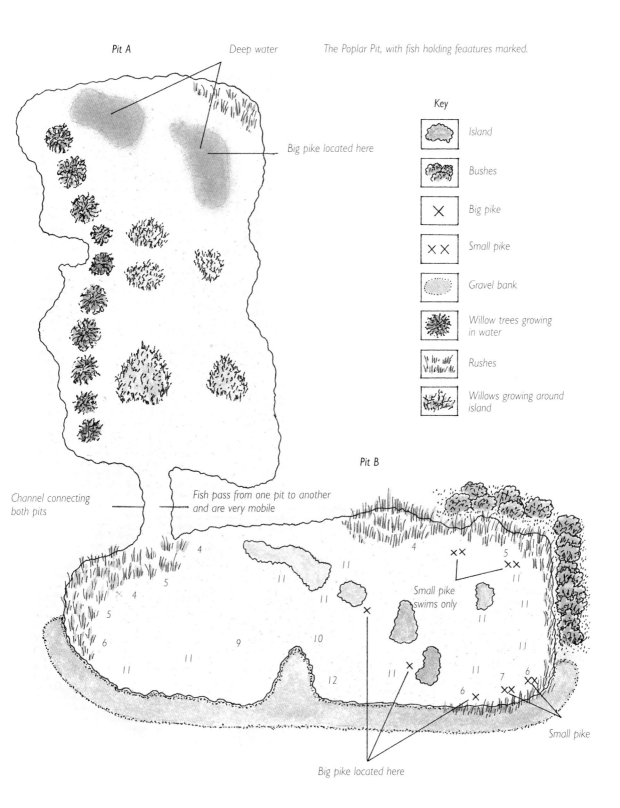

Pit A

Deep water

Big pike located here

The Poplar Pit, with fish holding feeatures marked.

Key

Island

Bushes

Big pike

Small pike

Gravel bank

Willow trees growing in water

Rushes

Willows growing around island

Pit B

Channel connecting both pits

Fish pass from one pit to another and are very mobile

Small pike swims only

Big pike located here

Small pike

westerly wind will have been blowing. It's also where any dead or dying coarse fish that float up in the water will be carried, and pike there will be on the look out for a free meal.

If that fails to produce, though it usually yields something, I head for the north bank and then work my way down into the corner again and along the east bank, which will be sheltered from

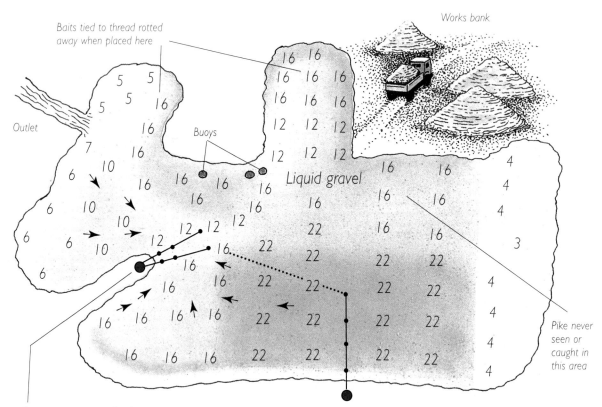

Baits tied to thread rotted away when placed here

Works bank

Outlet

Buoys

Liquid gravel

Pike never seen or caught in this area

Commanding point to fish from. Baits will be taken at range through the day, then at night as the bream move close to the shelf

Bream shoal located here. Match anglers have driven them out at range through the day by continuous pressure, but they do come in **close** after dark. They **rarely** stray far away from the lines shown above

cold easterly winds and their raw chill factor. The east bank can hold a deep gully that is home to large shoals of bream and roach, though this is by no means always the case.

The only time I will fish one of the other banks is when there is a fish-holding feature, like a series of islands, that may have drawn pike away from the usual holding areas, or if the water in the favoured corner is very shallow or extremely deep and unsuitable for pike to live in.

On the Big Coloured Pit, which is 120 acres and 22 feet deep, there were only four swims that produced fish. As an experiment, we tied baits to cotton and put them out in different areas. Many of these rotted away without being taken, which gives you an indication of how few swims are worth fishing, even on a big water.

If the water you are fishing is popular, there's always a chance that fish have been pushed into unlikely areas by angling pressure. That complicates matters because the fish are no longer

behaving naturally, and when working out their likely location you have to consider their need to escape anglers as well as their need to feed and find shelter.

My first line of attack would be to tackle areas rarely fished, at longer range and closer in than the norm using the least common baits at the least popular times, possibly at night. And when on a new water I would try to fish as many different swims as possible to get a broad picture of which areas are most productive.

Whatever the situation on a new water, start by breaking it down into several, smaller parts, to make it more manageable, and look at one area at a time, examining the features. The following places are likely to attract food fish and pike:

Ledges are used by coarse fish like bream and roach, which will follow them, coming in to them at night, searching for food and feeding at the bottom of the shelf, where they feel secure. Baits

have to be placed right against the ledge with pin-point accuracy, not just fairly near, as that is where pike will feed.

Drop-offs likewise. The smaller the water, the less pronounced a contour needs to be to attract fish. In a shallow water a drop off of a foot is a major feature, whereas in a deeper one it wouldn't necessarily be a spot to head for.

Buoys placed by sailing clubs are attached to their anchors by ropes, and ropes collect algae, which attracts food fish, which in turn attracts pike. On the Big Coloured Pit, if we could hit a buoy with half a mackerel we would catch fish.

Landing stages require a very stealthy approach. We used to creep to the end of one on the Education Pit and lower the bait straight down from the rod top and then stand well back.

When **islands** are created artificially on gravel pits they're often made by digging a deep trough alongside. These can be anything up to twenty feet deep and home to bream and roach, with the pike holding a little way off them, keeping in contact with the shoal.

I like to put a boat with an echo sounder on a new water if the rules allow, and look for contours that could attract fish. However, I won't fish from it because I don't believe boat fishing on gravel pits is in anyone's long-term interests. Pike need

Above: Wooded banks and islands harbour insects, which drop into the water attracting prey fish, which in turn attract pike.

to have some sanctuary where they can escape from the attentions of anglers, and on many waters the only way they can find peace is by getting out of casting range of the bank.

Feeder streams attract large shoals of fry and have large numbers of pike crashing into them. Water piped from another pit will often have the same oxygenating, fish-attracting effect, stirring up food on the bottom and cutting a hollow in the lake bed. Chub in particular seem to like these.

Sticks, dead trees and saplings growing in the water offer refuge and cover from open water. Perch in particular like them. Pike will often get right in among beds of sticks, and heavy tackle will be needed to get them out.

Small pike are fond of **rushes** as they suit their camouflage colouring, and this in turn attracts very big, jack-feeding pike. The best kind of rushes are the ones that have spaces between them so that pike can get in. If they're too densely packed, pike can't penetrate them.

Pike can get so far into them that they can't detect your bait, fished up against the edge. When you have tried putting a bait against the weeds, without success, you can then sometimes flush a fish out by disturbing it, and it is still likely to take a bait. As Fred Buller explained in his book, Tom Morgan's experiences of flushing pike out of dense weed beds by weed thrashing with an oar from a boat and then catching them on livebaits has been proven to work on other waters. John Bailey and Barrie Rickards know the same happens among the Norfolk reed beds in East Anglia, and no doubt this would work elsewhere.

Left: Fish hooked at close-quarters can whip the water into a foam. When fishing the margins, be ready for a surprise.

Gravel bars are sometimes inter-linked throughout a pit and pike, which know its layout intimately, will follow the contours. They will wait alongside a bar or at the bottom for the chance to attack their prey from below and ambush them without being seen. Gravel bars are a welcome sight as they break up the monotony of large strips of water and offer shelter and food for fish of all species.

Below: A fish of 21 lb 8 oz on a sardine freelined against a submerged island.

Wooded banks and **islands** harbour insects, which drop into the water, and they in turn attract roach and so pike. The best place to put a bait near an island is where the warmest winds hit its shores, which means the southern tip or western side. It's also worth a look at the steepest shore in wet weather, as land-based creatures like worms and slugs may fall into the water.

Why pike are easier in winter

A lot depends on the time of year that you are tackling a water. Locating pike is a great deal easier in winter than in summer. Throughout the summer, coarse fish can be seen dimpling on the surface, spread evenly around the lake. The pike are distributed likewise. If they want food it's right in front of them and there's no competition for it from other pike.

In summer, pike can satisfy their hunger easily. But come September and October and the first frosts, food fish begin to shoal in different areas, where the temperature is even and they can shelter in safety. Don't waste time locating pike in autumn, ready for their winter campaign... the fish will be somewhere else entirely come the harsh weather.

Wherever the food fish are, pike will be close behind, made hungry by the cold, and in the process of changing their feeding times from night to day. Some anglers struggle to catch fish until the first frost of winter, not realising that they are fishing by day for a creature that could be feeding at night until October and November.

When the weather is warm, pike become nocturnal feeders because it is cooler and quieter at night. The darkness provides cover for pike to stalk their prey successfully. But in winter the nights are too cold for feeding, so the warmest time of day becomes the time for feeding. And as food fish are tightly shoaled, pike can pick them off without the aid of darkness.

In raw, easterly winds, **bays** can offer welcome shelter from the cold, for you and the fish, and when the sun is on the water it is these that usually warm up first. If they're on the north bank, receiving warm winds, even better.

Whenever I fish a bay I cover the exit and entrance so that a pike entering it from anywhere on the water has to come across one or both of my baits. Normally it will follow the contour of the bank and not just swim into the

bay from open water, so you should cast on either side of the mouth.

Points and headlands are very important features from an angler's point of view as pike moving from one area to another can be intercepted by a bait cast from a point. A great deal of water can be covered from a peninsula – far more than when fishing from a straight bank, with a commanding view of the water. And if you

Above: Don't neglect the margins. This 22 lb pike picked up off a half mackerel head dropped just beyond the rod tops from a point on the east bank of the Poplar Pit.

have an island close by, even better. You can cast a bait between the two features where it forms a funnel through which food fish swim, and an ideal ambush site for pike to lie in wait. A channel that connects two pits is another good ambush point because it is narrower still.

But the biggest single feature on any gravel pit is **the bank**. Small fish take refuge in the margins, wave action disturbs the margins, dead fish get swept into the margins, and so on. And if a water doesn't have any islands or bars, like the Thames Conservancy pit for instance, the margins are even more likely to produce pike.

Walk along an undisturbed bank early in the morning and you will see small fish swimming out from the edge as you approach. Even in mid-winter you can often see roach topping in shallow water close to the bank, making the most of a warm, winter sun. Pike will be close by, and not in the deepest water – where you might expect them, given the time of year.

I once noticed that a mackerel head I had discarded in the margins had disappeared. I threw another in the same place and soon that had

disappeared as well. I didn't need any more hints. I reeled in one of the rods and dropped a bait in the same spot. Within five minutes it was taken and I landed a pike of 19 lb 7 oz. The moral of the story is don't neglect the margins. They are, perhaps, the most underrated feature.

Psyching out pike

When you've spent time fishing for pike and watching them in clear water you start to understand why they behave in the way they do and even learn to predict their movements and response to a bait.

After a while you can categorise pike according to their behaviour, and this way it's possible to capitalise on favourable situations and read the signs when a fish or group of fish are behaving in a way that makes them more catchable.

Here are the main categories that I have come across among pike I have observed.

Rovers are nomadic pike that travel great distances and turn up almost anywhere. They are opportunist feeders fond of scavenging and likely to pick up anything edible, dead or alive, in their path. This makes them among the first fish to be caught in a swim, but they are rarely the biggest because of the inconsistency of their food supply.

Shoal followers stay in touch with fodder fish at certain times of year, following their mobile larder and dipping into it when they need to. They stay at the same depth as the shoal, keeping just a short distance behind it.

Stayers are pike that have found a lie that suits them well, providing cover to spring ambushes and comfort out of any current, but with a ready food supply near at hand. These pike tend to be the biggest, and when one dies, its lie will be taken almost immediately by another, slightly smaller fish. If the lie is big enough, two or more pike may occupy one niche.

A **fierce** pike is one feeding aggressively and taking anything available – usually a small fish. Very big pike don't often feed as voraciously as small ones because they are not growing at anything like the same rate, but maintaining body weight and replacing energy loss.

An **interested feeder** is the kind of pike that we are fishing for most of the time because it is hungry enough to be tempted by a fresh, well-presented bait, though not ravenous and searching for food.

And the **satisfied** pike is one that has just fed well and is not interested in another meal. This sort will, however, reflex-feed, and grab a livebait to kill it if it finds it annoying. Often, when anglers catch these fish they find the remains of the previous meal still in the pike's throat. If your hooks are positioned correctly you can strike immediately and you will have a fair chance of hooking the pike before it lets go of your bait.

Feeding patterns can change each day, each week, each month and each year. That is why an angler who catches fish one week may not do so the next.

Above: Small pike often take refuge in the margins and bigger pike will never be far away, waiting for a chance to strike.

Choosing the method

You can save a lot of time when investigating a new water by choosing the right method to tackle it. By far the most successful method on gravel pits is the freelined or legered deadbait, normally a half mackerel or a whole sardine.

I would urge you to stick to sardines, but they don't lend themselves to long casting. Use them for close- to medium-range work or for boat fishing. Sandeels also have their day, and don't forget jack pike. You can use a free-roving livebait to locate pike on an open expanse of water, but a deadbait cast to a feature is just as likely to be successful. It all depends which bait you have greatest faith in, and whether you are prepared to try different baits and depths until you get it right.

However, you need to respond to what you see happening. If the fish are up in the water, because it is warm or there is a bar or a shallow area where they can bask, fish your bait up in the water, too.

A paternostered livebait just under the surface works well in summer. If you are legering and a fish follows your bait in to the edge as you reel in, that fish may have been up in the water when your bait came past and it could be worth changing over to see if that is true.

Novices armed with half-a-dozen mackerel and a pike bung often tether a bait three feet under the float on a nice warm day, cast it out and catch the biggest fish in the lake.

Above: The 23 lb 8 oz fish that created a calm patch and took the half mackerel I cast to the spot, on the drop. Bite alarms give you time to watch the water.

The lesson is that the bait has to be where the fish can see it, so if there's evidence of fish high in the water, put the bait there. I've caught pike five feet down in thirty-five feet of water in summer, and from the number of times I've seen dorsal fins break the surface, I know they like it up there in the sunshine.

One of the reasons I use bite alarms rather than just silent, drop-off indicators is because I like to keep my eyes on the water for signs of fish. I remember seeing a circle of oil-calm water appear in a ripple, where something had struck, and when I cast to it, my bait was taken on the drop by a pike of 23 lb 8 oz. I'm sure that if I hadn't been watching, I wouldn't have caught that fish.

And I always make a mental note of where I have just cast, lining the spot up with a tree or a telegraph pole on the horizon, so that I can put the bait in the same place again if this proves to be a hotspot.

At the mercy of the weather

The weather plays a big part in determining whether fish on the gravel pit you've chosen will feed. Frosts, for instance, are the kiss of death because gravel pits don't have sufficient depth to weather them without being badly affected.

I always wondered why the myth existed that a frosty morning – the classic piker's dawn, when the fields are white and the grass crunchy under

foot – was thought to be good for pike fishing. It certainly isn't good news on gravel pits.

The only explanation I can offer is that the idea that frost means good pike fishing is a throwback to the days when stillwater fishing was done on estate lakes, which are very silty and perhaps less susceptible to sudden changes in temperature. It could be that some warmth is created in the lake by the thick layer of decaying leaves on the bottom, or it could be that the fish are used to the low temperatures because most of the water is fairly shallow. But whatever the reason, it is certainly true that, of the few stillwaters worth fishing after a very hard frost, the old English estate lakes are worth trying

Not all gravel pits are typical, however. The Poplar Pit, which I mentioned earlier, produced fish irrespective of the weather, and in conditions when a session on another similar water would have been a waste of time. I don't know why this should be.

If frosts are bad news, surely, then, mild weather must be perfect for catching pike? Not necessarily so. I believe if the air temperature is 55 degrees Fahrenheit for too long, pike can feed when they feel like it, and they become so well spread out that they are difficult to tempt or find.

Above: The Poplar Pit produced pike irrespective of the weather, in conditions when fishing should have been a waste of time.

Right: Estate lakes like Bladon, near Woodstock, may hold the key to the popular myth of the frosty piker's dawn.

The answer, I'm now convinced, is to be on the water the day before a cold snap. The fish know that cold weather is on its way and that stimulates them to feed. They must feel the need to stock up in readiness for the lean spell about to descend, and feed very hard indeed for that one or two days prior to the change.

The cold snap may last for three weeks, especially when there is a full moon in winter – often accompanied by high pressure and sunny days, followed by frosty, clear nights. At this time pike will remain torpid and take little or nothing in the way of food. But as soon as the weather

breaks and a short spell of mild, wet weather takes its place they will go on a binge and feed hungrily again.

If you can anticipate the weather and be on the water just before or just after that cold snap, you may find pike queuing up to take your baits. My tackle is at the ready throughout the winter, and when the weather man says we're in for a change, I'm out on the water like a shot.

This happened once in November. I just knew that the fish were going to feed. I arrived with a friend at a gravel pit at about tea-time. I kept looking at my watch... 6.30 pm... 7.30 pm...

8.45 pm… 10.50 pm. Nothing had happened.

We were just thinking of going home when the fish switched on. The trip was transformed from a blank to an unforgettable evening. We had thirteen doubles that night. When you put a theory to the test and it comes up trumps it's particularly pleasing, especially if you were about to give up!

Above: Three twenties caught in twenty-five minutes as the first rays of light broke through at dawn, during a spell of mild weather in winter, followed by fish of 18 lb and 16 lb.

Warm spells in winter

Some waters respond to a change in the weather faster than others. It depends on the size and depth of the gravel pit. If the water is deep it can take three to four days for the temperature to rise in a warm spell in winter, and some waters, particularly big concrete bowls, are just too deep for even a prolonged warm spell to bring pike out of their winter torpor.

On the Big Coloured Pit, fishing in winter was a dead loss because it was so deep. The temperature didn't get high enough to make pike respond. But one winter we had such a prolonged spell of very warm weather that there was just a chance that the pike had been encouraged to feed.

The longer the warm weather went on the more we fancied our chances at the water, and when we went there, the fish were feeding, though only for the final day or two that the good weather lasted. If you know why the fish in your chosen water respond in the way that they do, you're in a much better position to anticipate good sport, and do so with surprising accuracy, and be in the right place to make the most of it when it happens.

Dawn and dusk

Pike feed early in the morning and late in the evening because these times offer a lot of advantages. Shoal fish are grouped together, grazing among the weed, and their preoccupation with feeding makes them vulnerable to being picked off by predators. As the light begins to fade and objects become silhouettes, pike can use this reduced visibility to press home their attack with least chance of being detected.

Flat as a pancake

I've never liked fishing in flat-calms. Given a choice between windy weather and still, I would go for windy every time. A gentle breeze will push the surface water down to one end of a lake, which shunts the water on the bottom back to the top end to take its place. This causes top and bottom layers to intermingle, and if the sun has been on the water, this will have the effect of warming up the whole lake.

I have found four or five degrees difference between top and bottom temperatures on a very deep water. Perhaps this is why a good breeze improves fishing so much in winter.

Wind in itself is a stimulus to fish to start feeding. It adds oxygen to the water and stirs up food. Pike in clear water respond to it well because it sets up a ripple, which refracts the light, breaking it into uneven patterns, and camouflages them with their gold bars and dappled markings, allowing them to creep up on their prey.

On the Norfolk Broads, it doesn't seem to be essential for there be a ripple on the water because many of those waters have a tinge of colour to them. I've discussed this point with Bill Giles and he is adamant that on the Broads, a flat calm is not necessarily a bad thing. But on clear waters, like many of those found around Oxford, a ripple is a distinct advantage.

Fishing in the rain

I've hardly caught any pike while fishing in the rain. In fact, now I come to think of it, I can't remember catching a single fish when it's been pouring. I've done well after rain, or before it, and before and after thunder, but not during rain.

It's not for want of trying. For the sake of experimentation I've sat it out, getting cold and wet, and still caught nothing. I find it depressing watching rain pouring down, especially if it's windy, and if that grey, drizzly rain descends that I know isn't going to go away, I'll pack up and come home. Confidence is all, and if I haven't got enough enthusiasm to sit it out, there's no point in staying.

Immobile pike

Other influences on a pike's feeding habits include wind direction, barometric pressure, light intensity and water clarity, and all have a direct influence on the feeding habits and moods of fish. On some days, particularly when the temperature is well down, pike will not move to a bait, even though they are hungry, and want the bait placed almost on their nose.

If I'm on a water at a time of day when they usually respond and I haven't had a run for half an hour, I will move my bait, sometimes putting it just five or six feet to one side. Whether it's the movement of the fish through the water or just that pike are rendered almost completely immobile, I don't know, but sometimes pike just have to be spoon-fed.

You can tell when you have caught an immobile pike because the flanks often have two or three leeches attached, where they have been lying still in weed, conserving energy.

There is an exception, though, and that is in Scotland, when it can do very little else but rain for long periods, so the stuff often can't be avoided. But even then it's not a highly productive time, and from the angler's point of view, it can be downright miserable.

Fishy preoccupations

If conditions are in your favour, and you know the water holds pike, and you've fished around features and things still aren't going your way, you could be dealing with a preoccupation. Pike can become very selective feeders, and sometimes unless you present them with the exact size and species of bait that they favour, nothing will happen.

I've known pike to become totally preoccupied with small tench, to the exclusion of all else, or tiny roach fry, and on other waters only jack pike used as bait will tempt a sizeable fish, so preoccupied are they with eating their own kind. Finding out what's on the menu is extremely difficult, and getting them off that food impossible. Preoccupation occurs more often than we realise. When we fail we usually put that down to other factors rather than the choice of bait.

At Theale Lagoon, the big pike preoccupied on fry wouldn't look at anything bigger, and at Blenheim pike were crashing into shoals of fry, stunning them with sweeps of their tails and coming back to mop up their victims. The frustrating thing is that preoccupations can change within days. No sooner have you found out what they are taking, and found a bait to match, than they're on to something else.

But sometimes preoccupations can last for years, perhaps only affecting one or two fish, often big ones, and these pike don't get caught. If they haven't been seen or caught for years, everyone has assumed they've died or been stolen. Then, after years of avoiding capture, their preoccupation ends and they start picking up anglers' baits and get caught, and everyone wonders where they've come from.

It takes only one or two years when the main food fish fail to spawn, or for predators to have made heavy inroads into their numbers, for pike to have to look elsewhere for their staple food.

Right: A fish of 19 lb 8 oz that fell for a tench.

Bottom right: Blenheim Palace lake, where preoccupied pike crashed into shoals of small roach.

There's also a possibility that old pike can no longer catch fast-swimming roach and dace, and turn to slower species. They don't need to feed so often as they are not growing, so they may become scavengers, restricting their feeding to dead and dying fish. Whatever the reason, preoccupations can strike at any time and should always be considered as a reason for lack of success.

Jack feeders

On one water that we discovered, there was a surprising lack of small coarse fish dimpling on the surface in the evenings, and no fry in the margins. When we explored with spinners, we caught three or four jacks, and it was only when we put one of these 3 lb fish on a hook that we found something bigger – a 26 lb 12 oz pike which had a 4 lb jack in the back of its throat.

In all we had nine fish of over 20 lb, every one on a jack deadbait. The water held some very big tench but I never saw a roach or a perch or any other coarse fish. Pike have got the ability to grow big on their own kind if they are left alone, and this was what had happened.

I remember seeing a little pike lying just off some rushes and looking very agitated. When he saw me, he spooked into deep water but came back almost straight away. I knew instinctively that there must be a very big fish about.

I put a jack bait out and within ten minutes it was taken by a fish of 25 lb 3 oz. When pike of that size are hungry and are actively seeking out jacks, they know the small fish will be in the margins, near the cover of rushes, and they come looking for them.

But ultimately this type of water is living on borrowed time because there are so few food fish.

When the last small pike has been eaten, the big fish will lose weight fast. There were no doubles... nothing below 24 lb. When we first found the water, we could catch jacks on spinners, but towards the end there weren't even those.

If you look at the shape of the pike you catch it will tell you a lot about the water's food supply. Ideally you want pike with deep bodies and heads that look small in comparison with their girth. If the pike have slim bodies and big heads then the chances are there isn't enough food to enable them to grow to their full potential, and some of them won't survive.

Above: Remote estate lakes can yield some very big pike as many are free from angling attention. Get permission to fish one that has been left alone and it could spring a surprise.

The pyramid of pike

To understand the balance of power of pike in your water, you need to know whether you have a pyramid of pike, with only a few big fish and lots of small ones, or an inverted pyramid, with the balance the other way around.

The normal balance is for there to be only one or two really big pike in a water, and then for numbers to increase in each size class. If you have one or two fish of over 30 lb in a water, the size of these fish will have an inhibiting effect on the growth of the 20 lb fish, which can't or won't reach that weight. I've even seen big pike push smaller ones out of the way before taking a bait themselves.

But if one or other of the biggest pike should die or be removed, there will be a surge in the size of some of those upper twenties, and the strongest and most aggressive will grow to take that big fish's place. It will even move into the prime lies that the big fish used to occupy. The queen is dead; long live the queen.

And the size that the new ruler attains will be more or less the same as her predecessor, as this is governed by the size of the water and the amount of food available. If the food fish suffer a disease and a drop in numbers, then the pike's weight potential will be reduced, or if it is a particularly remarkable fish with a genetic capacity to grow very big, it may reach a greater weight.

But in other waters there is an inverted pyramid, with lots of pike of the same, stunted size, nothing bigger, and only a few smaller. In this case the number of these single-figure pike of the same year class will have an inhibiting effect on each other's progress. Often there will not be enough food to enable one or two fish to grow bigger and faster than the others and to dominate the population.

But sometimes one or two will find the character and the aggression to begin feeding on their similar-sized brothers and sisters, and if they are successful, they will surge ahead in size. If they manage this leap they will have a vast larder of pike now smaller than them on which to feed, and the size they can reach can be awesome.

If you come across a water like that, where normal baits produce lots of single-figure fish but nothing bigger, and you suspect a few fish have become exclusively cannibalistic, waste no time in trying a jack pike as bait. You could be in for a big surprise.

RIVERS

Above: Bill Rushmer with his Thames record pike of 33 lb 6 oz from a punt on the tidal river at Teddington on 27 February 1987. It was 45 inches long and had a girth of 25 inches, and still holds the record.

Rivers are the last, unexplored frontier as far as pike fishing is concerned. Many stretches haven't been pike-fished for years. Some are privately owned, but some are just very inaccessible. You may only be able to get to them by boat, or they may run into wide open country that requires a lot of hard bank walking. So many pike anglers are just not prepared to walk for miles to find their quarry.

There's all that untapped potential, yet so many anglers huddle around gravel pits trying to catch fish that have been caught many times before.

Pike fishing on rivers is totally different from gravel pit fishing. Indeed, on the big rivers like the Thames, the Severn and the Trent, pike fishing is more akin to that of the big Scottish lochs. There's hundreds of miles of water offering endless opportunities, and as with lochs, they are an unrestricted environment, with the pike free to move miles.

There's a lot more of interest on a river. You never really know what's going to turn up next. And the fishing can be very straightforward if you know what to look for. It's very seldom that I come back from a session on the river having caught nothing.

Pike in rivers are more opportunistic feeders – they have to be, because if they don't make up their mind quickly, the meal is swept away in seconds. They need to feed more frequently than pike in stillwaters, to replace energy used up maintaining their position in the current, and searching for food that the flow tries to hide or take from them.

Rivers, especially the big ones, can be a daunting prospect to fish, but break them down into manageable sections and look for fish-holding features, and you'll get along fine. Rivers aren't easy to fish, that's for sure, but the fish are hard-fighting, athletic and a large proportion haven't been caught before.

There's no doubt that river fish fight much harder than stillwater fish. There's no comparison

Frightened of floods

Perhaps one of the reasons why rivers are neglected by pike anglers is the way they can change from one week to the next. A few days of heavy rain can transform a steady glide into a swirling mass of chocolate-brown water sweeping towards the sea with its cargo of fallen trees, household refuse and the odd, dead sheep.

You need determination to get to grips with them. I've driven all of the way to the Wye in September only to find it an unfishable torrent, having come up overnight, and had to turn round and come straight back.

But if anglers could fish a river as it is rising or as it is fining down, with a tinge of colour still in the water, they would find the pike in feeding mood and sport second to none. A rising river stimulates the fish to feed in preparation for the lean pickings when the water course is in full flood. When the period of fasting is over, as the river runs off, the biggest pike go on the feed, making up for lost time. There's a hunger there that gives them the same sense of urgency that they have just after spawning, and as the water clears so the pike can see their prey. The joy must be like a blind man slowly getting his sight back.

When the river is clear, and pike are able to hunt by sight, pleasure anglers and matchmen get plagued by them snatching roach and skimmer bream on the way to the net. A walk along the bank

Above: Heavy rain can turn a sedate river into a swirling mass.

during a match will give you a good idea of which swims hold numbers of pike.

The problem is at its worst in mid-autumn and winter, when pike are feeding by day. The clarity of the water makes hunting difficult, so pike are more likely to be hungry. In summer, the need doesn't arise because pike are feeding more at night.

Above: A rising river stimulates fish to feed in preparation for lean pickings when it's in flood.

between the two… a pike of 15 lb from a river will fight harder than, and in a different way from, one of 25 lb from a gravel pit.

The best fight I ever had from a pike lasted 15 minutes. This was a fish of 26 lb 12 oz that I caught in February, as the river was fining down. It tail-walked across to the other side and made one deep, boring run after another, taking 30

yards of line, and just wouldn't come in. When I looked at it on the bank, it was the muscle tone of the fish and the size of its fins that astonished me. English river pike don't quite match pike from the Scottish lochs and Irish loughs for fighting qualities, but they're the closest you're likely to get. Catch one in the peak of condition and you will have a fight on your hands.

Advantages of being on the spot

Living on the spot helps enormously because you can keep an eye on the condition of the river and get to know its moods. Living in Oxford, I can be on the Hampshire Avon or the Severn in an hour, and I can be fishing the Thames within five minutes of leaving my house, picking the tackle up from where it stands ready, with the rods already set up. The short sessions that this allows can produce big fish, often within the first few casts.

It's also handy for night sessions, fishing on into the evening and still being in bed at a reasonable hour so that I can get up for work the next morning. Regular sessions on a river just around the corner are an excellent way to get to know it.

But living on the doorstep is not absolutely essential. If you have contacts in the right parts of the country who can give you an insight into what the river is doing, you can keep in touch through them.

You need that kind of contact if you are to know where the fish will be because river pike are nomadic creatures and can travel great distances and follow food fish shoals for miles. They live in a totally wild environment with an enormous number of options open to them. I have caught the same fish two days running in spots a mile apart.

So location is the most crucial part of being successful on rivers. The swim that held fish yesterday could be empty today, and it could take hours of searching along miles of bank, fishing lots of swims, a livebait on one rod and a deadbait on the other, before you find them again.

I've covered five or six miles in a day, and you can lose up to a stone in weight in one winter. There's no place for moon boots, one-piece suits and rod pods – it's walking boots, bib-and-brace and bank sticks.

Don't get me wrong, when the river has burst its banks and flooded the fields you won't find me fishing it. When this happens I turn to a gravel pit like everyone else. In the depths of winter when some gravel pits freeze over, I go back to the river.

Rivers are much less vulnerable to rises and falls in temperature and the fishing suffers far less in really cold spells. The water is constantly

The benefits of boats

Having a boat is a huge bonus on a big river like the Thames. In summer, I head for the weir pools, which can only be fished properly by getting out on the water. And in winter, when the weir pools are often too fast to be fished, I use the boat to get to inaccessible places, mooring up and getting out to fish from the bank without disturbing the water.

But it's a great help having a boat when searching for features, or tracking down big bream shoals, using the fish-finder to locate underwater contours. I've covered miles of river devoid of fish and then hit a feature that's been black with them. There aren't as many hotspots as you might imagine. I know of three miles of river and only two really hot areas in the whole of that. There are ways of cutting corners, like finding out where matches are being won, but many areas don't have matches, and then it's down to hard work.

Having spend a lot of time in my younger days fishing for other species on the river I have learned a lot about their movements and this gives me a good idea of where they, and thus the pike, are going to be. And I'm lucky that many of my friends are match anglers and pleasure anglers and they can provide me with extra information that helps with location, and will do the same for anyone who bothers to ask.

Above: Weir pools are always best tackled from a boat.

changing, coming from small feeder streams, from springs deep in the ground and draining from neighbouring hills and fields. I've caught fish in minus eight degrees Fahrenheit – a temperature that would be the kiss of death on every gravel pit I know.

Above: In coloured water location is made easy because pike are forced into small areas, making a mobile approach the best bet.

There are times when fish really won't feed, because they are in a torpid state, and then it takes something with a bit of movement to get them to respond. I turn to legered livebaits, and there are days when these can be deadly.

Floodwater fishing

Covering several miles of river in a day helps you to build up an intimate knowledge of the river that will pay dividends when it is up and running, as you will know where to find the bays and slack water.

Many anglers will not fish chocolate-coloured, fast water, but this is a mistake because location has been made easy for them – the pike have been forced into small areas. They will be feeding mainly by smell, so legered deadbaits are the order of the day. You will be surprised just how good your results will be if you approach rivers in this way.

Keeping on the move, I like to give each swim about twenty or thirty minutes before moving on, dropping back in the same places later in the day. There may not have been a pike in them earlier, but as river pike are highly mobile, they may move in there later.

The mobility of pike is not random, though. They have a clear idea of where they need to be to intercept food and by their movements they are taking advantage of all of the opportunities that the river offers. They will visit various potential food sources during the course of a day in their search for sustenance.

Several sorts of river

Rivers can loosely be divided into four types – those that are big and slow, medium paced, fast, and small tributaries. An example of a big, slow river is the Thames, a medium river is one like the Trent, fast is like the Wye, Hampshire Avon and Dorset Stour, and a tributary, the Evenlode.

The Wye is turned a deep, red colour by the silty soil when it is in flood, while the Avon and Stour run over chalk and are supposedly clear, though trout farm effluent and pesticides and fertilisers from the land have banished any claim to true clarity.

The Trent is also subject to tainting by any number of substances from treated sewage and the by-products of industry to oil washing off neighbouring dual carriageways, yet still produces excellent sport. The Thames, however, is clear a lot of the time, even after rain, because the amount of water in it is strictly controlled according to the amount that is being held in reserve by sluices, and its level may bear no relation to the weather.

The Hampshire Avon is the richest of all of these rivers, as pike that live in its lower reaches have access to extra food from the sea, as well as a substantial run of game fish.

Left: The River Wye at Symonds Yat, a rich waterway quite capable of producing a pike in the upper 30s and maybe even a 40lb fish.

Mullet and mackerel, sea trout and grayling, and a big run of eels are all available, and couple that with the high-quality water and you have a river capable of growing a pike to 40 lb.

Large areas of the Hampshire Avon flow through private estates where all anglers are excluded, or through salmon beats, where anything other than game fishing is forbidden. The Wye has too many rapids and boulders to be navigable, and the Stour and the Avon have strict controls on the amount of boat traffic, all of which benefits pike and anyone fishing for them.

The Wye is also a rich river, with its run of migratory fish, and quite capable of producing a pike in the upper 30s. It wouldn't surprise me if it produced a 40 lb fish. In addition to the salmon there are plenty of roach, chub, trout and eels for food, and much of the river doesn't get fished for pike, so they are left alone to pack on weight.

The Symonds Yat area has produced good fish, but so many of the stretches look attractive that almost anywhere that you can get permission to fish and have the time to experiment and observe would be worth a try.

The potential of the Thames

The Thames isn't as rich a river as the Hampshire Avon or the Dorset Stour, no big runs of game fish or escapees from trout farms. There used to be dace shoals for which the Thames was famous, but cormorants have made huge inroads into them. Anglers on the lower Thames have counted as many as eighty cormorants in one spot, all looking very well fed.

As a result there are fewer double-figure pike on the tidal Thames than there used to be, most being either jacks or fish of over 20 lb, but with little in between. This points at a gap in the food fish stocks, for you need progressive sizes of food to feed a full range of pike, and if you miss out a food fish size then you get gaps in the ranks of the pike.

But on the middle Thames the picture is very different. The shoals of bream that led to a pike fishing bonanza more than a decade ago are back, and pike are getting bigger. Everything moves in cycles, and sport was excellent the last time bream were around in large numbers, until stocks dwindled or bream outgrew the size at which pike could eat them. Then roach took over as the dominant species, and the piking peak was over.

Now, once again, we have bite-sized bream in places like Medley and Northmoor, and lots of double-figure pike, a good number of 20s and a sprinkling of low 30s, helped by a balanced spread of age classes among the bream, roach and perch.

The way that river flows are being managed is in the bream's favour. These days, the Thames is often turned into a spate river, even when there is no rain, because the EA is afraid that rain is on its way and needs to prepare. So they let the water out, running it off very quickly, flooding the river and causing it to colour, instead of letting it go evenly, which does a lot less harm. However, the slower flows that follow these artificial floods, and the silt that they deposit, produce an ideal habitat for fish like bream to root around in. It's back to the days of the sixties, when big bream shoals were everywhere, and I don't think it will be long before the river produces a real monster pike.

Above: A Medley fish of 24 lb 7 oz. The middle reaches of the Thames hold shoals of bite-sized bream that enable pike to put on weight quickly.

Above: As long as the river remains sluggish, big pike will be caught in the Thames at Medley.

What price a monster?

If these conditions persist, a very big pike could soon grace someone's net. The current Thames record is held by Bill Rushmer with a fish of 33 lb 6 oz, caught from a boat at Teddington.

Other Thames monsters discovered include a pike trapped in the stanchions of Teddington Weir which weighed 35 lb and the body of a fish that weighed in the mid-thirties, found at Wallingford. I think the upper limit for pike in the river at present would be about 36 lb, without spawn, and at the right stage of the year, say late January or February, one could weigh 38 lb or 39 lb.

The upper Thames is a different river again – faster-flowing, with chub as the main food fish. There is much less food in the upper reaches than middle and lower middle. Lower down, around Medley and Mapledurham, a big fish is most likely to be found.

Left: A backwater of the Thames at Nuneham Courtenay with big shoals of bream, chub and roach. The numbers of food fish and its remoteness from roads suggest it could produce a huge specimen like the one below, or perhaps the next river record pike.

Both stretches are rich enough for coarse fish to thrive and grow in huge numbers, and the introduction of salmon smolts by the Environment Agency has boosted the larder. It wouldn't surprise me if a really big fish came from Molesey weir or the River Mole, where the salmon smolts are being introduced, but realistically, anywhere from Oxford to

Molesey weir could produce a river record. Most likely of all it will be caught in an area that rarely gets fished, and be a pike that has never been caught before.

The livebait/deadbait river theory

There's something about the speed of current that seems to govern whether rivers respond best to livebaits or deads. The faster and clearer the river, it seems, the more it lends itself to livebaiting.

The Trent and the Hampshire Avon and Dorset Stour are all livebait rivers, and don't seem to respond so well to deadbaits. The slower-moving Thames, on the other hand, responds as well to deads as to livebaits.

I have a theory that if a river is fast-flowing, a pike has less chance of picking up a fish from the bottom than on a slow river like the Thames. On the Thames a fish that has died is around for longer, and has time to rot and sink to the bottom, but on a fast river it will float to the top and get carried away before it has time to decay.

The main feature...

Location is the single most important factor on any water because if you can't find the fish you certainly won't catch them. So, where do you start if you want to find quality river pike. The following is a list of some of the places from which I have caught pike consistently.

Deceptive bends

Bends can be deceptive. Some ought to hold big pike but hold only jacks, while others always have a good double and a chance of a 20. I've often wondered why this is.

In my experience, a long, meandering bend doesn't produce as good a stamp of fish as a tight, elbow bend. In the latter, there's enough of an area scoured out by the current for pike to get

Trees

Usually these are very visible features, but sometimes a tree gets snapped off beneath the water line. The stump forms a barrier to the flow, and a slack area that will hold fish. A bait lowered into the slack, while standing well back out of sight, can often produce a sizeable pike.

Branches of overhanging trees trail in the water, and debris such as leaves and

Above: Fallen tree branches have great pike fishing potential. I like to trot a livebait tight to the branches and let my float stop, allowing the bait to explore the darkness beneath.

rubbish carried down in the current can get trapped, forming a raft of floating material that provides food fish with shelter from the sun and protection from attack. If there are grass and plants growing from this debris then so much the better as this will attract insects, which will attract small fish, which will in turn attract pike. Pike love these natural rafts as they offer cover in winter and shade in summer.

Any fish that die and float to the surface will get buoyed up by the raft, and flies will lay their eggs on the fish producing maggots that will fall into the water to be eaten by fish.

However, you must present your bait dangerously close to the raft. It's no use being three or four feet

away, as pike will not always move to the bait. I like to trot a livebait tight to the branches and will often allow my float to be trapped momentarily at the front of the raft, allowing the bait to explore the darkness beneath. You can also float-leger a deadbait, keeping as much line off bottom and out of snags as possible.

Willow roots often reach underwater to form a canopy, and pike like to hide among them. I know this from people who go scuba diving and have seen pike tucked in there, right under the bank.

under the bank. However, when a long bend does hold fish, there are generally more of them because there is more room for food fish.

Pike like deep water, and so do other big coarse fish, particularly bream and chub, which will tuck in tight under cover of the bank. On the inside of the bend, you will find small fish in the shallow water, out of the main flow.

Bends are two swims in one – deep water, and undercut banks. If there is a very strong flow hitting an elbow bend, the fish may move out from the bank to where the shallows begin to drop into deeper water. A legered livebait can prove deadly.

If the flow is less strong, the fish may be right across, and if I can't get access to fish the far bank I will point my rod high after casting out and keep as much of the line out of the water as possible, to stop the bait being dragged out of position.

If the river isn't too wide or fast, I like to cast a fluted float in at the top of the bend and use this to take my bait down to the pike. However, this type of swim could be too difficult to fish if there is debris like leaves and dead weed coming down as this will give false indications.

If you can reach the bank on the outside of the bend you are in a perfect position to work a

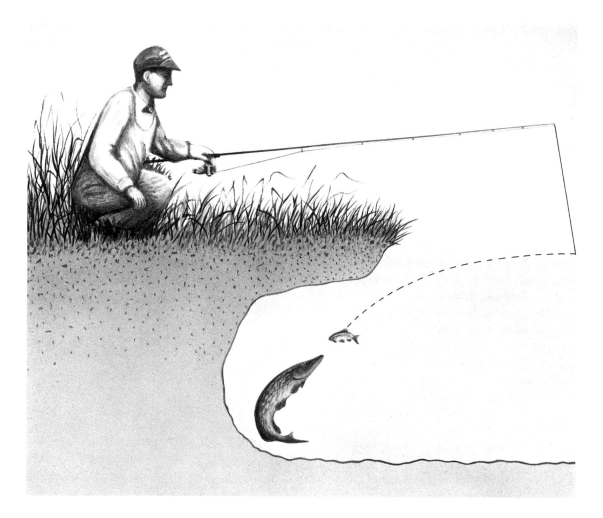

wobbled deadbait, sink-and-draw style, almost anywhere. This will often outscore any other method.

Start at the top of the bend and systematically search the whole of it. Cast well out from the bank and let it swing in an arc downstream to cover the deep water, which should hold fish, and bounce the bait across the river bed before letting the current pull it right under the bank to where a pike should be lying.

Reel it in slowly, occasionally drawing it up. Allow it to bounce on the bottom or trip back, covering the whole swim.

The rate of retrieve is crucial. Bring the bait as slowly as you can through the pike's striking zone, allowing a really big fish enough time to make up its mind. Big fish don't move quickly unless they have to, and for one of any size to accept the challenge of chasing a meal, it needs to get a good look at what's on offer.

Above: Tight, elbowbends scour out an area under the bank. A bait allowed to be pulled under the bank by the current will find pike lying in wait, and a slow retrieve will give a big fish time to make up its mind whether or not it wants the bait.

Bays

When viewed from the bank all bays look alike, but some produce quality and quantity of pike whereas other yield little or nothing. It is only when you examine them with an echo sounder and can see the big difference in the bottom contours, or topography, of each bay that you realise why they differ greatly in what they hold.

Deep bays usually contain a good head of bream, while other bays have gravel beds and weed, which attracts roach. There are nursery swims that hold only very small fish and others that have quantities of good-sized food fish. Generally, it is the bays that are of between two and five feet deep that hold the small fish.

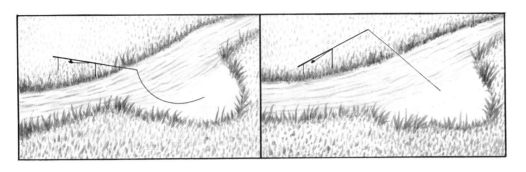

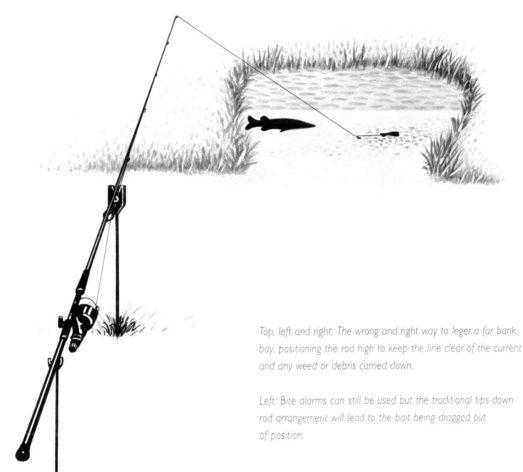

Top, left and right: The wrong and right way to leger a far bank bay, positioning the rod high to keep the line clear of the current and any weed or debris carried down.

Left: Bite alarms can still be used but the traditional tips-down rod arrangement will lead to the bait being dragged out of position.

However, on the Hampshire Avon the slacks of between two feet and nine feet produce the better fish, whereas on the Thames, I prefer slacks of between nine and thirteen feet.

Islands

Islands make perfect ambush points for hungry pike. The eddies at the back of them create havens of slack water for shoal fish, and pike can pin these fish against the island, or funnel them in between picking off their prey.

I know of one swim on the Thames that could produce the next river record. It has two islands through which pike come to ambush the fish moving upstream towards the shallows at the head of the run.

This is the only feature for hundreds of yards and acts like a magnet for the coarse fish in this stretch, luring them into the lair of the pike. It has the perfect features to produce big pike and will continue to do so as long as the islands remain.

Reed beds

There's a certain type of tight, green reed with a round nodule on the top that always seems to attract pike. It acts as camouflage and allows them to strike from cover. Find a bed of these leading into deep water, with gaps between the reeds for the pike to get in and out, and you will have found a favourite haunt of pike.

Above: Tight beds of reeds allow pike to strike from cover.

Above: A 21 lb 9 oz pike from a Thames marina on float fished sardine while fishing from a boat, part of a 300 lb-plus haul when the river was in flood.

Slacks

When a river is in flood, all of the fish will have been driven into slacks areas, out of the current, and any obstruction that holds up the main flow should hold fish.

The best way to find these spots is to walk the bank when the river is at normal or below-normal level and you will see the areas with little or no flow. These are where you want to be when the river is high, with a strong-smelling deadbait like a sardine.

Marinas

Take an athletic river pike with a healthy appetite and put it in a backwater such as a marina, where coarse fish stocks are high and there is no current to fight against, and you have the potential for producing a very large fish.

River pike use up a lot of energy maintaining their position in the current, but put them in with populations of big bream like the ones you find in places like Abingdon marina and at Dean's Farm, Bray and Windsor, and on the River Kennet, and 30 lb plus is easily achievable. I have had big 20s and have seen a fish of 32 lb 8 oz caught.

The problem with marinas is getting permission to fish. The banks are often private so you have to fish from a boat, and the summer is a waste of time because of the amount of traffic on the river. But get permission to fish in winter and get there early before the boat owners have got out of bed, and you can have some excellent sport.

Some of the pike in marinas are ones that have learned to avoid the bits of river that anglers are allowed to fish, and have moved into these areas to get away from them. I've had a haul of 300 lb-plus from a marina, including fish of up to 21 lb 9 oz and 13 mid- to upper-doubles, all on sardines floatfished from a boat when the river was in flood.

Pike move in there to get out of the flow, up the man-made channels that run at right angles to the river, and when the main flow is high and the fish hungry they are queuing up to take a bait. But if they find it to their liking they may stay there permanently and forget that some meals come with treble hooks attached.

Moored boats

On parts of the Thames, the Environment Agency moor their dredger boats for the winter, and these provide cover for food fish like chub and roach and a dark place for pike to stalk their prey.

House boats on the tidal Thames provide havens for roach and dace shoals, offer shelter from the sun and frosts, and from cormorants, as well as enjoying scraps of food thrown over the side.

Lock gates

One of the best places to find pike is just below lock gates, which are very slack areas in winter. The main flow goes over the weir, while the water below the gates is only disturbed when a boat comes through, which is seldom in winter.

The action of the gates being opened frequently in summer for boat traffic scours out a deep channel, creating slack water that attracts shoals of food fish. When the boat traffic eases in winter, fish will head for this deep hollow and can often be seen rising when the sun is strongest, at midday.

The sides of the channel become silted, are shallower and come into their own early in spring when the pike move on to them to spawn.

You'll need special permission from the lock keeper as fishing is not normally allowed within thirty or forty yards of the gates. I like to tackle these spots from a boat, tying up to the wooden mooring poles from which I can cover all the water.

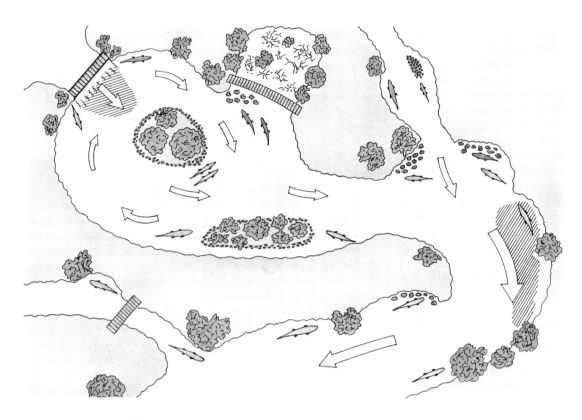

Weir pools

These are wonderful gathering places for fish of all species, which live side by side in the areas that suit them best, benefiting from the extra oxygen in the water and foraging for food items that swirl round in a giant eddy on the edge of the current.

Above: A Hampshire Avon weir pool showing the flow of water and fish-holding areas. The angler who can read the pattern of flows will be the one who catches the most fish in any given condition.

In summer and winter, weir pools hold food fish and pike of various sizes, and the angler who can read the pattern of flows will catch fish in most conditions. Big pike will have taken up the prime lies, where they are in the best possible position to intercept food fish as it passes or is brought to them on the back eddy or over the top of the weir.

Left: Marlow Weir, the largest weir on the Thames, overlooked by the famous Compleat Angler Inn, frequented by anglers since the days of Francis Francis.

Finding the bars, the submerged banks, the snags and the hollows has to be done by sight and 'feel' through the rod, as a fish finder won't work due to the clusters of bubbles rising from the bottom in the white water.

Where the main line of foam forms on the surface is where the fast water meets the slow, and this will be home to food fish, with pike on guard nearby.

At Mapledurham weir on the Thames, the water travels round in a big eddy and pike like to lie on the crease between fast and slack water. Pike also lie under the stanchions of the weir, out of the main flow, and over the shallow silted areas

on the sides, where food fish gather to spawn. If there are obstructions, like mounds of rocks and debris, they also like to lie behind these, where they can lie tucked in out of the current and strike from cover.

Above: Food fish gather in weir pools and pike like to lie behind mounds of rocks and debris, where they can tuck in out of the current and can strike at prey from cover.

Left: Pike will live happily, in really fast water. Anglers must be brave enough to fish it and adapt their methods accordingly.

In summer many of the really big pike can be seen in the reedy bays on either side of the weir. I have seen two or three 20 lb fish basking there in warm sunshine in no more than three feet of water. These fish will move off to feed elsewhere and come back at night.

In summer they may be right under the main part of the weir, which carries too much water for them in winter but is slack enough for comfort when the flow is a little less. It's a mistake to think that big pike will not be found in the main flow of a weir as they like to feel the push of the water on their backs and are streamlined and athletic enough to cope with surprisingly fast flows without any problems.

Getting to grips with weirs is an apprenticeship because each one has its own, unique contours and obstructions. The first time you fish there you will hit snags, and if you are fishing from a boat — the only way to do a weir pool justice — that means moving the boat to free your tackle, which disturbs the swim.

Weir pools have their own features. Some have salmon ladders to help migratory fish running the river pass the weir on their way upstream to spawn. Small fish can't get up these ladders and food gets washed down them, so pike lurk at the bottom waiting for something of an edible size to have a momentary lapse of concentration.

Some weirs are prone to silting and have reed beds encroaching on the main pool and red buoys positioned to warn boat users of shallow water. Both are worth investigating. Pike enjoy basking in the sun, and the shallow edges of the main weir can be real hotspots, especially in summer, when weir pool fishing is at its best.

Look along the ledge of a weir, which can get choked with weed in low flows, and if there is a

gap in the weed
somewhere in the
middle, there will be
fish waiting below this
spot for whatever the
current may bring.

Look at the debris on
the surface; if this has
been carried to one
place, the same may
have happened below
the surface.

My favourite tactic
for weir pools is a sink-
and-draw wobbled
trout, freshly killed, or
if the pike are in a
choosy mood and not
looking at deadbaits, a
12 oz roach or chub
livebait under a float. I
wouldn't choose to use
baits of this size, but
sometimes, in certain
weir pools, pike won't
look at anything else,
and even reject only
slightly smaller
livebaits.

There's no need to
cast; just send the bait
down one line in the
current and after a
pause, pull it back up
on another, against the
flow, which is easy from
a boat. I like to hold
the float back, so that
the bait rises up in the

Left: Bringing a mid-double
caught on a sink and draw
bait to the boat while
anchored in a Thames weir
pool. A multiplier forces you
to retrieve the bait at just the
right speed.

Below: Getting to grips with
weirs is an apprenticeship,
but they will yield rich rewards
for the anglers that persevere.
Each one has its own unique
contours, character and
obstructions to be discovered.

water almost to the surface, before letting it
go again. Sometimes you can't control a float in
the flow, and then a big, legered deadbait is
the answer.

But when a wobbled bait works it is a dream to
use, cast out underarm and brought back on the
crease of the flow, fished deep or allowed to flutter
up near the surface, covering lots of water at a
complete range of depths. A multiplier is the tool
for the job as it forces you to retrieve slowly, and

this is crucial. A big pike is a sluggish fish and it
needs time to make up its mind as to whether it
wants that bait. The longer it takes to bring that
bait through the pike's striking zone, the better.

On some days pike will take the bait gently,
just plucking at its tail, but on other days they
will lunge at it, scattering scales like confetti.
With a multiplier you are in touch with what is
going on and feel every tap and twitch through
the line.

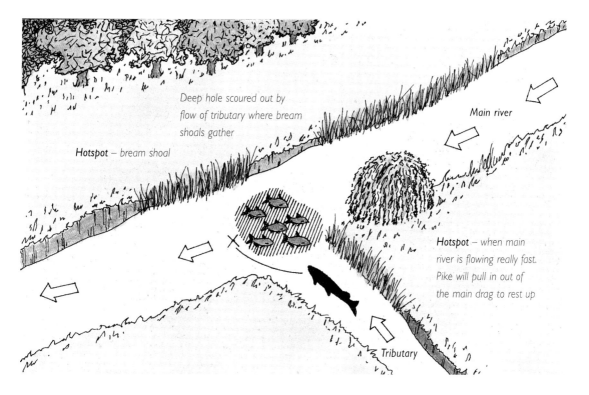

Deep hole scoured out by flow of tributary where bream shoals gather

Hotspot – bream shoal

Main river

Hotspot – when main river is flowing really fast. Pike will pull in out of the main drag to rest up

Tributary

Above: A bream shoal is usually in residence where a tributary hits the main river, holed up where the current has eroded the bottom.

There are exceptions to the success of wobbled deadbaits on weirs. The weirs on the Thames at Marlow, Temple and Hambledon do not respond as well to moving baits. I have tried to catch pike on livebaits, wobbled baits and spinners, but they respond far better to deadbaits.

It just goes to show that you shouldn't let appearances deceive you. While the surface may look very fast, all white water and spray, things will be a good deal slower beneath the surface.

Trout farms

Anywhere with a trout farm above has the potential to produce big pike because escapees from the farm will enrich the food source just downstream. Trout farms on tributaries of our major rivers reduce water levels and cause pollution through waste products. But bite-sized escapee rainbow trout are one of the benefits.

Warm water outlets

Temperature plays a huge part in dictating the movements of coarse fish, especially when the weather is extreme. When it's very hot, fish will head for well-oxygenated water just below a weir, and in extreme cold, fish will find somewhere deep enough not to be affected by frosts and sudden drops on the thermometer. If a river has a warm-water outlet from a power station, it will attract fish of all sorts in winter. The temperature difference may be no more than a degree or two, but that's enough to attract food fish, which attract pike, and keep all of them feeding when fish in neighbouring stretches have stopped.

Tributaries

February and March are the months to take a look at the places where tributary streams enter the main river. Bumper catches of big fish are possible from them at the back end of the season as specimen pike in the mid twenties gather prior to spawning in the shallow water, or come on the feed straight after. The ethics of catching fish just before or just after spawning are another matter.

In the past on the Thames I have had several 200 lb-plus bags from where a tributary joins the main flow, made up of fish of up to 25 lb, all taken on trotted livebaits.

Usually there's a bream shoal at the point where the tributary hits the main river, holed up where the current from the feeder has scoured out a small depression in the river bed, which will have

partly filled with silt. Bream will use this to rest out of the main flow and to feed, and even if there are several side streams in a row, they may all hold bream and have pike waiting nearby to move out of the main river.

If you fish a swim that usually produces lots of moderate pike and yet find there's no response on one visit, that's often a sign that there's one, very big fish about. It's well worth persevering.

Try fishing in the mouth of the tributary. Also try a little way up the tributary, especially if the main river's flow is strong. Pike wait there before spawning, while others may be leaving after spawning. Whichever way they are going, there's bound to be a lot of pike in one small area.

Gravel pit pike can be tracked down to their spawning haunts just like river pike, but river pike are opportunists and more likely to be tempted with a bait, particularly a livebait.

When fishing in the tributary, there may be so many pike in one area that they have to compete for any food that comes their way, like a flock of birds chasing a few morsels of bread. Each one that picks up the bait will run off upstream with it before another fish can take it away.

But contrary to popular belief, that kind of competition will make pike grow bigger instead of putting a ceiling on their weight. Experiments with trout in a pond showed that a shoal of 20 or 30 pike grew bigger than one on its own, because they competed for food rather than living aimlessly.

Shrunken side streams

Some small side streams become shrunken through abstraction, yet they are still very attractive to pike at spawning time. Reeds may have encroached and mud and silt built up, like on the Pot Stream near Oxford, which Dick Walker used to fish, but if you can overcome the difficulties of soft mud banks extending into the margins you can get among a lot of fish.

You need to stand well back from the reeds and use a bait that gives out plenty of vibrations; draw the pike to you, and stimulate them into feeding. Failing that, if you can waft a freelined deadbait under the reed encroachment and let the bait settle right in under the near bank, this can work well. You can do this with or without extra weight, depending on the flow, and you should have the rod facing straight toward the bait so that you get an immediate indication of a fish picking it up.

I use very light bobbins as bite indicators so that the bait isn't dragged along the slippery silt bottom after being cast. Long bank sticks are needed to get through all of the mud to the firmer ground that will give you a grip, yet with enough bank stick above the surface to keep the line above the reed stems.

But the most important thing to remember on these side rivers with unpronounced banks is not to walk on the floating rafts of reed and mud in the edge. When trodden on they shudder, and this vibration will put pike down.

Estuaries

On the estuaries of rivers like the Hampshire Avon pike have an incredible larder of back-up food in the form of mullet from the harbour. Stamp your feet on the estuary shore and the surface of the water will erupt with the bow waves of alarmed mullet.

Some of the biggest pike in the river live in the mouths of these estuaries, only moving upstream once a year to spawn, in February or March. This is the one time that they are vulnerable and it is this life cycle that is likely to produce a real leviathan.

History repeats itself

As I stated in the chapter on gravel pits, if big pike die or are removed from a swim, the few that are the next biggest will compete to take over the old queen's status and prime position. The one

Above: A 30 lb 4 oz South Cerney gravel pit fish caught at range on a half mackerel, followed by one of 26 lb the next day.

that inherits the throne will be found in the same location as its predecessor, so any location that has produced a big pike will, provided things don't change, produce another within a few years.

I know of a swim on the Thames that produced a fish of 34 lb 3 oz many years ago, and then five years ago, a 34 lb pike was found dead in the same place, a sharp bend on a long, straight section.

If pike are left alone, history will repeat itself, and in this case it's a good couple of miles walk from the nearest main road. Even in a boat you have got to pass through several locks to get there. I've had fish to 25 lb and another of 24 lb from this swim since, and given time, I know it will produce another pike nudging the 35 lb mark. The locations mentioned in pike fishing books published as much as eighty years ago and said to hold big pike are the ones likely to produce big fish now, because many of them have not changed and still offer the same unique advantages.

RIGS

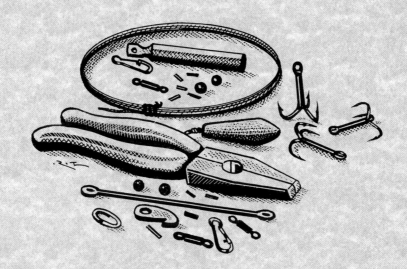

The best rigs are solutions to problems. Perhaps you want to put a bait in a certain place and present it in a certain way but you can't achieve this with any of the methods at your disposal. So you find some way of overcoming the problems by experimenting with terminal tackle until it does what you want, doesn't tangle and, above all, catches you fish.

Eventually you refine the rig to the extent that it probably can't be improved upon and if it includes items not commercially available, as in the case of my Deadbait Support Links and Wobble Bars, you find a firm prepared to produce them. But the strength of the rig lies in its simplicity – a straightforward solution to a common problem – for the more simple a rig, the better it works.

The rigs shown here are open to interpretation. Make of them what you will, and experiment with them by adding to or subtract from them according to your preferences. I offer them simply as working examples of ways of presenting a bait, live or a dead, in a certain way to suit a certain type of swim.

Armed with these you will have a few solutions to potential problems and a trick or two up your sleeve for when the need arises.

The following is a rough guide to when and where to use the rigs described:

Gravel pits and lakes
Deadbait Support Rig/Legered Deadbait/Wobbled Deadbait/Pop-up Deadbait/Floatfished Deadbait/Float Paternostered Deadbait/Free-roving Livebait/Float Paternostered Livebait/Trailing and Trolling

Rivers
Legered Deadbait/Wobbled Deadbait/Trotted Deadbait/Float Paternostered Deadbait/Float Legered Deadbait/Trotted Livebait/Legered Livebait/Float Paternostered Livebait

Lochs and loughs
Legered Deadbait/Wobbled Deadbait/Floatfished Deadbait/Float Paternostered Deadbait/Float Legered Deadbait/Free-roving Livebait/Float Paternostered Livebait/Trailing and Trolling

Legered deadbait

A legered deadbait is the best method when you want to anchor a bait in one spot. It is useful when you are fishing the far side of a river and your float keeps getting dragged out of position, or if the far bank is too far to reach with float tackle. You want a heavier, more streamlined rig to get the extra distance.

On gravel pits a legered deadbait is the first choice for distance casting, especially when presenting a small bait like a sandeel or smelt as an alternative to a mackerel. The added advantage of legering a small bait rather than freelining one is that you can tighten up harder to the bait and so spot runs earlier.

The lead is attached to a Cox and Rawle boom and this slides on the main line stopped by a bead above the trace swivel. The top treble or Parrot Beak single goes through the root of the tail, with fuse wire or freeze spray to hold it if it is a sardine, and the end treble is pinned loosely into the flank of the bait.

Wobbled deadbait

This is a deadly way of finding fish and covering a large amount of water. The deadbait, usually a rainbow trout of about 6 oz, is hooked through top and bottom lips with one point of the top treble and very lightly nicked in the flank with the end treble. Alternatively a Parrot Beak single can be used to seal the lips.

The stainless steel wobble bar is attached to the eye of the top treble or Parrot Beak by an inch and a half of crimped wire. Carbon Kevlar braid can be used as an alternative, knotted instead of crimped.

The wobble bar is pushed into the back of the throat of the bait so that only the top is visible. If it isn't pushed down far enough, it may come out through the gills and the bait won't come back in a lifelike manner.

Similarly, if the bar is pushed too far down into the fish it will inhibit the action of the rear half of the body as it moves through the water.

In the situation where the bait is only hooked through one lip instead of both, it will spin awkwardly as it comes back on the retrieve, whereas in an ideal world I want it to wobble enticingly.

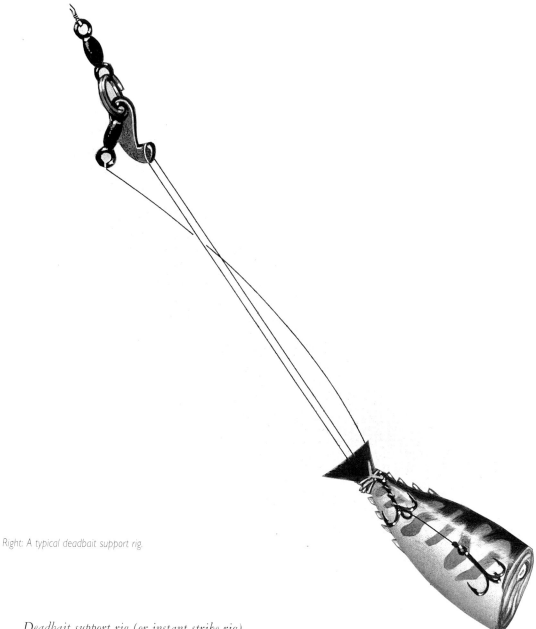

Right: A typical deadbait support rig.

Deadbait support rig (or instant strike rig)
I've explained the background to this rig in previous chapters. It is simply an excellent deadbait rig for freelining.

A plastic bait support link attaches to the bottom eye of the trace swivel by an oval split ring. A loop of 8 lb or 9 lb line sits on the flat ridge of the link and the other end of it is lassoed around the tail root of a deadbait with two half hitches.

The loop should be about 17 inches long, roughly three inches shorter than the wire trace. If I use a longer trace, because I'm fishing over gravel bars or snags, the loop will be longer, too.

The loop falls off the ridge of the bait support link as soon as the bait hits the water because it is only held in place by the tension provided by the weight of the bait. If you pass your wire trace through the loop of line before the cast is made, the loop catches on the trace on the retrieve and the bait comes back even if it's worked its way off the hooks.

Pop-up deadbait

On waters that are particularly silty or weedy, a bait that falls slowly and settles gently, or sways in the current at a predetermined height off the bottom is an advantage.

Injecting air into the side of a deadbait will lift it off bottom, making it more visible to pike and keeping it clear of debris. I always go for a bright bait like a roach or a dace.

I aim the needle at a spot close to the lateral line. Don't go for the gut cavity underneath because air will escape through the mouth, and you risk puncturing the swim bladder, which will make the bait less buoyant.

I like to test my baits in the margins prior to casting to see if they are doing what I want them to do. An air-injected bait can be fished anywhere between bottom and surface, anchored in place with a lead sliding on a Cox & Rawle boom and a back-stop of pole elastic and bead. Tighten to the bait gently when it is in position to avoid reeling it down to the bottom.

Some anglers favour putting lead shot on the trace because that takes the bait a little further away from the main line and lessens the chance of a bite-off.

The treble hooks can be positioned in the bait to make it face head up or head down, and the direction doesn't seem to make any difference to the number of takes.

Despite the dangers of sharp needles, I prefer to inject deadbaits with air rather than stuff polystyrene down them. If a bait is lost, any polystyrene will end up in the stomach of a pike, which can't be good for it.

Floatfished deadbait

Floatfishing a deadbait allows you to present the bait at any depth. If you want a bait close to the surface, to lie on top of tall weed for instance, it's easier to suspend it below a float than try to pop it up.

The rig I use is a straightforward one with a float running on the main line above the trace. Various hooking arrangement can be used, depending on the size and type of deadbait chosen. The top treble through the root of the tail and the end treble in the flank will make it sit tail up, and top treble through root of dorsal and end treble through flank will make it sit upright in a natural manner.

There doesn't have to be tall weed for the method to work. Sometimes a bait fished a couple of feet below the surface over deep water will take pike cruising in the upper layers. A good way of searching a big, open stillwater for near-surface cruisers is to go to the upwind shore and drift a bait, set shallow, out under a balloon attached to the line with a paper clip. The balloon will come off on the strike and can be retrieved from the down-wind shore at the end of the session.

On lochs and loughs I use big, bright, self-cocking floats that will be visible through waves as much as three feet from peak to trough A hefty float is needed to get any distance on the cast with a multiplier, and a good cast is often needed to avoid spooking pike or fouling the anchor rope.

My floats are four or five inches long with a stem made of a brass rod inserted in the body. They are attached bottom end only with a snap-link swivel that runs on the main line, stopped by a bead and a knot of pole elastic.

Trotted deadbait (rivers only)

Trotted deadbait is a deadly method for finding fish. The kind of swim you are looking for is somewhere with a clear, gravel bed or one that is weed-free. Any obstacles on a stretch make it difficult to fish effectively, but if you can find a length of water about five or six feet deep and of fairly uniform depth, with a bottom that is clear you will have perfect water for trotting .

Ideally you will be able to trip the bait along the bottom and then hold it back so that it rides up in the water before letting it go again. It's often the sight of the bait doing something different that triggers the strike. I like to trip a bait through on the far side and come round in an arc across the river, do the same again on lines closer in and then retrieve it and work it down the near bank.

You can also trot a deadbait off bottom if you have weed or other obstacles in your way simply by shallowing up. If you trot a bait down to a weed raft under overhanging branches you can let the float trap itself momentarily on the front of the raft and the bait will lift up into the darkness beneath.

Right: Float-legered deadbaits suit loch fishing, where baits need to be anchored despite strong surface drift, and line needs to be lifted clear of those waters' notoriously boulder-strewn bottoms.

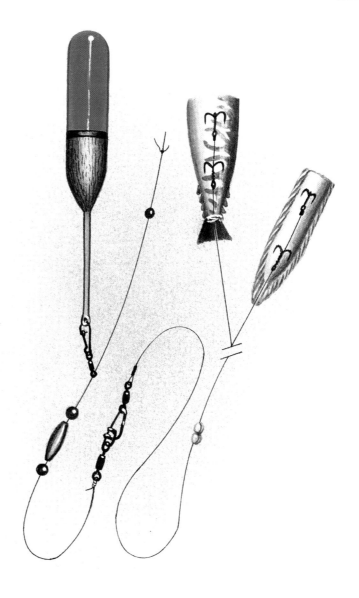

Whatever the deadbait used, the top treble should be hooked in the root of the tail and the end treble in the flank, so that it sits head down with the hooks clear of the bottom. This allows the bait to travel through the swim unimpeded.

The float can be a fluted balsa or a cigar shape, depending on the flow, or even a round polyball.

Float-paternostered deadbait

See float-paternostered livebait, below. The method is the same, but a deadbait is hooked with the top treble in the dorsal root and the end treble in the tail.

Float-legered deadbait

This is generally used from boats, where alarms can't be used but you need visual bite indication and a static bait. I use it only on lochs and for fishing marinas and weir pools. The float provides extra casting weight and lifts the line up.

My floats are attached bottom-end only and the weight is provided by several swan shot pinched on the trace. The top treble goes through the root of the tail and the end treble is pinned loosely into the flank of the bait.

On a loch, there is a lot of drift to be countered to keep the bait in position on the bottom, and a float-leger rig allows you to anchor the bait firmly but with all of the advantages floatfishing has over legering. Loch bottoms are strewn with snags, but this rig keeps the line away from them. Even so, I often use traces two- to three-feet long to prevent damage to the line by jagged rocks and boulders.

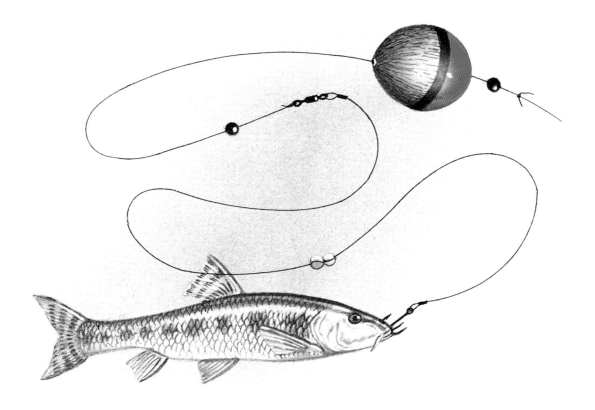

Floatfished and trotted livebait
(or free-roving livebait)

Floatfishing covers large volumes of water a lot more quickly than legering, keeps the bait away from bottom weed or snags, and makes a welcome change from sitting behind alarms.

When I am floatfishing livebaits in gravel pits, I hook the top treble in the tail root and the end treble is nicked just under the adipose fin in the case of a trout or the dorsal root in the case of coarse fish.

When I am floatfishing a weir pool, I will put the top treble through the upper lip to make the bait face into the current. I will also use the top lip hookhold when I am fishing a very small livebait for which only one treble is needed. But lip hooked fish are more likely to fly off during the cast, so I locate the hooks elsewhere for long-range styles.

For long-range casting with trout livebaits, for instance, I put the top treble in the adipose fin and the end treble in the flank, which offers a good hookhold and makes the bait much more streamlined.

Above: Float-fished and trotted livebaits cover large volumes of water a lot more quickly than legering, keep baits away from weed and snags, and make a welcome change from sitting behind alarms.

When fishing a livebait in rivers, everything depends on whether you are letting the bait trot downstream or making it work upstream against the flow.

If you are trotting downstream, a pike will expect a bait to be facing downstream when it is travelling in that direction if it's going to look natural.

To do this I put the top treble through the tail root and the end treble in the adipose fin in the case of trout, or in the tail root and the dorsal root for coarse fish.

But when a bait is being brought upstream it should be facing into the flow, so you will need to place the top treble through the top lip and the end treble in the flank to make it look natural and be streamlined when being brought back against the current. It will last longer like this and can be made to rise up in the water and fish at different depths.

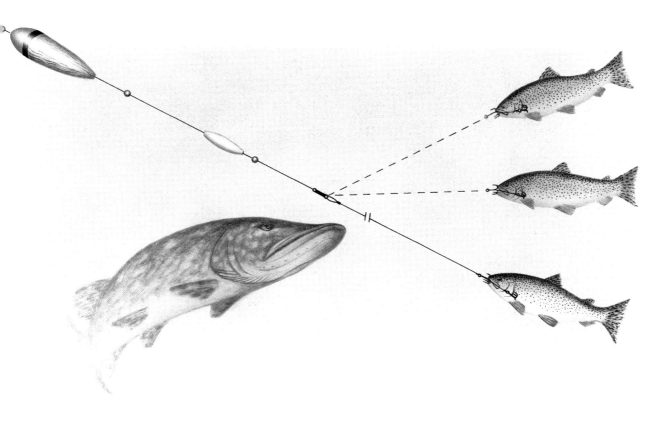

Make sure you put the hook through one lip only, though, for if you seal the lips together, the bait will drown. And use the top lip, so that it can open and close its mouth without being impeded by the hook.

Use as little lead as you can get away with, to avoid tiring the bait; a couple of swan shot pinched on the line for a small dace, or a streamlined barrel lead for something bigger. The trace should be about 16 inches long.

Free-roving or floatfished livebaits are particularly deadly used up against the beds of Potamogeton weed in lochs, and in rivers when pike are moving into the mouths of tributaries ready for spawning.

If pike are only in a mood to reflex feed, and let go after a second or two, the hook position for an instant strike is top treble through the dorsal root and end treble through pectoral root, to aim the hooks at the centre of the body so that they will find a hold instantly. With this hooking arrangement the strike can be made instantly, as soon as a sign of a take is noticed, and hopefully before the jaws are opened and the bait discarded.

Above: In weir pools I like to explore different depths of water by holding back the bait, and then letting it travel on and ride up and down. A cigar-shaped sliding float and barrel lead have the type of streamlined profile that does not catch in the current and offers little resistance to taking fish.

Legered livebait

When pike are on the bottom, in rivers after a heavy frost for example, and are in a torpid state and reluctant to respond, a legered livebait is the best bet. If you know of a deep hole where pike are likely to be, you can use this method to hold a bait in place.

There are days when a deadbait won't be looked at, but a livebait creates just enough of a stir to provoke some interest in pike, and then this method will outscore any other. There have been times when a floatfished livebait has been ignored but a legered livebait has been successful.

Brown trout or rainbows are the first choice baits, though chub also work quite well. It doesn't matter how they are hooked, but I prefer to put the top treble through the tail, and end treble in the dorsal root for ease of casting.

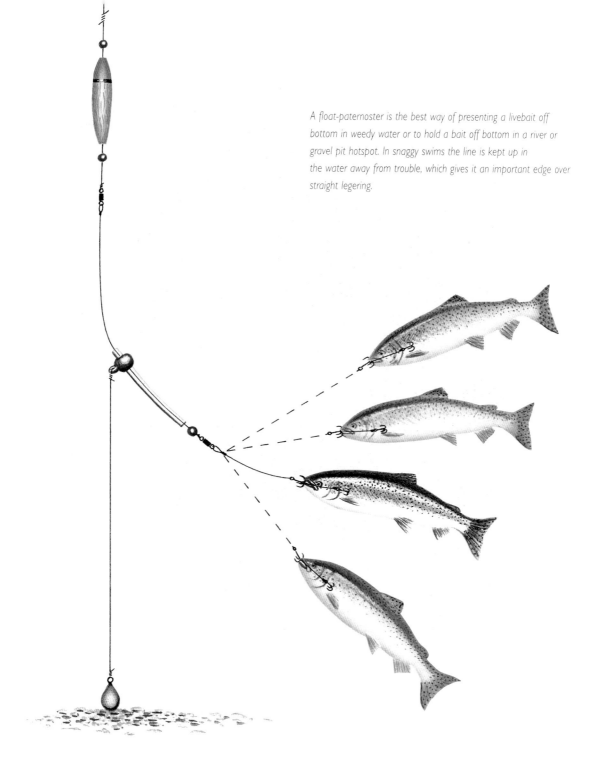

A float-paternoster is the best way of presenting a livebait off bottom in weedy water or to hold a bait off bottom in a river or gravel pit hotspot. In snaggy swims the line is kept up in the water away from trouble, which gives it an important edge over straight legering.

Float-paternostered livebait

This is the best way of presenting a livebait off bottom in weedy water or to hold a bait off bottom in a known hotspot in a river or gravel pit. It is particularly useful if the chosen spot is close to a snag, where the repeated casting necessary with roving float tackle would be a disadvantage. In these spots, leger tackle can't be used because the line has to be kept up in the water and away from further snags.

A green, sunken float or a standard balsa that shows above the surface goes on the main line, stopped by a knot of pole elastic and a bead. I always use a 13-inch uptrace of wire below the float to prevent bite-offs, as a pike can catch the line in its mouth as it strikes.

A John Roberts Pike Paternoster Boom keeps the 10-inch hook trace and bait away from the main line, while the lead is attached to an 8 lb nylon weak link in case it gets snagged.

Rudd and dace tend to ride up in the water and can spin around the float, so I don't use them for this, but roach, rainbow trout and brown trout work well.

Two things to remember – always make sure the hook trace is shorter than the uptrace to avoid bite offs, and always keep a tight line to the bait so that it is working constantly. As soon as you let the line go slack, the bait doesn't have any resistance to pull against and stops moving around, making it less visible and attractive to pike.

Trailing and trolling

Trailing with a float works particularly well on estate lakes and trout waters and enables you to cover a lot of water. I use the same set up as for free-roving livebaits but with the top treble through the upper lip and the end treble in the flank. Trout and roach are the best.

To work well, though, trailing must be carried out slowly, using a small electric motor and lines paid out behind the boat. Many anglers trail too fast to cover water effectively, and do not give a big pike enough chance to make up its mind whether it wants the bait.

The float acts as an indicator and a means of controlling the depth at which the bait is fishing, which is usually shallow. A fairly heavy lead is used to hold the bait down.

A special float is used, with a length of bent plastic tubing protruding from the top through which the line is threaded, before going through the centre of the body. The line in this tubing is bent at an acute angle, which stops the float from sliding down to the bait and shallowing the rig.

Trolling, on the other hand, is very different and involves the use of deadbaits and lures over deep water in large lakes like Scottish lochs. There is no float on the line, but a downrigger takes the bait to the desired depth.

The hooking arrangement for trolling is top treble through top and bottom lips and end treble through flank. I use mackerel, chub, trout or any sizeable fish, but the lips must be sealed to stop it from spinning in the water and allow it to run on

an even keel. Trolling is another a good method for searching water, and uses the same electric motor and lines paid out behind the boat, but it is carried out at a slightly faster speed.

Traces

My standard trace is 20 inches of 30 lb Berkley Steelstrand wire. Two, size 8 trebles are crimped on, two to three inches apart. These are Partridge Extra Strong Outpoint trebles for deadbaiting and Partridge Grey Shadow trebles, which have a wider gape and a more rank barb, for livebaits.

I always make sure the top treble on the trace is fixed. Some anglers like to leave it sliding, so that they can move it up and down the trace to suit the size of bait, but if it slides when you move it, then it will slide when you strike, and you won't get a proper hookhold.

Sliding trebles also have a habit of damaging traces, making them coil like a spring and reducing the breaking strain. If I'm using different sizes of bait, I will take a number of different traces with trebles firmly attached at different distances apart and match them up, changing traces if I change bait size.

To attach the top treble so that it won't slip, pass the wire through the eye of the hook and back through again while allowing a loop of wire to be drawn tight between the three prongs where they separate as they leave the shank. Then wrap the wire three times around the hook shank, go through the loop formed at the shank and pull the end through.

Check that the wire is pulling against the hook when it is drawn right, not against wire, which will make it kink. I find it easier to attach the top treble first and then add the end treble a suitable distance away.

To attach a single Parrot Beak hook, do the following. Slide a crimping sleeve on the wire and pass the wire through the eye of the hook and back through the crimping sleeve again. Double the end over and bring it back through the sleeve for a third time, making sure not to pull the loop you have just made right back out of the sleeve. Adjust the size of the loop next to the eye of the hook and then crimp once in the middle. You can then put the end treble on the loose end of wire and the trace is complete.

NIGHT FISHING

and the neuromast system

If I'd been writing this book little more than a decade ago, a chapter on night fishing for pike would have been treated with derision. Pike were thought to hunt by sight, and fishing at night for a species that chases fish and flashy plugs would have been laughable.

Above: A fish of 22 lb 8 oz. There is no doubt that some of the biggest pike on any water feed at night.

Left: An upper double from the early days of experimenting with night fishing for pike, when we were arriving as other anglers were packing up to go home as it got dark.

Early manuals on pike fishing wrote off night fishing as a waste of time, but how wrong they were. Slowly we've come to realise that when the sun goes down, pike go on the prowl, and in summer the cool hours of darkness are the ones in which most of the feeding takes place. What better time for a pike to stalk its prey in the underwater alleyways between the weed than when everything is cloaked in darkness?

How it all began
The first pike I caught at night was by accident, while legering a gudgeon head for eels on the Coca Cola stretch of the Thames, and I don't know who was more surprised, me or the pike.

It came at a time when it seemed that pike stocks in gravel pits around Oxford appeared to be dropping after several years of successful fishing. Initially we had thought the fish were feeding beyond our casting range, but after the Coca Cola fish we had other ideas.

We decided to try close in at night, and sport was amazing. It seemed the pike had learned not to accept food items during the day, but at night they came into the margins to feed and pick up baits discarded by anglers.

In the course of our experiments, we found that pike fed most freely on dark nights when you could hardly see your hand in front of your face, in particular between one and three hours after dark, but often well into the night.

As summer turned to winter, the feeding period took place earlier, in the first few hours of darkness at first, rather than the middle of the night or early morning. And the most productive method by far was a static deadbait.

However, on bright, moonlit nights, the pike responded best to moving baits, twitched or retrieved or on the drop, and we reasoned that if it was a moving bait that they wanted, perhaps livebaits would be a better bet than deads. We made some floats for the job, with Betalights glued into the tops, and the results were even better than with deadbaits.

This was exciting fishing, watching isotope-topped floats race across the black surface of the dark water and disappear suddenly as they plunged under with an audible plop.

However, while livebaits were three times more effective than deads when there was a big moon, deadbaits still outscored livebaits on the darkest nights. This suggested that the pike's sense of smell played a bigger part in finding food when visibility was poor.

Pike that feed only at night

As we broadened the scope of our experiments we discovered that pike were feeding at night even on waters that had very little angling pressure, so their nocturnal activities weren't just to avoid capture. And we started catching fish no one had seen before, which suggested that they were exclusively night feeders and had been so for a long time.

We also noticed that the average size of the pike that we caught at night was much higher than during the day. There's no doubt that some of the biggest pike on any water feed at night. Most of what we caught were 12 lb and over, and there were none of the jacks that turned up regularly in the day.

The transformation in our fishing was amazing. Fisheries that had produced next to nothing for several seasons now yielded pike up to the upper 20s at night.

We were arriving at waters as other pike anglers were packing up fishless, and by staying until 10 pm or 11 pm we were catching a fair few fish, some of them big. On the Big Coloured Pit, I had three twenties in quick succession one night, yet fishing there was very slow during the day. It wasn't that we were better anglers than the others, just that we were fishing at a time when the pike were feeding.

We were also fishing at night on the river, as it was there that the whole idea had been born, and livebaits presented correctly in flowing water produced a lot of fish for us early in the year.

Mostly in the margins

Stealth is essential at night because often the fish will be almost under your feet. On mild nights, pike come in close on gravel pits to feed on the small fish that take refuge in bankside reeds and tree roots.

Other coarse fish move into the shallow margins in late afternoon, when the threat of attack from birds and animals has decreased, and stay there for the night, foraging for food. When the sun rises, both they and the pike will move out into deeper water, where they feel more secure.

But it isn't just food that pike seek when they move in close after dark. They are looking for shelter, as well. On one water where scuba divers were studying fish movements at night in winter they found that over seventy per cent of the big pike spotted were close to the bank, many swimming right under wooden platforms. They watched them cat-nap for ten minutes or so and then move on to patrol the margins.

In Scottish lochs, pike will only move in close to the bank during the day if they have cover from weed. Bays without cover are unlikely to be visited until the sun begins to fade, though once the strength has gone from its rays, these could be as good as the weedy ones.

And if you catch a fish from one swim it's often a good idea to move to another straight after, to let things settle down before trying there again.

Summer and winter

The milder the weather, the more chance there is of action close in at night. In summer the nights can be light and warm and pike will feed because

Location is the key

But going night fishing without deciding in advance where you are going to fish is a short cut to failure. It's no good adopting a chuck-it-and-chance-it approach, because if your bait ends up yards from the hotspot, it could go unnoticed.

Left: Walking the bank in late evening before the sun went down paid off with this upper double catch.

I like to walk the bank in the evening on a river and pick out features on the far bank to mark swims for when I return later. Reconnaissance trips are a must, and information built up by fishing during the day and talking to people who know the water well will lead to success at night.

Tributaries and the points at which they join the main river are ideal places to try, especially if there is a lot of water flowing through and fish have moved a short way up out of the flow. Static deadbaits will outscore livebaits in these conditions as pike feed more by smell than sight in coloured water.

But all of the usual, fish-holding features listed in the rivers and gravel pits chapters will also be well worth a visit, as will any noted swims or known hotspots.

Then when you return at night you will have a good idea of the characteristics of each swim and where to cast to avoid snags and get results. It's surprising how different waters look at night, and the degree of technical difficulty is greatly increased.

Just knowing your way around the swim without stumbling over tree stumps and scaring fish will be a big advantage. An absolute must is a small headlamp, preferably a Petzl, for mounting the bait on the hooks, for positioning the bait when casting, for unhooking pike and for finding your way around. A torch is not enough, because you need both hands free when casting baits, netting fish and unhooking them. Over use of lights can have an adverse effect on sport, but so can blundering around because you can't see what you're doing.

Pick two or three swims so that if your first choice is unproductive you can move on to another. It is easier to fish deadbaits because they pose no problems of transporting them to the water. A dozen or more sardines wrapped in bubble wrap and pushed into a Packaseat with a few odds and ends of tackle and a camera is all that you need.

Bank sticks can be wrapped up in your landing net and carried in one hand and your rods will go in the other.

it's cooler than in the heat of the day and quieter. But in winter, the darkest nights are the best because they are the warmest.

At this time of year the nights are a lot longer. There are no people around to disturb the peace and quiet, and no boats on the river to disturb the calm. It's a perfect time for any secretive angler to catch fish. Big pike are landed, weighed, photographed and returned without another soul knowing what has happened.

This is the magic of night fishing. It is totally unlike anything you will experience by only

fishing during the day. The atmosphere is completely different. Every sound is magnified and the imagination runs riot at every noise nearby, as unseen creatures rustle through the undergrowth just inches from where you are sitting.

When a fish swirls it sounds like a body being dropped from a bridge, when a fox calls it sends a chill through the night air, and when you get a take, it makes your heart beat so fast you don't know whether to run towards your rods or away from them.

Playing an unseen creature that is wrenching the top of the rod over from somewhere out in the deep, dark water, lunging to the left and to the right, you can't help wondering if you've bitten off more than you can chew. It's fishing in a different world, and as exciting a branch of the sport as any I have experienced.

The big chill

In September, when the weather is still mild, I will fish moving baits at night, but come October and November and those first frosts and it is static baits most of the time.

Runs can be no more than gentle twitches. On a particularly cold night on the Thames, with the mercury in the minus, I saw one of the tips of my rods move slightly and the line between tip and water quiver and twitch. This happened for 10 or 15 minutes without a take developing so I moved the bait about six inches.

At once there was a steady pull on the rod and I tightened into a fish. It shot 40 yards down-river and took a lot of landing. It weighed 23 lb 8 oz.

I believe it had been guarding the bait but was not hungry enough to eat it, until it thought it was going to lose it. The line twitching may have been caused by the pike's pectoral fins and gills vibrating slightly and displacing water as it held itself steady.

The neuromast system – a pike's secret weapon

The great barrier to night fishing for pike has always been that pike were traditionally believed to hunt entirely by sight, so what was the point of trying to catch them when they wouldn't be able to see the bait?

When my friends and I started to catch pike at night, we began to discuss how they could find a live fish, and take it swiftly and cleanly when they couldn't see further than the end of their noses.

When you start pondering this question you realise that pike also manage to do the same in dirty, flooded rivers, and in gravel pits that are still being worked and remain cloudy.

When a scientist in Holland conducted an experiment whereby he blindfolded pike and found them still able to catch their prey, it became obvious that pike possess a secret weapon that we know very little about.

Top: A trotted trout livebait under a luminous float about to be tried on a bitterly cold night on a River Thames backwater.

Middle: Tripping the bait through close to the bank while sitting quietly to avoid any potentially fish scaring vibrations in the swim.

Bottom: First cast a 20 lb pike, which took the bait confidently and headed off across the pitch black river with its prize.

Further research has revealed that the special fish-detection powers pike possess are a remarkable, vibration-sensitive perception known as the neuromast system. It is vital to the survival of pike, and one of the prime ways in which they detect food, yet few pike anglers have even heard of it, let alone understand how it works.

Above: A very cold night on Dorchester Lagoon and a heartwarming 22 lb 8 oz fish on a half mackerel.

Left: A quick snap of the two 18 lb fish because the low temperature threatened to freeze their fins.

Since finding out about it, my approach to livebait presentation has changed radically, as I now know how easily pike can find a bait located in weed or at great distance from them, no matter how dark the night or coloured the water. Furthermore, I know that the livelier the livebait the better the chance of it being detected by the pike and taken, especially in a flooded river or a silty gravel pit.

The perfect predator

The neuromast system consists of a group of cells running in a row along the lateral line and others above and below in horizontal columns, like large 'plus' signs. The lateral rows pick up lateral movements, and the horizontal ones horizontal movements, working independently to provide the pike with a complete picture of the source of the activity.

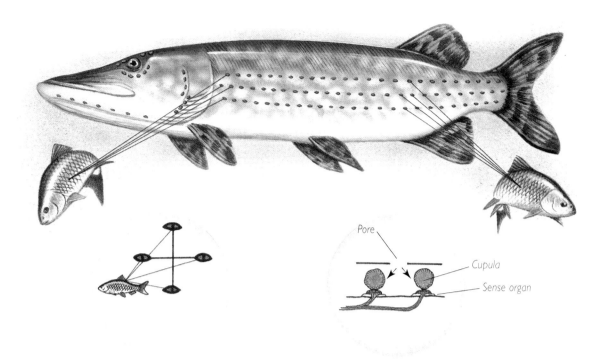

Pore

Cupula

Sense organ

Each cell has a structure called a cupola which is positioned in the epidermis of the pike's skin. Each cupola is linked by a short hair to nerve endings, and as water is displaced from around the pike's body the cupola and the hairs bend, stimulating the nerve endings and telling the pike that something nearby is moving.

There are other sensitive cells along the underside of the jaw that can be seen as a series of shallow pits, and some that run across the top of the head. All of these combine to provide an accurate picture of the location, direction and speed of whatever has caused the disturbance.

I think the nerve cells on the lower jaw are sensitive to the electrical impulses that every living creature gives out, and it is these that help a pike to find fish in the densest of weed beds. There is a species of shark that can detect its prey even when it is hidden in sand, and the pike's ability is akin to this.

The cupolas are so sensitive to water displacement that even the movement of the pike's own fins can prevent it from detecting prey fish. For that reason the neuromast organs are positioned well away from its own pectoral and dorsal fins, so their movements do not 'deafen' the pike's sensory system.

Above: The neuromast organ in prey fish. Note the cupolas are positioned in the dermis and are not exposed to the external part of the fish's body. Prey fish can muffle pressure waves or nearby movements around them and can differentiate whether the movements are caused by the flow of water around them or the approach of a predator.

Moving water can also deafen a pike's vibration detection system, forcing it to hunt more by sight and smell than by vibrations. But even when forced back on these two food-finding aids, pike are still deadly fish catchers, as they have very good vision and sensitive olfactory organs in their nasal cavities, able to detect even slight scent trails.

They have remained almost unchanged for millions of years while other creatures, ourselves included, have evolved. Nature got it right first time, and created a design classic and a perfect predator that could be improved upon only slightly over millions of years.

THE TRAVELLING ANGLER

The writing is on the wall for pike anglers everywhere. More people are turning to pike fishing; fewer gravel pits are being dug, and rivers are shrinking as populations grow. The obvious conclusion is that if you want to continue to enjoy quality fishing in the future, then you need to be prepared to travel.

On the plus side, roads have improved enormously in the past ten to twenty years, and with a half-decent car and an early start it's possible to travel over one hundred miles each way for a day's fishing. For a long weekend you could get to a water in an unspoilt part of Britain as much as three hundred miles away and still have your baits cast out by lunch time.

When you're away for a few days, the trip becomes well worth the effort and something that can be repeated often enough, providing funds allow, to get fully acquainted with even the remotest of waters.

A long-distance trip also means that the cost comes down as you drive away from the crowds. As a general rule, the more far-flung the location, the more likely that the ticket price will be more of a token amount, out of proportion to what's on offer.

Above: The River Wye, just one of many unspoilt waters throughout Britain just waiting to be discovered by the travelling angler.

From the wide open spaces of the Norfolk Broads in the east to the untapped potential of the River Wye in the west, and from the countless lochs of Scotland in the north to the estuaries of the big south coast rivers – there are a wealth of fishing opportunities for anyone willing to travel.

And if you're prepared to venture abroad, you can fish for pike of a very different size and species from our native British variety. There is excellent pike fishing in the Baltic, Holland, France, Germany, Denmark, Russia and Poland. In America there are muskellunge, which grow to five feet long and can weigh more than 60 lb.

Muskies are found in the northern states of the USA and Canada, where they thrive in the cool climate. The record stands at an ounce short of 70 lb, a fish caught in the St. Lawrence river in 1957. Even that is dwarfed by earlier monsters, the biggest for which photographic evidence exists weighing a staggering 110 lb. It measured seven feet four inches long and was landed in Michigan in 1919.

North America is a pike angler's heaven. Besides the mighty muskie (Esox masquinongy), anglers can also fish for our own species (Esox lucius), and three smaller cousins, the chain pickerel (Esox Niger), redfin pickerel (Esox americanus americanus) and grass pickerel (Esox americanus vermiculatus).

All five species are capable of producing hybrids, the most prized being the tiger muskie – a pike/muskie cross with all of the tackle straining attributes of both parents.

The Great Lakes in Canada are home to big, tail walking muskies, and the rivers of Alberta and Manitoba's Winnipeg River are home to the great northern pike, the same species as our own.

The heart of musky territory is Ontario, where the Ottawa and St. Lawrence rivers and the countless lakes that supply them have some of the biggest examples of this exciting species, while Minnesota is a region with as much water as land and a reputation for breeding some of the biggest and hardest fighting muskies of all.

But if you feel that America is a little far to travel, then the countries of Scandinavia, with their expanses of brackish water that hold huge stocks of pike to a size that would make a British angler's eyes bulge, are an obvious alternative.

The only other pike species outside America is the amur pike (Esox reicherti), found in the Amur River in eastern Asia on the border between Russia and China. It grows to just over 20 lb and lives mainly in flowing water, though it migrates to lakes and shallow backwaters to spawn.

Inch for inch, though, British pike are heavier than their American and asian cousins. A typical forty-inch pike on the other side of the Atlantic weighs in at around 16 lb, while any self-respecting British pike of that length would exceed 20 lb.

At forty-eight inches an average American pike weighs 28 lb, while if you catch one of those in Britain it would be of record-threatening proportions.

What all pike have in common, though, is a predatory habit. They are natural-born killers and anglers from Boston, Massachusetts, to Boston, Lincolnshire, use similar tactics to tempt them.

In recent years there has been a cross-fertilisation of ideas across the Atlantic. Many

Above: Chris Tarrant fishing in Manitoba. (Picture courtesy of Anglers World Holidays.)

Above: Fishing Athabasca Lake in Alberta. (Picture courtesy of Anglers World Holidays.)

American anglers are now using our advanced livebait and deadbait techniques to deadly effect, while we in turn have learned how to catch big pike on their excellent plugs and artificial lures.

Be prepared

But before you throw your tackle in the back of the car and set off for somewhere few anglers' feet have ever trodden, it's worth knowing that the single factor that will influence your catches more than any other on a remote water is preparation.

The more homework you do before you leave, the more trouble-free and so the more enjoyable the trip will be, and the greater the chances of success.

If you know where you are going to stay, where you are going to fish, how much the permits are, where you are going to get them, what bait you are going to use, what the weather is going to be, what the usual feeding times are and where the local hotspots can be found, you will have increased your likelihood of success many times over.

If you are going to build up an accurate picture of what is happening on a big lake, you need to establish a contact with someone who lives close by and is in touch with what is happening on a daily basis. I got to know a salmon and sea trout angler in Scotland, Neil Buchanan, and he tells me when pike are being drawn into one area of a loch because of a natural food source, like a heavy fly hatch or the perch population spawning. This kind of information gives you an enormous advantage, especially if you can only visit that water half a dozen times a year.

The aim is survival

At this point I should make a couple of admissions. First, that the majority of my fishing trips away from home have been to Scotland. I have fished in Wales, in Southern Ireland, in the East Midlands and in Norfolk, but Scotland is my first choice, and most of what I have learned has been picked up while north of the Border for a week or two at a time.

But the principles apply whether you are spending a fortnight in Inverness or two days in Stoke Poges.

The aim is a dual one, to fish and to survive. If this sounds a little melodramatic then I should explain that by survival I mean having everything you need to make yourself comfortable so that nothing will interrupt your concentration and, as a result, your fishing.

I'm not suggesting that you might not come back alive, only that some anglers come back from trips when the trip ends, and others when they are soaked through by inclement weather, when they are cold, hungry and too miserable to care about catching fish.

If by day two you are dreaming of a hot bath and a big meal, you haven't got it right. There's no reason why you should feel any less comfortable while away than when sitting in your favourite armchair with your feet up in front of the telly.

Left: A sheltered bay on Loch Awe where perch spawn at a given time each year, attracting large numbers of pike.

Above: Irish Pike fishing can be spectacular but choose your guesthouse with care if you don't want to be still waiting for breakfast when the pike have had theirs and moved on.

The second confession I have is that, when it comes to preparation, I'm something of a perfectionist. I used to say I don't do things by halves, but it would be closer to the truth to say I don't do things by three quarters or even nine tenths. It's all or nothing, and what I take with me reflects this. If there's a chance it may be needed, I've got it with me. I don't overburden myself with items that I don't expect to need. I know by now what is required, and streamline what I carry to match this.

However, my streamlined tackle is more than many anglers take, right down to spares for an outboard motor or tools to repair it. What you consider essential is entirely between you, your bank manager and your conscience. I am simply laying before you what I do, and you must decide whether and where you wish to cut corners.

But I should point out that hardly a trip goes by without me having to help someone who's

stranded miles from anywhere without some vital outboard motor part, and less than a snowball in Hell's chance of finding somewhere in the Glens that's likely to stock one. One forgotten or overlooked crucial item can ruin a trip. Like the best boy scouts, I like to be prepared.

Problems are multiplied

If the water to which you are travelling is bigger than the one that you usually fish, or you are spending longer there than you would normally, you need more gear.

For two days, you need twice as much bait as for one, twice as many rigs and twice as many leads. If the water is a loch rather than a gravel pit you will need bigger floats, stronger line and hooks and tougher wire. Everything is different and you must realise this at the start.

If you're catering for yourself – and believe me, it's the best way – you will need twice as much food for two weeks as one, twice as much fuel and twice as much money. And if you are sleeping under canvas on the bank, you'll need twice as many spare clothes for the times when the weather makes you wet through.

I rarely spend two weeks away, now. One week I can prepare for comfortably, but two weeks brings logistical problems that start to reduce the chances of fishing effectively in the second week, and make calculations unnecessarily complicated. By the time you've loaded up all the essentials you look more like the driver of an aid vehicle on a mercy mission to a war zone than an angler going fishing. I try to keep it simple now, having learned the hard way.

The problem with guest houses

Why not simply stay in a guest house, with meals and accommodation laid on, and a place to dry out when the weather turns bad?

Unfortunately pike and landladies don't keep the same hours. When the sun rises at 4 am in mid-summer, pike will be feeding as the first faint rays penetrate the water, and that spell may only last for about twenty minutes. You will need to be up before 3 am and in place before they start. Try asking for your breakfast to be served at that time of the morning and you're more than likely to find your bags on the front drive.

The good food guide

Left: No self-respecting travelling angler will leave home without a tin opener. A metal cup allows you to brew up directly over a flame, and a Coleman Multi-fuel is a joy to use.

Anyone who's ever been out for a Chinese meal and felt peckish on the way home will know that there's food that gives you a quick burst of energy that's soon over, and there's food that will keep hunger at bay for hours.

Meals eaten in between fishing sessions are best described as refuelling. You need something to satisfy your hunger and provide you with energy until the next fishing break, but you don't want to spend your time peeling spuds and scrubbing pans.

No self-respecting traveller will leave home without his tin-opener. Forget Delia Smith and her little squirt of lime juice and her sprinkling of fresh herbs. Tinned potatoes, easy-to-cook rice and tinned ravioli or spaghetti are what you want. You need carbohydrates for energy and plenty of them. You can mix in some tinned meat if your taste buds require it, but the important thing is to have something hot and filling. If you can raise your body's core temperature or at least keep it constant, that will greatly add to your feeling of well being, after a cold day spent fighting the elements.

Fred J. Taylor once wrote that the only use for a frying pan was to bang someone over the head. A couple of saucepans is all you need for cooking food as fried items will take too long to digest and cause cleaning problems. I save on the washing up by using a metal cup and brewing up with it directly over a flame.

Cooking will become less of a chore and more of a pleasure if you've got a stove of which you're proud. I've tried a few and the Coleman Multi-fuel that I've settled on is a joy to use. It will run on leaded or unleaded petrol, meths or turps, making it easy to replenish and very reliable. The price is about £30 to £35 for a single burner, and I wouldn't use anything else. Oh, and take a lighter rather than matches, as matches and water don't mix.

Despite what the adverts say, a bar of chocolate won't help you work, rest and play, and nor will junk food like crisps and biscuits. They will give you a boost of energy but not the sustained flow over several hours that you need. If this is starting to sound like an episode of the Good Food Guide, then I should say that I can't emphasise strongly enough that if you aren't well fed then you won't be able to concentrate, you're more likely to lose a big fish and will be seriously reducing your chances of success.

If you are going to fish for 13 or 14 hours a day, you need to look after yourself better than you would at home, where you have all of the comforts of familiar surroundings. It's hard work to be alert and fishing at 4 am and still be concentrating at 11 pm for one day after another, no matter what you do in between.

One corner I do allow myself to cut is in never taking fresh water with me, but just boiling up the water I am fishing in. I can imagine people wrinkling their noses as they read this but I've been using the same method for twelve years now without ill effect.

The water that comes out of the taps here in England has probably got more nasties in it than a fresh scoop of water from an unspoiled loch, and until I experience problems, I'll carry on. Perhaps in built up areas or near heavily-farmed land it wouldn't be wise, but in Scotland, at least, most of the water is just melted snow that's come down from the hills, and provided it's boiled there's no reason why you and I shouldn't drink it. I've no wish to carry a gallon container of water around with me unnecessarily, but if you don't like the look of the stuff where you're fishing, then it would be wise to err on the side of caution.

The motto is, choose your guest house carefully, in the case of Ireland with advice from Paul Harris, who is angling advisor to the Irish Tourist Board. That way you shouldn't have a problem.

And having achieved the ideal of getting up in the dark and enjoying the excellent sport that first light can bring, I like to come off the water for breakfast and a wash and brush up and maybe even a couple of hours kip just at the time when bed and breakfast owners want you out so they can clean the place and make the beds. I don't need to tell you that fishing on into the first hour of dark and getting in after 11 pm, tired and hungry, isn't exactly popular with non-angling landlords. Find a place run by an angler if you can, as tourist guest houses and successful pike fishing do not produce a marriage made in Heaven.

Bedding down on board

There was a time when I used to sleep under canvas, but the kind of weather that Scotland can dish out and the problems created by packing up and moving, as well as the security aspect, have persuaded me that the best way is to sleep on a boat with a cabin.

It's the perfect answer to all the problems created by tents. I now have a sixteen-foot Quayline with a proper cabin, complete with bed and cooker, and with this I don't need to leave the water at the end of the evening or take shelter from continuous, heavy rain.

I used to use a cuddy with an awning thrown over it but this was far from an ideal arrangement. With a boat that has a cabin you can sleep in, you're totally self sufficient. You don't have to rely on shops and garages, and if you get cold there's a door you can use to shut yourself in where it's warm in the cabin.

However, if you opt for sleeping under canvas, and plenty of anglers do, don't be tempted to take a bivvy. Faced with seven days of heavy rain you will realise that you can't to mess with Mother Nature. A proper tent's the thing, and a strong, well-waterproofed one, at that. Those of the dome design are light and compact and can be erected in seconds, which is important when you may move from one area to another or even from one water to another several times in quick succession.

The two essentials when choosing a tent for fishing trips are enough room to store everything and also sleep inside, and a sewn-in ground sheet to stop water from creeping in underneath. The stove makes a very effective heater inside a tent if used with care, especially just before going to sleep on very cold nights. It's important to be warm when you climb into your sleeping bag. I always have a hot drink before turning in, to raise my body temperature.

Peg it down

The best tent in the world won't keep you dry if it gets blown away in the first gale. Bivvy pegs are vital, and you should try to get the ones that are nine or ten inches long to get a secure hold, and push them in as far as they will go. A friend of mine had his tent and its entire contents hurled into a loch after he failed to peg it down in strong winds. Everything was soaked through and it took him two days to dry it all sufficiently to be able to get back to his fishing.

I helped him sort it out but I drew the line at his request to share my sleeping bag because his was still wet. Angling comradeship can be taken too far.

When fishing from the bank you can sit beside your tent, but when you set off in a boat each day and leave the tent behind, it's worth taking steps to ensure that nothing gets pinched. You may think that when you go to a place like Scotland to fish you will have the loch to yourself, but Loch Lomond in high summer can become extremely busy with sightseers, and boats will be going to and fro all day. If you are camping, try to set up somewhere where you can see your gear from where you will be fishing, and if possible store it on an island, which is a little more secure than the shore. Even then it's worth hiding valuable items like spare tackle in nearby bushes, for if someone is snooping around, the first place they are going to look is inside your tent.

And on the subject of hiding tackle, when you go to the shops to stock up on provisions, never leave rods on view in the back of your car. If you haven't got a sealed boot, buy some one-way security film and stick it over the back windows so that people can't see in, or at least cover things with blankets. Valuables have been stolen from the most remote and beautiful places, and many a trip has been ruined by the loss of large amounts of tackle.

The best sleeping bag

A good bag is worth its weight in gold. The one I use is a minus-20, down-filled model with sewn-in waterproof ground sheet and built in pillow. You can get them from army surplus stores for about £40 or made by the same company for anglers and sold by Fox. You need more than a standard sleeping bag for everything except high summer if you are going to get a good night's sleep and be able to stay awake the next day.

I never used to bother with bedchairs, but that wasn't because I'm one of those Crocodile Dundee types who can sleep on bare ground. I used to use a thick, Israeli, closed-cell-foam sleeping mat, which doesn't absorb water and cut down on the amount I had to carry in my days of sleeping under canvas.

Warm, dry clothing

Clean, warm, dry socks are the basis for fishing in comfort, for me. All the other warm and waterproof clothing is just as important in principle, but until I've got my feet happy I don't feel comfortable.

Modern waterproof materials have brought outdoor clothing on in leaps and bounds in recent years. Gone are the days of heavy waxed-cotton raincoats or nylon overalls that made us sweat so much we might as well have not been wearing waterproofs in the first place.

Now we have Aquatex, Ventile and Goretex garments that are light and very waterproof and don't make a noise like a bag of crisps being opened every time you move in them. They're not cheap but are worth the outlay for the freedom and comfort they offer.

The warmest way to dress is with several loose layers under a waterproof outer one, which has an added bonus that if the weather warms a little you can take a layer or two off until you feel right, unlike a one-piece suit, or straight-jacket as I call it. You won't find me in one. I can't move freely in them and think they could be dangerous if you fell in, because of their weight when soaked with water, which could pull you under.

Watching the weather forecasts

Weather forecasting is something else that has made great strides in the past decade. Now we are offered a far more accurate picture during periods of settled weather than we used to get, and the movement of high and low pressure fronts bringing changes in conditions can often be predicted up to a week ahead.

My trips to Scotland happen mainly in the summer because the weather is so unpredictable once winter sets in. I see no point in spending days at a time battling through heavy rain and gales and water whipped to a fury for what is usually a meagre reward under those conditions. What I'm looking for is a period of settled weather with overcast skies, even light drizzle. I don't want the weather to be too bright as pike tend to shun strong sunlight, which tends to restrict feeding spells to dawn and dusk, whereas we want pike to be on the lookout for food throughout the day. The longer the feeding period the greater the chances of catching a number of fish.

Above: Settled weather is the key to success in Scotland.

Best of all is the bib and brace, made by Abu in Goretex or Ventile, with several warm layers beneath. It is the ultimate combination of lightweight, warm, waterproof clothing that doesn't restrict arm movement yet covers you from ankle to chest.

Spare sets of clothing are a must in case of an accident. Even when you wear waterproof tops, heavy rain can still find its way in, and there can be more few more certain ways of feeling uncomfortable than by braving the elements.

Above: All you need to know about waters north of the Border.

Just the ticket

Ticket information is something best sorted out in advance, and here a phone call to a local tackle shop should help. It's useful to buy the licences and permits you will need on the day you arrive, for the length of time that you need, to avoid losing a day's fishing while you go in to the town. With an early start when travelling, the shops should be open when you arrive.

I used to have problems finding out who controlled what fishing in Scotland until I discovered an excellent booklet called *Scotland for Game, Sea and Coarse Fishing*, published by Pastime Publications in association with the Scottish Tourist Board. This will tell you all you need to know about waters north of the Border, including maps, details of which club controls what, where you can get tickets and how much they will cost. It is available from the Scottish Tourist Board, 6 York Place, Edinburgh EH1 3EP.

Transporting livebaits

If your pike fishing success depends upon the quality of your bait, then it is worth spending some time putting together a means of transporting them that gets them to your destination in good condition. Getting enough live fish to last you a week from one end of the

country to the other in the height of summer without them keeling over is quite an achievement, and it has to be done if you aren't going to risk wasting your time.

On the trips I have made to Scotland, a lot of the fish I've caught have been on deadbaits, but I always take livebaits for the odd times when pike won't look at anything else.

Trout bought from a trout farm, which are free from disease, are what you want. I favour brownies of 3 oz to 6 oz. If I can get some chub of 4 oz to 8 oz as well, I will also take these.

You may need as many as forty if the fishing goes well, and the pike seem to prefer them to deadbaits. Even with forty baits I've been known to run out within two days. There are times when you must have livebaits, so it pays to know somewhere where you can catch them to order in an emergency. I take a float rod and a pint or two of maggots in the cool box and head for one of the burns that flow into the loch or one of the boatyards. These potential livebait sources are among the things I look for when scouting around for new waters in the close season.

All hands to the pump

To transport livebaits successfully, air pumps are a must. Get one that will plug into the cigarette lighter of your car – Shakespeare make one and an American firm make another called Bubbles. I run the aerator cable from the dashboard to the back of the car and, provided I use it while driving, it won't flatten the battery.

The fish are kept in two big plastic fermenting bins with snap-on lids, ideally with trout in one, and chub in the other. The water level should be about three quarters full.

I stick the aerator to the lid of the chub bin with Velcro to stop it sliding around, pushing the air pipe in through a tiny hole punched in the top, with no room for water to splash out. Air stones are fitted at the end of the tube.

Make sure all of the connections are secure. A friend of mine had an aerator pipe come away from a pump, and by the time he got to Scotland all of his baits were dead.

The water in the trout bin is kept fresh with a cylinder of oxygen, which you can rent reasonably cheaply from British Oxygen and which will last a long time. Trout need a lot of oxygen to survive and it's worth the investment if you want baits to stay healthy.

A good tip before setting out is to put a lot of ice in the water, which brings down the temperature. When I reach the loch, I put three quarters of my baits in a keep sack in a couple of feet of water, and the other quarter in a bucket with a battery-run air pump. If I'm going out in a boat, I will put them in an American wire bait bucket, which is G-clamped to the gunwale and dropped over the side.

Fish moving orders

When transporting livebaits to any water it's as well to obtain a fish moving order in advance from the Environment Agency. Great damage has been done to individual waters' ecology by the illegal introduction of species which do not belong there.

I certainly wouldn't tip any live fish left over at the end of a trip into the loch if they weren't indigenous to the water. It's one of the advantages of using brown trout for livebait. Anglers have no idea how much damage they can do by the simple act of releasing non-indigenous species into a water.

Transporting deadbaits

Keeping deadbaits frozen can be as much of a problem as keeping livebaits alive if you haven't got the right equipment. The best invention from the deadbait user's point of view is a mobile freezer that plugs into a car's cigarette lighter and which runs off a twelve-volt battery when I am out on the water.

Cool bags and boxes are an alternative, are fairly cheap and will keep baits frozen if well-lined with ice packs. Wrap the baits very tightly in layers of newspaper and bubble-wrap plastic to insulate them. However, you can't expect baits to stay frozen for more than a couple of days in the summer.

It pays to take plenty with you because they help keep each other frozen. I take four kilos of sardines, a couple of dozen mackerel and a couple of dozen eel sections. They're cheap, and you can throw them away or re-freeze them if you don't use them.

Go on a recce

Some anglers would turn up their noses at travelling hundreds of miles just to look at a water and not wet a line. They'd happily stroll down to the local river in the close season to look for fishy features and hotspots but they draw the line at a full-blooded trip. But the truth is, the more homework you do, the better your chances of success will be.

Whether it's combined with a family holiday or a detour en route to somewhere else, reconnaissance trips can provide a wealth of valuable information, provided you know what to look for.

If I'm looking around a loch that I've never fished I will try to find where the main feeder streams come in, and see if there are signs of bait fish. Fishy looking features can be sought out and pin-pointed for future attention, and tackle shops, garages and boatyards can be found, saving time when there's fishing to be done.

And one of the richest sources of information can be the local pub. It's surprising how much you can learn over a pint. I like to talk to the salmon anglers who troll the loch and often hit big pike. Usually they are fully prepared to divulge information on the whereabouts of pike, as it's a species that doesn't interest them.

Locals know about the runs of game fish, the routes they take through the loch and where and when the coarse fish, like perch, spawn and they can save you a lot of time for the price of a couple of pints of Heavy or a few wee drams.

This will give you an intimate knowledge of what is happening on the loch throughout the year and put you in an excellent position to make the most of your time on the water.

But no matter how much you learn from a close-season trip, you will need to back this up, and get to know the water and its changing moods by making regular visits.

The daily routine

Most things in life are made easier with a regular routine, and fishing away from home is no exception. The pike and their feeding spells dictate what you do and when, and you will need to monitor these so that you can pace yourself and take rests and catch up on necessary chores in the slack periods in between.

On the lochs in the summer when the weather is warm the majority of the pike feed early and late. I like to get up before dawn, have a quick cup of tea and have the rods cast out ready for the dawn feeding spell. This can be very short lived, so it's worth making the effort and being there before it starts.

When the feeding stops I make breakfast and have a quick clean up. This could be still early or it could be mid morning, but even if the fish carry on taking baits until lunch time, which is rare, I will have a break at midday.

Lunch time is the chance to get a hot meal down me and maybe have a siesta if the evening looks like being a long one.

Afternoons can produce sport but generally the fish are not overactive then, so I use that time to get myself together. I'll sort through my tackle, checking the line and trace, tidy up the boat and get ready for the evening session.

A couple of years ago I was determined to make the most of every minute and fished so intensely that I was down to having one meal a day. I wouldn't recommend that method. Sooner or later

Above: The head of Loch Awe pictured at sunset in high summer.

you have to take a break, no matter how ambitious you are or how many miles you've travelled to be there.

It's better to force yourself to have a rest even when you want to carry on than to have to come off the water because you've overdone it.

And you will find that the first couple of days of a trip are usually the best in terms of catches. If someone else has just fished the bay you intended to try, it won't be worth fishing there because that bay will have been disturbed and won't produce fish until it has had several days' rest.

And the longer that you fish in one spot, the more disturbance there is in the water and the more wary the pike become.

So it pays to take a break, and if you know that the biggest pike will be around at dusk, you can time your evening meal for about 6 pm and that way you will be in place and alert when they go on the rampage.

BOATS

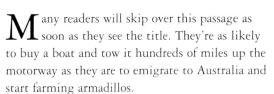

Above: The 16-foot Orkney Strikeliner has a deep draught and the size and strength to weather any storm that whips up a big water.

Left: Boat fishing is a unique experience akin to walking on water, and no one should turn their nose up without giving it a try.

M any readers will skip over this passage as soon as they see the title. They're as likely to buy a boat and tow it hundreds of miles up the motorway as they are to emigrate to Australia and start farming armadillos.

Which is a shame, not because I dislike armadillos particularly, but because boat fishing can add a new dimension to your angling. Fishing from a floating platform brings its advantages and disadvantages, joys and woes, but is, even at its worst, a unique experience akin to walking on water, and no one should turn their nose up at it until they've had a go.

Whether you hire a boat to see how you get on, or cajole a friend, angling or non angling, into letting you join them for a day, I would urge everyone to try it once, just in case you find it as wonderfully liberating as I do.

If you enjoy the experience enough to want to own your own craft, that enthusiasm should see you through all the preparation and expense involved in boat ownership, which I will be discussing in this chapter, along with how to approach fishing from boats.

Owning a boat can be costly and inconvenient, but it can also be as liberating as getting a car.

What boat to buy?

There's never been a better range of suitable boats available to the angler... from glass fibre to the traditional wood.

Glass fibre, or GRP, is my first choice. It combines strength with lightness and is virtually maintenance free. Wooden boats are very heavy, take a lot of looking after and are not as towable because of their weight. Someone once said wooden boats are like women – they need a lot of care and attention – and I wouldn't argue with that.

I have two boats for different conditions. I have a 13-foot Orkney Dory with a cathedral hull – three keels close together – making it very stable. This is used for most of my slack-water fishing, from navigating the Thames and anchoring in weir pools, to fine-weather fishing on Scottish lochs. It's the ideal boat for fishing sink-and-draw style, which calls for a mobile approach.

I used to have a 16-foot Orkney Strikeliner, which has a simulated clinker hull and a much deeper draught than the Dory, but I've recently changed it for a Quayline Reefrunner of the same length. It has plenty of floor space, a deep draught and a self-contained cabin that sleeps two people. Orkney produce a range of fishing boats, in particular the Spinner, the Coastliner and the Strikeliner.

You need a boat with plenty of clearance above the water for when strong winds whip up huge waves. It's ideal for fishing static deadbaits, when a solid platform is needed. I can tow either on a trailer behind my diesel four-wheel-drive, which I can also sleep in if necessary.

I prefer the Dory because it's flat-bottomed, which makes it easier to stand in, and very manoeuvrable, but it's not good in strong winds and certainly not the boat to be in when a storm is brewing. You need a bigger boat, one that is capable of getting through waves three or four feet high and crossing from one side of an expanse of water to the other.

To tackle the big Irish and Scottish lochs you need a boat of no less than 13 feet, and if I knew it was going to be rough or I was going there at a time when the weather could be bad then it would be a 16-foot craft every time.

· To make fishing half way passable, any decent boat should have a cuddy – a fibreglass shelter bolted to the bow, under which you can sit and be dry and warm, out of the wind and rain, while watching rods mounted on outriggers. If you're out of the wind, you won't suffer from the chill factor and you can stay out there longer and be more alert if something happens.

Choosing an engine

Until you have experienced a storm blowing up out of nowhere on a big water you can't imagine how quickly the weather can change. Water can turn from flat calm to a raging sea in ten minutes, and when that happens you need to get yourself to the lee shore or on to an island and out of trouble very quickly.

Top: Flat-bottomed Dory boats are easy to stand in and very manoeuvrable.

Bottom: A 30 Hp Mariner engine will get you out of trouble in rough weather.

To do this you will need a reasonably powerful motor. I have a 30HP Mariner engine, which gets me out of trouble, but I always take a back-up motor slotted on the back of the boat in case the main motor breaks down.

I can think of few things worse than being stuck on a big loch in bad weather, miles from where you started and faced with the prospect of having to row home. I've been known to motor fifteen miles to reach a good spot, and if I break down, I've got this distance to cover to get back.

You may think the chances of something going wrong are slim, but you would change your mind if you looked off the front of a boat into the water of a big loch or lough. The bottom can be fifty feet deep one minute and a foot down the next.

I've damaged props, motors and hulls when I've been caught unawares because these features – called skerries – are so unpredictable. Some of the Irish and Scottish waters have pointed boulders jutting almost up to the surface that can tear a hole in the bottom of a boat with ease. When you're exploring new lochs, accidents are going to happen to even the most experienced anglers.

But the Scottish countryside isn't exactly over-endowed with specialist stores selling spare parts for various makes of outboard motor. One bad bump and you could be going home early or fishing for the rest of your stay from the shore.

The sort of size of engine needed on a big loch can get through a lot of petrol. I take two tanks of fuel and plenty of oil – enough for several days' use. Large, remote pike waters are desolate places when you are stranded. Rarely does a trip go by to one of the more popular lochs without me ending up towing anglers back who have run out of fuel. Others have to cut short their session to come ashore to refuel. The very least you should do is find out in advance the whereabouts of the nearest place that sells it.

The second engine that I carry is 3HP to 4HP, which doubles as a trolling motor. It has an integral petrol tank, and is very compact and light.

Also, I always carry a basic tool kit with a spare set of spark plugs, so that if the fault is minor, I can tinker with the engine and maybe fix it.

Extending the handle

My own, personal contribution to boat fishing comfort is an outboard motor extension arm. I offer you this information without any attempt at personal gain as the item is not sold by a tackle firm under a fancy name, but by DIY stores in the form of lengths of plastic tubing.

The idea came about because I found that when I was trolling, I was continually reaching back, and sitting at an uncomfortable angle. To watch the rods, check the echo sounder and see where I was going meant looking in three directions, one after the other, for long periods of time, which was literally a pain in the neck.

The problem was that the standard length tiller handle on the motor was too far back to reach. But with a two-foot length of plastic tube slotted over the handle of my trolling motor, I can sit facing forwards, watch the rods in front and the echo sounder to the side, while steering, without looking round.

Two types of anchor

Anchors come in two sorts – heavy, flat-bottomed mud weights for holding on smooth bottoms of silt or sand, and traditional, lightweight folding hooks, like giant trebles, which grip debris and rocks.

I have home-made, non-folding, anchors like grappling hooks, with four prongs slotting into a two-foot length of scaffold tube half filled with lead. These are the only design capable of holding a big boat in a powerful swell. A specially-built anchor is needed to keep a boat still on a big water.

Mud weights are only used to stabilise the other end of the boat or to anchor up in a very sheltered bay. You can't present baits properly if the boat is yawing, or not stable. My mud weights weigh 50 lb to 60 lb and have large surface areas to stop them dragging along featureless lake beds. I've customised mine by gluing carpet on the bottom to stop them clattering against the front of the boat on the way in and out, and scaring fish.

The drawback with any kind of anchor is that it can get trapped in snags and be can difficult to get out. If this happens, you will need to wrap the rope around a cleat and back the boat up until you have pulled it free.

Each rope needs to be forty feet long, as you could find yourself fishing in thirty-five feet of water, but more importantly it needs to be at least 3 cm in diameter so that you can get a grip on it

Above: Anchors come in two types – flat mud weights and ones with prongs that grip.

without it cutting in to your hands. I use polypropylene yachting rope, which floats, a useful feature if you're absent minded and prone to dropping anchor without attaching the other end to the boat.

I carry two shorter lengths of rope, about ten or twelve feet, which I use when I'm fishing shallow water, so that I don't have lots of coils of spare rope trailing around my ankles. To change over I use caribenas, which are sturdy, snap-on metal links used in rock climbing.

Some people believe a length of heavy chain is a substitute for a well designed anchor, but no amount of chain will hold an anchor that is prone to slipping when a strong wind gets up.

Always anchor with the bows – the pointed end, for anyone not familiar with such complex nautical terminology – facing into the wind. Anchoring across the wind is asking for a bumpy ride, for waves to break over the side and for the anchor to be dragged out of position. And be prepared to change position when the wind changes, as it can do frequently on a big water, or you could find yourself facing in the wrong direction despite having anchored with care a little earlier in the day.

All hands to the bilge pump

No matter how hard you try to keep it out, water has a habit of finding its way on board. It could be rain or spray or seepage during overnight mooring, but hopefully it's regular use of a landing net laden with one big fish after another.

However it gets in, though, it needs to be got out. I have an electric in-line bilge pump and I've

Outsmarting lively fish

The problems don't end with a securely-anchored boat. Once you have presented a bait properly and hooked a fish, anchor ropes become a liability, as does the propeller. I like to get the prop up out of the water in advance, but if a fish goes around an anchor rope, you've got problems.

You can't stop a fish from running under a boat. Believe me, I've tried. I've broken rods sinking the tips and holding on while trying to turn a pike. There is a way of outsmarting a fish, though. The best way to beat them if they've gone under the boat is to put the multiplier on free spool. The fish will carry on for a while but when it feels no resistance it will stop. You can then pass the rod under the anchor rope, tighten up and you are back into the fish.

The more you pull against a strong fish, the more it will go away from you. If you slacken off you can usually get away with it, and the hook hold is usually strong enough to let you do this because you've already tried stopping the fish with rod pressure. Slack lining isn't an infallible technique, though. The odd fish hasn't read the rule book and just keeps going.

known it rain so much I've had it going all day to keep the boat dry.

Electric pumps are very compact – mine is about 20 cm long – and will clear out any water that has collected inside overnight in minutes, through a length of plastic piping. You can use a bailer, but this is much simpler. I attach mine to the battery that I use to power the fish finder.

Lost without a fish finder

Maybe it's a slight exaggeration to say I'd rather leave my rods behind than my fish finder when out on a loch, but it comes a close second. Loch Lomond, for instance, is over twenty-five miles long and five miles wide. It comprises thousands of acres of water and you don't need me to tell you that represents an awful lot of man hours of depth-finding with a float rod and a plummet.

If you are trolling without a fish finder, you are working blind. Looking for needles in haystacks doesn't come close when compared to one angler pulling a pair of baits aimlessly behind a boat in a vast loch in search of pike.

Lochs are huge sheets of water, more akin to the North Sea than a gravel pit or a big river. They have dramatic, fish-holding features that are invisible from above the water line, and you need a fish finder to pin-point these underwater contours. But they won't find you pike, and will work against you if you try to use them in that way.

Above: A 20lb pike caught from a feature found with an echo sounder. Big blank waters like the Wiltshire gravel pit that produced it really require a fish finder to do them full justice.

Use them as contour finders and feature finders, or to locate shoals of food fish, and look for drop-offs and shelves, holding areas and stream beds. Anglers caught pike before they were invented and will probably always succeed without them, but against the odds. I only know that I wouldn't be without one.

I run the sounder off a large, twelve-volt leisure battery, which is about eighteen inches long. This also powers my small-water trolling motor, which is a little Minn Kota electric outboard, which trolls at just the right speed and is almost silent. But for bigger waters I use the 3HP petrol motor mentioned earlier, because it copes better with the larger waves and longer distances involved.

If the leisure battery needs to be recharged after prolonged use it can be taken to a boatyard, many of which will charge it overnight for a small fee.

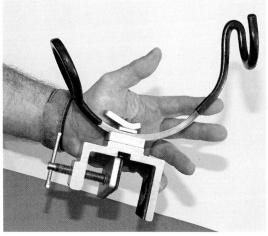

Above: A Minn Kota electric outboard makes an excellent small-water trolling motor, moving the boat at just the right speed to present the baits attractively while remaining almost silent.

Top: Outriggers make useful rod rests, taking the tackle clear of the boat.

Bottom: Lengths of two-inch diameter tubing prevent the rods from getting trodden on.

Outriggers make things easier

Like fish finders, outriggers aren't essential for trolling, but they make the job a great deal easier. Mine are bolted on to the sides of the 16-foot boat.

Outriggers are front and back rod rests all in one, that will hold the butt of a rod securely and in a position that keeps the line well away from the boat. They are also useful as rod rests when not trolling, as they get the rods out of the boat to leave plenty of room on board.

There are two varieties – under and overs, which should have a deep U rest because lochs can be choppy places and rods have a tendency to bounce out and get lost, and the American sort, imported by Bob Carolgees, which are more sophisticated and grip the rod so that there is no chance of it coming free. Both types allow the

rods to be spread further out to cover areas away from the boat . They're well worth having.

On my under-and-overs, which a friend made for me, I have plastic tubing covering the rear U to protect the rod handle from damage and a length of rubber over the top of the front U to prevent the rod from bouncing out and sliding into the water.

On the subject of rod holding devices, I use lengths of two-inch diameter tubing bolted to the boat, pointing upwards, to hold my rods upright when I'm moving from one bay to another. This avoids a tangle of rods in the bottom of the boat that can get trodden on if you should trip over or tips broken because they protrude beyond the end of the boat.

Splendid isolation

At this point it's time for another confession. I don't like fishing with other anglers in the same boat. Call it selfish or anti-social, but I don't believe there's room for more than one angler in one boat. With another person on board I have to consider them all of the time.

For instance, I'm very meticulous about keeping everything in the right place. When I put something down, like a pair of forceps, I expect it to be there when I go to pick it up again. I like to have everything to hand, and when I fish with someone else they put things down in another place and I can't find them.

To some people it's an acceptable nuisance – the price you pay for having company. To me it's just annoying.

Besides this, two people create twice as much disturbance in a boat as one, no matter how quiet they are, and that reduces the chances of success. I know people are going to say I should be more tolerant, but I just don't find two in a boat conducive to catching quality pike.

Floor space is another reason. It's important to have plenty when fishing, so one less angler means double the space. With this in mind, I also make sure I leave everything that I don't need on the shore. The less clutter in the boat, the more room I have for manoeuvre.

Covering the floor

Having claimed the space in the bottom of the boat as my own, I like to kit it out for maximum comfort – the pike's and my own.

I Velcro three big Wychwood unhooking mats to the floor, cut to fit the bottom of the boat, to protect the fish and help keep noise and vibration in the bottom of the boat to a minimum. By way of a bonus, if you feel like a lie down then they are just the thing – warm to the touch, being made of closed-cell foam, soft and springy and offer complete insulation from cold coming through the hull of the boat and up through your feet.

I customise my boats whenever there is a feature that is unsuitable for my needs. The bottoms of many big boats are curved, so they are uncomfortable to stand up in, but that can be solved by putting flat boards in the bottom. And

on the Dory I've taken out the big bench seat storage area so that I can walk the length of the boat without tripping over it. It's now possible to buy the boat without that seat, for a considerable saving.

I allow myself one rucksack of non-essential items, which will hold spare clothing and valuables, and this goes in the stowage compartment along with engine spares and tools. The main bag carries the Coleman stove, food, bait, my favourite metal cup for brewing up, trace tidies, forceps, tackle box, scales and weigh sling, plus my camera in a watertight box packed with foam. This is so that if it goes overboard it will float (I've tested it) and it should stay dry. This keeps out the rain as well. I used to rely on the maker's camera case to keep out water until one £500 camera began to sport mildew and the man from Nikon examined the circuitry and declared it a write-off. I vowed it would never happen again.

The much-neglected trailer

If I had to name the biggest mistake that boat-owning anglers make it is neglecting their trailers and the biggest area of neglect is wheel bearings. They are forever getting wet, as the trailer gets rolled into the water, and if they aren't greased regularly, they can give out at any time. I do mine with a grease gun every time it has been in the water, and I use marine grease, which stands up to high temperatures and being submerged in water, unlike standard, car-axle grease, which turns thin and milky.

The bearings take an incredible amount of weight, as even the Dory weighs more than a Mini and takes four or five people to lift. Every time you go over a bump in the road they take the full force.

It's surprising how many people expect it to be easy to tow a trailer. They picture it trundling along the motorway behind the car and don't give the matter another thought. But when they need to be backed down a narrow jetty at a sharp incline, perhaps in the dark, it's Jeremy Beadle time.

It looks easy when it's done by someone experienced, but if you haven't done it before you'll find out it isn't. It's well worth practising reversing your car with boat and trailer attached through narrow gaps before the day of the trip, daft as it may feel. And take it round a few corners while you're at it.

Also make sure the vehicle you use to do the towing is man enough for the job, if you don't want to get stuck on a hill in the middle of nowhere.

Trailers should be as well made as the boats that go on them. If you're getting one, make sure it's galvanised and has waterproof lights permanently attached. A trailer board is too much trouble. Everything should be welded on so that it can't be stolen or fall off.

Wheels should have locking wheel nuts and the spare should also be locked on, and the trailer should be locked to the car. I carry a spare set of keys in case of an accident, and these are attached to a small plastic bottle so that they will float if they should go over the side.

On the subject of time saving, always load the boat with gear while it is still attached to the car, to save walking back and forth into the water. It's surprising how many anglers do it the hard way. When travelling between waters I stash the rods on top of the car, full length, tied to a rod rack.

A trailer with docking arms, which guide the boat on when you are winching it out of the water, can be a great asset, especially when the flow on rivers or the tow on lochs pushes the boat out of position.

Mooring overnight

There are two types of disaster to avoid when choosing a place to moor your boat overnight; natural and man-made. Natural disasters take the form of holes worn in the bottom by sharp rocks as the craft shifts at anchor. The others involve people with designs on your property.

If someone is going to pinch my boat while I'm away, I'm going to make them work for it. I put it somewhere where it's necessary to wade out to get it, right up to their chest. But even when there's no security risk, never moor a boat in shallow water or near any rocks as that's asking for a hole in the bottom if the wind gets up. Choose as sheltered a spot as you can, and always moor the boat at both ends to keep it from swinging.

Above: Docking arms are a great asset on a trailer as they help guide the boat when it is being winched out of the water.

If something goes wrong and the boat gets a breach, I carry a tube of fibreglass marine filler for small holes. If you put a big hole in your boat there's not much chance of doing anything out in the wilds. The advantage of the Dory is that it has a double skin of fibreglass, so you can puncture the outer skin and carry on fishing. You just take it to the shore at the end of the day, empty out the water from the chamber between the skins and fill in the hole.

Some bits of a boat's hull are more vulnerable than others, and if you get to know which these are you can built them up with fibreglass to protect them. Best of all, fit stainless steel skid rails under the boat so that if you hit rocks or are regularly pulling your boat on gravel they will reduce wear and double the life span of the hull.

I like to moor where I intend to fish the next day, so that when the new day dawns, I can just climb out of bed and I'm ready to fish. If the boat needs to be moved a little I will sidle gently into position using an electric motor or oars to avoid disturbing the swim. I then drop anchor slowly, without any clattering.

Sleeping on the boat means you are on the spot and can catch pike unawares in the bays where they have been sheltering for the night or as they come in to feel the sun on their backs.

Essential extras

A lifejacket is a must. If you make regular trips it's inevitable that sooner or later you will have a mishap, and if you want to be around to tell the tale you'll need a lifejacket. I never go out without one, having witnessed a near fatal accident.

A friend of mine was fishing alone in a boat in Scotland when he lost his balance while leaning over the side in very rough conditions. He fell into extremely cold water without a buoyancy aid. Fortunately, I was fishing within earshot and heard him go over. I pulled up anchors and went and got him out.

He was an experienced angler and boat user, and a big, strong chap, but it was still quite a shock for him. He was having a job to struggle back on board when I got to him; his clothing was saturated and weighed him down, and the cold was numbing his arms and legs. He would probably have made it even if I hadn't been around to help, but it was still a predicament he wouldn't ever want to be in again. He also wears a lifejacket on the water, now.

The best garments I have come across look no different from normal fishing jackets but have a gas capsule that makes them inflate on contact with water. They also have a whistle to alert other water users. But whatever the make or type, any buoyancy aid is better than none.

Waders or a wetting

Launching a boat is a wet business, even in the height of summer. You need to get into the water to get it off the trailer, and if the water is very shallow close in, you may have to walk out quite a way before you can get the boat afloat.

Thigh waders are no good. It's chest waders every time. I've even tried wearing wellies and standing on the trailer, but the water always comes over the tops and gives me wet feet. Once you're in the boat, of course, the chest waders should be taken off, for safety reasons, in case you go over the side.

Above: I never go boat fishing without a life jacket under my coat, having seen a friend come close to losing his life after falling overboard. Even strong swimmers can soon get into difficulty.

When to go

I used to think that you could go pike fishing in Scotland or Ireland at any time of year in any weather, and it was just a matter of having the right clothing to overcome bad weather.

But I've since learned from the example of friends who went to Scotland in open boats at the wrong times and were drenched day in, day out until they came home early vowing never to go at that time again.

Spring can be a wonderful time of year, and pike are catchable on their way to or from the spawning grounds, but when their time comes they are very reluctant to take a bait. When they are grouped together to spawn and preoccupied with the urge to reproduce, I won't fish for them.

And when they have spawned they are in the poorest condition that they will be in all year, and at their lightest weight. Sport can be hectic as the newly spawned fish replace lost energy by taking advantage of the natural larder of salmon smolts on their spring migration downstream, but I'm just not interested. I don't want to catch them when they are out of condition, but by May and June they are fighting fit and well worth the angler's attention.

Also, the weather is very unpredictable in spring. By early summer the air and water temperatures are higher, hours of daylight are at their maximum and fish have reached a feeding peak.

Above: Multipliers are the first choice for boat anglers for bait control, superior presentation and an ideal rate of retrieve.

My favourite month is June, when pike have a faster metabolic rate and are more active, so they are feeding more frequently. I'm convinced that it is the increased hours of light that is the critical factor. The longer the hours, the greater the amount of feeding. And it's a bonus that the weather is at its most pleasant at that time.

Where to go

Vast areas of Scotland, which is a honeycomb of freshwater from north to south and east to west, have yet to be explored by pike anglers. Doubtless huge fish lurk up there, and the easiest ones to catch will be the ones that have never seen an angler.

When searching for new waters I look for a location that will suit pike and have a suitable environment in which they can find sufficient food and in which they can go undetected for many years.

I look for a water that has extra riches being brought in from the sea, a good run of game fish and a head of Arctic char, a native population of brown trout and perhaps a fish farm where rainbow trout and salmon are reared and from which a number escape. All of these factors tip the scales in the pike's favour and increase the chances of such a water holding an extremely big pike. If the water is prone to flooding, making

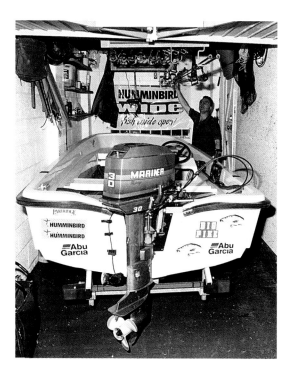

Above: A spare garage makes an ideal boat store for between trips.

feeding by sight impossible, or without extensive shallows then the potential is reduced. I want to find somewhere where pike can live out their lives without disturbance, from man or from nature, and then the chances of a fish growing to a big weight are very much increased.

LOCHS AND LOUGHS

Above: The view across Loch Lomond is breathtaking – and the prospect of catching pike from there daunting.

Left: Loch Awe in early spring surrounded by snow-capped mountains.

To stand on the shore of a vast, natural expanse of water in Scotland or Ireland is a breathtaking and daunting experience for a pike angler. You cannot fail to be moved by the rugged, unspoiled beauty of the landscape, but at the same time as you are marvelling at the scenery a voice inside you is asking 'Where on earth do I start?'

But the truth is that as much as two-thirds of some of these enormous waters can be ignored without greatly reducing your chances of success because it is far too deep. And by concentrating on the few areas that will produce fish and approaching them with the right tackle, tactics and bait, success is almost guaranteed, weather permitting.

The weather, of course, is the one big drawback to these huge, beautiful expanses of water, for when it decides to rain or blow it can do so with such awe inspiring fury and persistence that survival, and not catching fish, becomes the prime concern.

But go there in high summer, when even the locals can look tanned, and you can experience the countryside at its most welcoming.

A *stable environment*

The great advantage that lochs and loughs have over rivers and gravel pits is their stability. Loch Lomond is twenty-six miles long by up to six miles wide. In a water like that, pike can live out their lives without being disturbed.

Natural catastrophes are much less likely to occur on such a vast volume of water than on a river that flows through towns and cities, being drawn off in one place and pumped back in another with waste products and chemicals added along the way. Gravel pits, too, are vulnerable, being artificially created and often located close to towns, where some people see them as rubbish dumps, or near to industrial estates where oil and other waste products get into the water table.

The pike in Scotland and Ireland have access to rich feeding at intervals throughout the year, helping them to grow quickly and stay healthy, and unlike river fish do not use up energy fighting a fast current. In the right environment with as much food as they can eat, no anglers around and no current to work against, a pike can wax fat in a wild water in one of the more remote parts of the British Isles.

I've fished north of the Border and across the Irish Sea, but originally it was to Scotland that I went when I felt the urge to fish further afield. It was there that I learned to fish wild waters, though most of what I learned and have written about here will apply equally well in Ireland. For Lomond, Tay, Ken and Awe, substitute Conn, Corrib, Mask and Derravaragh and you won't go far wrong.

The stuff of legends

The Scotland I went looking for was the one described in Fred Buller's classic book *Pike*, in

Above: Dawn on an Irish lough. The unspoilt waters of Ireland and Scotland offer almost limitless opportunities for first-class fishing in beautiful surroundings.

which he recounts the most desperate moment of his angling career. He hooked a fish in excess of 50 lb while fishing with Dick Walker at Port Nellan Bay on Loch Lomond and after playing it for several minutes lost it when the trace knot broke.

He says he has relived that day in his mind countless times over the years and slowly come to terms with what happened. The pike was found dead a few weeks later, his trace still in its mouth.

I went up there to fish from those places he talks about: the Endrick Bank, Rossdhu Bay, where the Falloch enters the loch, Ardlui, Port Nellan Bay, the mouth of the Finlas Water, Fruin Bay and Balmaha Lomond is the pike angler's Mecca, and no self-respecting pike enthusiast can drive past without stopping and standing on the banks and thinking of other anglers who have made the pilgrimage. Places like Lochs Garry, Woodhall and Loyne have great potential and are well worth exploring.

But I soon realised that every angler who heads for the Highlands visits the famous-name places, and these popular haunts were being fished too heavily to ever produce anything spectacular. They still provide anglers with 20 lb pike, but I realised that if I wanted really big fish – I did and still do – I would have to explore

Above: Loch Lomond's Port Nellan Bay on the south-east bank, where Fred Buller hooked and lost his legendary big pike, and where big fish lurk to this day.

and find new areas. There are still places that are fished very sparingly, and with a loch as big as Lomond, there's no excuse for not breaking new ground.

It's not a bad idea when you first go up there to start with the famous haunts until you've familiarised yourself with the surroundings, and get a feel for the type of fishing that you will be doing. Many an angler has headed off into the mist on the loch, lost his bearings and spent a long time finding his way back to base.

First find the food fish

To find pike in untried areas I knew I would have to understand why pike are attracted to one place, so that I could seek out areas that offered the same advantages. That's where the really hard work starts. You need to build up a detailed knowledge of the water on reconnaissance trips. I still go up just to have a look at a few new locations and assess the potential of other, less popular, lochs.

And you have to find yourself local contacts and get close to the people who live on the loch and get them to trust you. My salmon-fishing friend Neil Buchanan has a friend who nets the loch regularly for eels, and when he's doing that he's catching powan, important food fish for pike.

I contacted the fisheries improvement people at Pitlochry Freshwater Fisheries Laboratory, who were able to tell me which lochs had decent runs of salmon, sea trout and char, and also which held good numbers of perch, roach and other food fish. That gave me a head start. Find the food and you'll find big fish.

Loch Lomond Angling Improvement Association, who are based at 29 Vincent Place, Glasgow, operate tagging schemes which monitor the movement of all fish through the loch, and their work is still going on.

I got to know game anglers on Lochs Awe, Lomond and Tay who encounter big pike when they are trolling. The information they passed on over a pint or two gave me a pointer as to where pike may be at different times of the year.

Getting to know these people provided me with location information for several different lochs, and by corresponding with contacts made during visits I was able to build up a picture of where to be and when. Without their help it would have been a very long and drawn-out affair of trial and error, and being six hundred miles from the waters, I wasn't prepared to waste precious time. The more that can be achieved in advance of fishing in terms of location, the greater the chance of catching the fish you are after.

Pike with a purpose
By breaking the loch down into small areas, the task is made a great deal less daunting. A lot of people try to fish too much of one water at once. Even before I leave for Scotland, I have decided where I'm going to fish and why. To fish blind and decide what to do as you go along is a mistake.

Once you know what draws pike to an area and when, you know where to find them. Pike know they need to be in one place at one particular time to take advantage of a food source when it becomes available.

They don't swim around haphazardly, and aren't spread evenly throughout a loch like currants in a bun. There's a deep-seated purpose in all of their movements. They have an intimate knowledge of everything that goes on in the loch, and they know when and where to be to capitalise on any situation from which they can benefit.

Salmon and sea trout smolts run back to the sea about three weeks after pike have spawned, when the pike are desperately in need of a rich food supply to replace the energy they have lost. It's perfect timing. You can plot the movement of the pike to take advantage of this, and if they are there one year, they will, more often than not, be there the next, depending on the weather.

Where two rivers run into a loch close to each other, like the Orchy and the Strae at head of Loch Awe, pike sit in the mouths of them and wait for salmon smolts to come down, picking them off as they pass. When runs of salmon and sea trout are held back at the mouth of rivers in

Above: I got to know game anglers on Loch Awe and their information about the movements of other fish gave me a pointer toward location of pike.

autumn, due to lack of rain, pike will be there, looking for a free meal.

On Loch Lomond there are many well-known islands, such as at Inchcruin, but there's also a submerged island at the McDougal Bank that many pike anglers don't know about. In late May and early June there is a massive fly hatch on the loch, and the trout and coarse fish know that there are rich pickings over that island. And anywhere where there is a gathering of food fish, pike will be there to pick them off.

And in May, Loch Tay's perch population comes out of its deep water haunts and moves into the same area of shallow water in the same week of the year. For three or four days the water comes alive with pike from every corner of the loch, hounding the huge numbers of perch collected in that one area.

I've seen it countless times, but it still amazes me that in a sheet of water perhaps twenty miles long, pike know the exact place and the exact week that perch will be there, year in, year out, without fail. It must be passed down through the generations and become something akin to an internal alarm clock that tells them the time has come round again.

Survival of the smartest

It's not just pike that are opportunists. In Lake Windermere the eels wake up from their winter hibernation just as the char spawn. They feed on this rich and plentiful food and then go back to sleep until the spring. Pike are there as well, feeding on the char and the eels, both of which are preoccupied enough to be vulnerable.

The fish in these wild places owe their survival to their instinct for where the next meal will come from. They are in tune with the movements of the food fish because they have to be, and they have honed their knowledge down to finely-developed intuition as to where these opportunities will arise.

I have located perch in 40 feet of water at another time of year, using the fish finder, and the pike have been close by. Success on these lochs is very much a matter of location, and if you know where there is going to be food for pike, the hardest part has been done.

Make a note of where and when these things happen because until there's a marked change that upsets the loch's ecology, the general pattern will persist. Loch Lomond pike are very long lived and they've been visiting these locations for many generations, and will continue to do so for at least the rest of our lifetimes.

Visible signs of pike

Very early in the morning, Loch Awe pike sometimes come to the surface and swirl, showing their back, dorsal and tail fins. Often they will do this over exactly the same spot for several mornings running, in close proximity to a drop-off, always at first light. I really can't say why they do it, but whatever the reason they provide anglers with a visual sign of their location, so it pays to keep an eye on what's going on.

There's a place on Loch Awe where the depth of water drops from four feet to seven feet, and in one small spot down to fifteen feet, and it's there that you see this swirling activity occurring. Loch Awe pike are very mobile, yet this behaviour takes place in this spot more often than anywhere else.

A word of warning

As you'll have gathered by now, to fish large, wild waters and do justice to what they contain you need a boat. If you don't own one you need not despair for they can be hired from the Portsonachan Hotel on Loch Awe or at McFarlane's boatyard at Balmaha on Loch Lomond or at Ardlui.

Some of the best bays are bordered by private land, as in the case of Rossdhu Bay on Loch Lomond, which is surrounded by a golf course and the country estate, putting the banks out of bounds. A boat will take you to areas inaccessible on foot.

A map of the water you intend to fish is well worth the small outlay. Trevor Moss at The Tackle Shop, in Gainsborough, Lincolnshire, sells an Admiralty one for Loch Lomond, the best map you can buy. It has everything from depths and contours to bays and islands, sunken and visible, and is essential for anyone with serious designs on big pike from this water.

And when you're fishing big waters, the tackle you use should reflect the terrain – 30 lb to 35 lb trace wire, 20 lb main line, 3 lb to 4 lb test curve rods and float fishing, rather than legering. Too many times I've seen bank anglers new to Scotland legering on the lochs in standard, gravel pit style, and every run they get wraps their tackle around so many boulders they end up playing the bottom and having to pull for a break. Conventional deadbaiting is a nightmare, and losses are all too common when that method is used.

On the subject of being prepared, don't leave home without the insect repellent in summer. Scottish mosquitoes are as pleased to see you as the local people, only the small Flying Scotsmen's welcome carries a lot more bite.

Another visual sign happens when pike come up out of deep water over a shallow sand bank to move into a bay. As they do this their dorsal fins come out of the water. I have sat in my boat and watched them and know from experience where they're going. I've caught them on the drop-off and I've taken my boat round the back of a nearby island and caught them in the deeper bay.

Left: A fish of 23lb 12oz caught from deep water in the heat of the day. At midday, loch pike are inclined to take cover in the safety of the deeps. This one took a sardine on the bottom in twenty feet.

But I'm sure that if I hadn't seen them breaking the surface one day as they moved over that sand bank, which is so shallow you'd have expected them to beach themselves, I would never known where they were going.

Sun loving species

When the sun is warm, loch pike like to bask. At midday, when it's rays shine directly into the water, though, they will be at their most vulnerable from attack from above, and are inclined to take cover or drop into deeper water. But early in the morning and in late afternoon, when sunlight is slanted and not straight into the water, pike move into shallow areas. They usually stay there for the night, as they don't feel in danger because they can't be seen.

All lochs have shallow bays, the most famous on Lomond being Rossdhu Bay and Port Nellan, and pike will visit them to get the sun on their backs. I once caught a pike which had a lighter back than the rest of its body from basking in the sun in a shallow bay, and I've caught mid 20s that were lying in just eighteen inches of water.

Pike are not lovers of deep water but prefer to be in areas that are at least close to somewhere shallow with weed for cover. The Endrick Bank is a flat, sloping, sandy bank that has been made shallow by the constant lapping action of the waves. The waves put colour in the water, and pike are so well camouflaged that they can sit happily in it.

But they will move out into deep water to plunder the depths and return to the shallows in the late afternoon to spend the night sheltering in the weed. I have caught them in just two feet of water on plugs cast to the edge of these beds of Potamogeton weed. On Loch Lomond this is broad leafed, with runners branching off underwater, and keeps pike covered through the day.

Pike still have an instinct for avoiding places where they feel vulnerable to attack from birds, even though the species most likely to pose a threat, the osprey, has long since ceased to do so. Only the odd dorsal fin breaking the surface in the weed or a sudden splash of water gives these pike away.

The most exciting way of fishing for them is to cast a floatfished or float-legered deadbait against one of these dense beds of Potamogeton from a moored boat and wait for something to happen. I have sat twenty or thirty feet from the weed and seen a pike come out and take a bait and move back into cover.

To do battle with a big, hard-fighting fish in shallow water and to see it break surface through the long strands of crisp, green weed on a bright day is as exciting as anything in pike fishing. Loch pike are known for their tail walking and powering out of shallow water down into the deeps in one unstoppable run. Their reputation for fighting qualities goes before them, and it is well deserved.

My best catch while fishing next to one such weed bed was made while returning from a fruitless trip to another water.

I was a little downcast after a blank vist and only dropped in for a day on Lomond on the way back on the off-chance of a fish. It just shows you what can happen when you least expect it.

The total catch weighed 137 lb and included three 20s and lots of double-figure fish, all from what I thought would be a brief distraction from my earlier disappointment.

If they won't come out of the weed to take your bait, then a wobbled trout, which is much more visible and easier for them to detect, can be an excellent alternative. The method used is the same as described in previous chapters, perhaps with a lighter wobble bar inside.

Top: The dense Potamogeton beds in Loch Lomond's Port Nellan Bay.

Bottom: This Loch Lomond twenty took an eel section tight to the Potamogeton weed.

High water hunger

High water is a stimulus for pike to feed. They realise it will bring salmon and sea trout up from the sea, and they seem to relish the total

transformation of their environment that high water brings.

With the water level now regulated by power companies, it can be raised or run off artificially at night, creating fishing opportunities or leaving boats moored in shallow water, or high and dry at a whim. You can never be quite sure quite what you will find in the morning, no matter what the weather conditions.

But when the level is raised there is something different happening in the lives of the fish. Their world is expanding, and this encourages them to feed.

Be sure to explore bays because that is exactly what pike will be doing when the level is higher than normal – finding their way around places that were previously out of reach and searching for food among vegetation reclaimed by the rising water.

High water is a welcome sight at spawning time, too, because it creates more spawning areas, which can be in short supply in even a large loch. In years of high water at spawning time good numbers of pike are born, providing another plentiful source of food in a year or two's time when the offspring are big enough to make a meal.

Above: The Quayline 16 fishing boat provides an ideal means of exploring lakes for pike.

When to fish wild waters

I've said that I prefer to fish the lochs in summer because of the weather, but another reason is that feeding reaches a peak in mid-summer, linked as it is to light and temperature. I would rate June as the best month to catch a big loch pike.

By then they have got over the exertions of spawning, the water temperature is high and the days are at their longest. The longer the daylight hours, the more time pike have to feed in the rich areas of deep water and then in the warm shallows at night.

When winter arrives they are unlikely to move into the shallows because the water is too cold, and the shortness of the days means they are feeding less in deep water as well. It's is easy to see why summer is a better bet from the angler's point of view.

Having said that, there are other times of year when you can catch big fish, the next best being spring when smolts migrate to the sea and pike move off their spawning grounds. On Loch Awe I have had bumper days as pike have come off the shallows at Kilchurn Castle.

Left: A downrigger, with its 5 lb lead, will take a trolled bait or plug down to the desired depth – and keep it there. I have caught pike in over thirty feet of water while trolling.

How to tackle them

Most of my fishing in Scotland is done by floatfished or float-legered deadbait, as mentioned earlier, but trailing a livebait under a float behind a boat or trolling a dead trout is also successful, especially over deep water.

Both are good ways of covering a lot of water if you are having trouble finding fish, especially if the pike have moved out from the margins into the main loch. I often have a trout or coarse bait on one rod and a deep-running plug or spoon on the other. An Abu Toby or Hi-Lo, particularly a fluorescent one, or a Kuusamo spoon seem to work best. Fluorescent lures are particularly good in water with poor clarity but, taken overall, a trolled fish seems to produce better pike.

The difference between trailing and trolling is that trailing involves the use of a float to set the depth at which a livebait will work and is best suited to water of up to 15 feet deep. Trolling has no float but uses a downrigger to hold a deadbait at the right depth. The main problem with trailing on lochs is in getting a float big enough to cope with the waves and in finding a weight heavy enough to hold the bait down and stop it riding up to the surface. A downrigger, with its 5 lb lead, will take a trolled deadbait down to the desired depth and keep it there.

Pike drop into deep water through the day and I have caught them in over thirty feet of water while trolling. Any area with a drop-off into deep water and nearby rocks and boulders and petrified tree stumps washed down from feeder streams is particularly good, and so is a narrow channel between two islands.

Trolling also helps you to get to know the loch a little better. Sometimes I just drift around with the fish finder and have a look at contours. Even now, after I've been doing that for many years, I still come across features that I didn't know were there.

A fish finder is essential for this type of fishing, and an outrigger and downrigger very useful for regulating depth. But all in all I don't do a lot of trolling, preferring to fish less speculatively. I believe the best way of catching a big pike is to find the fish and then sit it out with a deadbait. It's very slow and laborious, but it's what the pike want, or the biggest fish do, and it's those that we're after.

Pestered by eels

Scottish lochs have a vast eel population, and because there's so many of them and they're so rich in protein I'm sure they play an important part in a pike's diet.

But the smallest ones can be a real nuisance to anglers when they rip soft deadbaits like sardines to shreds in minutes on days and nights when they are active. It's usually when the weather is overcast and it's wet, and then they are everywhere. I've even had them come into the

shallows and take livebaits, following them in as I retrieve.

But the problem can be solved by using eel sections for bait, brought with you frozen or caught by putting an eel rod out. Balmaha bay, on Loch Lomond, is particularly productive.

One small eel will make five or six baits. I've caught plenty of Scottish pike on them, though I won't use them over 1 lb 4 oz because eels are so slow growing.

A fresh trout or roach will also get around the problem, but put a soft, saltwater bait on and the eels will have it, spinning the trace into a knot in their efforts to tear the flesh and leaving just the bare bones.

Above: Trailing baits or plugs on large expanses of water will cover a lot of ground. If pike have moved out from the margins and taken refuge in deep water, this is a good way of tracking them down.

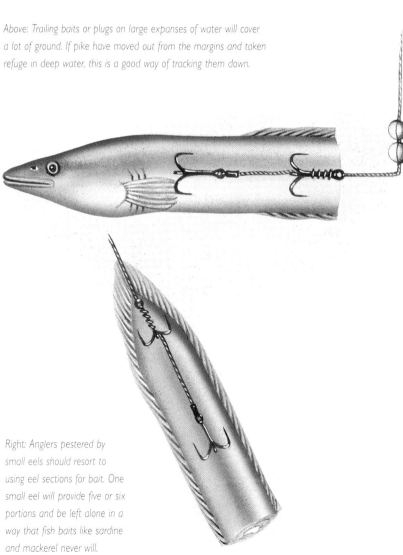

Right: Anglers pestered by small eels should resort to using eel sections for bait. One small eel will provide five or six portions and be left alone in a way that fish baits like sardine and mackerel never will.

Things ain't what they used to be

Unfortunately, Loch Lomond is not as good a water as it was in the 1950s and 1960s. Powan numbers have dropped dramatically, though they have made a comeback in past two years since eel trappers started returning ones they caught by accident.

But runs of salmon and sea-trout are not as good as they were three decades ago, so the loch we fish today is a different, much poorer water in terms of the resources available to pike, and this has an effect on their size. To catch a pike in excess of 25 lb these days is an excellent angling feat.

Anglers have only themselves to blame for part of the problem. They have taken ruffe and other non-indigenous species from English waters to use as livebait and, without intending to do so, have enabled them to colonise the loch, upsetting the water's ecology.

Vast shoals of ruffe now swarm all over Loch Lomond where there wasn't one to be found a couple of decades ago, and pike are eating them instead of the richer, natural food fish, the powan. And the ruffe population explosion has had its effect on powan stocks, as they are probably responsible for eating powan eggs.

It doesn't take an expert in fish ecology to realise the damage that a non-indigenous species can have on a delicately balanced ecosystem. I'm strongly against the releasing of non-native species of fish into these lochs because the effect they have is, at best, unknown.

Take livebaits back with you or knock them on the head, or better still take only brown trout and those coarse fish already present rather than species that don't belong. And if you can catch livebaits while you are up there, use these wherever possible.

Considering how successful deadbaiting can be in Scotland, there shouldn't be any need to take so many livebaits that you have to resort to transporting ruffe.

Loch Lomond now attracts thousands of boats each year, particularly in the summer when the holiday season is in full swing. The oil from their engines and the rubbish from their occupants can't be good for the loch, and water quality isn't what it was twenty or thirty years ago.

Litter strewn around the islands from picnickers who don't clear up after them is a sad sight on such a beautiful water and an indication of the pressure now on these once remote places and the creatures that live there. Scotland was once a world away from the south of England, but motorways and railways have meant that someone living in London will think nothing of travelling there to spend a long weekend on the loch.

The roads that brought these places within our reach have done the same for other water users, and all we can do as anglers is try to leave the place as we found it and hope that others will be responsible enough to do the same.

Fish farms – friend or foe

Rainbow trout and salmon farms have had a marked effect on the ecology of Scotland's lochs in the decade or two since they first appeared. Thousands of 'inmates' have escaped over the years, and in some cases this has led to the spread of disease to the native fish population and interbreeding with wild salmon that have navigated their way back to their birthplace to spawn. But on the plus side, pike have had an extra source of semi-tame food.

From the pike angler's point of view, when looking for a rich water capable of producing a big fish, cages for rearing trout and salmon for the table should be considered as they are... a feature that will enhance pike size, along with good runs of wild salmon and sea-trout. Anywhere with either is worthy of attention, and somewhere with both should be worth a great deal of time and effort.

But avoid lochs with high mountain ranges that drop off steeply straight into water, creating deeps close to the shore. Unless a loch or lough has extensive shallows it is unlikely to yield big pike, no matter how plentiful the food sources.

Conservation not annihilation

The more nets that are bought off by salmon angling interests to allow migratory fish largely unhindered access to their spawning grounds, the better for pike anglers, so long as estate management doesn't involve coarse fish culls.

The benefits of reduced poaching and regular game fish restocking programmes will be enjoyed by pike anglers on lochs adjacent to game rivers, but on certain waters where pike are seen as vermin, whole populations may be all but wiped out in pike removal operations.

In Scotland, I'm pleased to say, the message that pike bring people who want to catch them and who spend money while trying to do so is slowly filtering through, and the species is beginning to get the respect it deserves, if for reasons of tourism rather than informed fishery management. But in Ireland the thinking seems to be less well advanced, and tales filter through to me of huge fish culls on Lough Corrib wherein a dozen or more 30 lb plus fish are slaughtered to protect the trout, which is what, they are told, the visitors come to catch. These people know when the pike spawn and so by longlining and gill-netting at this time in Cushlough Bay they can almost rid the lough of pike in two or three days.

Above: Looking down on Lough Corrib in Ireland, the home of great pike.

Surveys have proved that most of the time pike feed on perch and roach, which are much slower swimming than agile game fish, which take a lot of energy to catch. The only time that pike feed heavily on game fish is during the annual run of smolts towards the sea through narrow river mouths. But even then nature has arranged for the rush of fish to happen in a short space of time, ensuring a large number get through safely.

Yet pike are still trapped and culled because they are believed to be killing game fish. So long as local people with influence labour under this misapprehension then wonderful, wild waters with healthy populations of pike and some very big fish will continue to be plundered at regular intervals in the name of fish conservation, or fish extermination. And while this happens, fisheries in Ireland, and the few where it still happens in Scotland, will be much the poorer.

ANGLING
ethics and the future

Left: The Baltic Archipelago, Uppland, Sweden.

Below: A weir pool on the River Evenlode that has been reduced to a trickle by abstraction. Yet licences continue to be granted when what we need is more water, not less.

Pike fishing is under attack from all sides. Two legged, four legged, six legged – you name it, all are having a strong influence on the sport and will slowly change the face of fishing as we know it.

The major threats

They say that the best way to win a battle is to know your adversary. We ought to be aware of the major threats to our sport so that we can speak out against them when the opportunity arises and recognise them when we meet them face to face.

The afflictions endangering the future of fishing generally and pike fishing in particular, should not be underestimated for the threat that they pose.

Abstraction

It's become something of a cliché to say so, but there are streams where I fished as a boy that are now no more than dry beds of stones and weeds. We hear of water supplies to households being cut off and people having to use standpipes at the end of the street in winter and summer, but it is perhaps only when we go back to somewhere we haven't fished since our youth and see how dramatically the river has changed that the full force of how much less water we have is brought home to us. The stark fact is that there are more of us demanding our share of a resource that can never increase. Pesticides and nitrates trickle into the river from adjacent farmland with the first rains in September, adding to the colour and the weed growth. It has become a regular feature for

the Thames to fish badly straight after the heavy rains of autumn as the summer's accumulated agricultural pollutants pour into the river in one foul slug, choking the fish with chemicals.

Cormorants

The fact that cormorants have moved inland from the sea says a great deal about how commercial fishing has destroyed the ocean's resources. Starved of food around our coast, cormorants have moved on to our rivers, lakes and reservoirs, where they have settled in colonies as large as six hundred on a single water, breeding successfully and working their way through the population of fish of takeable size. They even attack fish as big as 20 lb, spearing them in the side, often fatally, in their frustration at not being able to eat them.

I have seen scientific figures which indicate that an adult cormorant will consume in one year the equivalent of the entire edible fish population of one mile of river. If this is true, there could soon be little left that a pike or angler could want.

Mink

Also here to stay are mink, another of nature's least loveable creations. Even someone with a seriously underdeveloped sense of irony cannot fail to appreciate what an own goal animal liberationists scored when they gave hundreds of captive mink the freedom of the Great British outdoors.

Having spread and bred successfully for a couple of decades they have wiped out moorhen populations on some stretches of river and canal. They are not averse to taking on the odd human being, either, and possess a bite that any ferret would be proud of.

How long can we carry on livebaiting?

Considering the amount of good that anglers do in getting polluters prosecuted, and caring for Britain's waterways and everything that lives in and around them, we still have a poor reputation in the eyes of the public. Their image of angling comes from occasional documentaries about swans and lead shot, pictures of dead birds tangled in discarded line and debates on whether angling is cruel and fish able to feel pain.

But it must be said that we don't help ourselves. As pike anglers we are responsible for one of the least easy practices to defend, namely livebaiting. There may well come a time when mounting a live fish on treble hooks and casting it out to catch another fish for sport is outlawed, if not for humane reasons then at least to limit the spread of disease – and we will be unable to argue a case for avoiding a ban.

Artificial livebaits

Perhaps the ever more sophisticated world of electronics will provide us with a suitable substitute in the form of an artificial lure capable of swimming on its own and sending out high frequency impulses that mimic a fish in distress.

If such a lure could be devised, I, for one, would welcome the passing of the need to carry buckets

Above: My heart sinks when I find suitable perches for cormorants on a new water. They will only leave when there are no fish left to catch.

of baits in favour of a small box of realistic, rubbery creatures and batteries to bring them to life.

As lures become more lifelike, and soft rubber plugs as common as plastic ones, there could soon be a suitable artificial alternative to a deadbait for wobbling and sink-and-draw. Some American lure patterns have semi-permeable membranes that you can inject with a scent and retrieve to leave a trail. Lure fishing could be a major beneficiary of the march of new technology.

The first fishing reels with alarms built in are already being manufactured, and the ultimate in rod rings that are strong, light and won't wear, no matter what, are available now. They are made from titanium by Hopkins of Holloway, and at the moment sell for well over £100 for six.

Electronics will play an even greater part in fishing in the future, with fish finders getting still more sophisticated. There may come a time when they can tell you what species of fish you are looking at.

But really all that I want in the way of improvements is for a manufacturer to produce a large reel with a Baitrunner facility with a nice big handle that takes the knocks. When they do this, I'll be happy.

North American crayfish

But perhaps an even greater threat to fish stocks is posed by the six or seven separate varieties of non-indigenous crayfish that have found their way into Britain. Armies of the creatures are spreading across southern England unseen by anyone except anglers and wiping out whole year classes of the fish population as they devour the eggs laid by coarse and game species.

There are few natural waters that the interlopers have not penetrated. Northern Britain now has its share, and they have found their way over the Border into Scotland.

On some stretches of the Thames and many southern gravel pits it is no longer possible to fish with bottom baits as they get torn to shreds soon after being cast out, especially at night, when crays are most active.

On other waters, pike that were once plump are now

Above: Foreign crayfish could one day make legering impossible.

painfully thin because crayfish mop up any dead or dying fish that fall to the bottom, and then wipe out a whole year's spawn. When eggs aren't allowed to develop into fry, it's the predators at the top of the food chain that are the first ones to suffer.

Anti-anglers

Anti-anglers are now as much a part of the face of modern fishing as national rod licences and echo sounders. With regular reports of attacks on fishermen, we ought not to be surprised to find them bobbing about in the water in front of us in frogmen's suits.

Retaliation is never the answer, as huntsmen have found out in the courts, but we ought not to be afraid to point out that as anglers we are unpaid watchdogs of Britain's waterways, performing a quality monitoring service and ensuring food and shelter for the birds and fish that live there, completely free of charge. Thanks to our vigilance, ordinary people can enjoy a walk by a river without the smell of sewage, and can see kingfishers and herons at the water's edge, not shopping trolleys and matresses. We do it for our own ends, of course, but everyone else benefits as

well, including anti-anglers, whose spare time is not spent making the countryside a better place but hindering the work of conservation.

Close season – friend or foe?

Only time will tell whether removing the close season on stillwaters has cost us dear among a number of influential friends. We certainly can't have endeared ourselves to conservation groups by scrapping the annual period when we left the birds and fish in peace and gave the banks a chance to grow back.

You could say that the close season doesn't affect pike anglers much because the best of their fishing is in the winter, Scotland and Ireland excepted, and many pike spawn before mid-March anyway, so they have always been catchable.

But before spawning, the females are in a delicate state and in need of protection from

Above: How many anglers are there in Britain? There was a time when we could boast of four million and rising – but not any more.

Above: A 30 lb pike from a trout water caught by Steve Kilbee. Jaws would drop if some of these waters opened their doors in summer.

anglers for the sake of future pike stocks, for if they are mishandled there is more than one life at stake. And after spawning they have used up an enormous amount of energy, are thin, vulnerable and in the worst state they have been in all year.

You may have gathered by now that I am in favour of a close season, but it is not just concern for the welfare of fish and nesting birds that has swayed me. I fish very hard during the eight or nine months of the open season, and when it closes, the break gives me time to spend with my wife and son.

I need a break to look back on the season just ended, and to retrace my steps, evaluate my strengths and work on my weaknesses. There will be reconnaissance trips and days spent sorting out tackle and carrying out essential, close season tasks. In short, I need the break as much as the fish, and was sorry when the change was brought about and the magic of 16 June was lost.

I would like to see the close season reinstated. This has happened in Europe, where some countries, including the Netherlands, scrapped it and then brought it back. Maybe we should learn from their example.

Commercial fisheries

You have only to look at how popular heavily stocked, man-made carp waters have become to realise that they are going to play a big part in the future of fishing.

A commercial pike fishery is surely a contradiction in terms. Yet there are already large waters that get stockings of pike netted from trout reservoirs. Perhaps we will see more of this practice and in smaller waters, where pike can be fed artificially. And when the supply from trout waters runs out, there may be farm-bred pike.

Improved fish-rearing techniques have already enabled fish farmers to offer fishery owners carp and rainbow trout of well over the British record. Perhaps pike won't be far behind. Given a rich diet and careful temperature control, a 60 lb or 70 lb pike may be possible, to be sold to the highest bidder to boost ticket sales on his water.

Why wait for a fish to grow to that size when they are already available from other countries? It can only be a matter of time before we follow the example of the carp and catfish people, and bring muskellunge or Baltic whoppers into the British Isles.

Whether they would be suited to our waters is another matter, but that is hardly going to trouble the sort of people who legitimise alien's stocking as commerce. The trade in illegal imports is one of the few growth industries in angling.

Left: The World Record pike of 55 lb 1 3/4 oz caught in October 1986 by Lothar Louis, from Buhl in Germany, on a spinner. It was 55 inches long and was brought to this country to be set up by Peter Stone.

I can't help wondering why import laws and fish movement regulations are not upheld in this country. Every week – according to the angling press – fish are brought in and stocked illegally, they are moved from water to water, and illegal sites for crayfish farming are set up, but when do you hear about a prosecution? Yet the Environment Agency will happily hand out a summons to an angler without a licence to fish, or fine him for standing too far from his rods, which is an excellent way of driving people away from the sport

Piking on trout waters

If there's one development that pike anglers can truly look forward to, it is the opening up of more trout waters to coarse fishing. It will have to come about as revenue from a dwindling number of trout anglers falls below acceptable levels and those in charge seek income from other sources.

When you consider that the British record pike and its predecessor came from a trout fishery you begin to realise the untapped potential that many of these waters represent.

Alternatively, pike anglers after a Red Letter Day can venture abroad. Every year British anglers catch huge foreign carp, catfish and exotic creatures like Nile perch and mahseer, but so far pike haven't figured much in these holiday catches. Before long, though, British anglers will become more adventurous and visit the Baltic, for example, to get to grips with outsized Scandinavian pike.

So much for the future. If it seems a little pessimistic, then I apologise. My intention is merely to forewarn, not to deter.

I hope I'm proven wrong in my pessimism, for if I'm not we could lose what little unspoilt fishing is left in a country where concrete and tarmac are taking over.

If there were nowhere left to go pike fishing except to commercial fisheries where all the fish have names and turn up on cue like performing dolphins, I, for one, would hang up my rods and find some other way to spend my evenings and weekends. I wouldn't want to fish if commercialisation was all there was and neither, I believe, would you.

INDEX

Page numbers in *italics* refer to illustrations.